ECO-EMANCIPATION

Eco-Emancipation

AN EARTHLY POLITICS OF FREEDOM

SHARON R. KRAUSE

PRINCETON UNIVERSITY PRESS

PRINCETON & OXFORD

Requests for permission to reproduce material from this work should be sent to permissions@press.princeton.edu

Published by Princeton University Press
41 William Street, Princeton, New Jersey 08540
99 Banbury Road, Oxford OX2 6JX

press.princeton.edu

Library of Congress Control Number 2022950382
ISBN 978-0-691-24225-5
ISBN (e-book) 978-0-691-24226-2

British Library Cataloging-in-Publication Data is available

Editorial: Rob Tempio and Chloe Coy
Production Editorial: Jill Harris
Jacket Design: Heather Hansen
Production: Lauren Reese
Publicity: Alyssa Sanford and Charlotte Coyne
Copyeditor: Kathleen Kageff

Jacket image: *Southwestern Abstract* taken by Landsat 8. Courtesy of Earth Resources Observation and Science (EROS) Center / USGS

This book has been composed in Arno

10 9 8 7 6 5 4 3 2 1

This book is dedicated to the memory of my mother, Barbara Ann Krause,
who showed me how to love life and live it fully;
and to Tayhas, who brings me to life.

CONTENTS

ACKNOWLEDGMENTS

LIKE ALL BOOKS, this one has incurred many debts in becoming what it is. I am grateful to the colleagues, friends, family, and students who have listened and argued with me, read drafts, passed along references, and helped me find my way. I thank Rob Tempio and the staff at Princeton University Press for their expert support; and Brown University for sabbatical time and research funding, and for being as rich and collegial an intellectual home as one could ever wish for. My mother, Barbara, who died of cancer while I was writing the book, cheered it on even through her lowest days, as she cheered on (almost!) everything I ever did. Lucky me to have come into being in the ecosystem of her love. My greatest acknowledgment, as always, is for Tayhas, whose love and light make everything possible for me; and who, thirty years on, still runs through me like a current, "rich, deep, and warm."

Parts of several chapters were published in earlier form as "Environmental Domination," *Political Theory* 48, no. 4 (August 2020): 443–68; "Political Respect for Nature," *Philosophy and Social Criticism* 47, no. 2 (2021): 241–66; "Agency," *Political Concepts: A Critical Lexicon* 3, no. 5 (2016), https://www.politicalconcepts.org/category/issue-3/; and "Creating a Culture of Environmental Responsibility," chapter 4 in *Cultural Values in Political Economy*, edited by J. P. Singh (Stanford, CA: Stanford University Press, 2020), 65–86.

ECO-EMANCIPATION

1

Awakenings

A SPECTER MOVES among us—shadowed, indistinct, silent; it hovers at the edge of vision and then is gone, shape-shifting unrecognizably into plain sight. It lives in the quiet of a woods where birdsong used to be, in the chemicals that course imperceptibly through our soil and water and bloodstreams, in the long, low, windowless buildings on the outskirts of town that supply our insatiable appetite for cheap meat. It is at the dinner table with us, seated across the aisle on the flight to Chicago, sewn into the bags we carry, the mattresses we sleep on, the down jackets that keep us warm in winter.

This shadowed shape-shifter is a constant companion in modern democratic societies; like the air itself, it is everywhere and unseen. It is the specter of a domination that shapes every aspect of our lives while being virtually invisible to us: the domination that human beings exercise in relation to nonhuman nature. People are a part of the natural world, of course, and consequently the human domination of nature entraps and exploits us too, albeit in different ways depending on who we are and where we fall in human hierarchies. Yet whereas modern democracy establishes principled constraints on power in relation to persons, constraints that are intended to check arbitrary power and exploitation, it entails few such protections for nonhuman beings and things. This structural condition of vulnerability to insufficiently constrained power and exploitation is the essence of domination.

The domination of nature is not unique to democratic societies, of course; it permeates regimes of all types in most every part of the world. Yet democratic domination is especially troubling because it cannot be blamed on a thug or a political strongman. We all play a role. Most of us do not see the role we play in the domination of nature, or the ways it circles back to entrap and exploit other people and ourselves. And even if we did see it, this domination is not a condition we can rectify as individuals. A distinctive feature of domination in this form is the forced complicity in which it holds us. On the one hand, poor and marginalized people are made to be the tools of a "slow violence" exercised over nature and themselves by extractivist industries and corrupt governments.[1] On the other hand, the relatively privileged masses in even the most prosperous societies are enlisted, through the promise of consumer satisfactions and misguided notions of freedom, in their own entrapment and exploitation by a system that makes sustainable living essentially impossible, compromises health and well-being, and feeds the slow violence of environmental degradation abroad and at home.

To speak of the human domination of nature may seem to imply a stark divide between people and the Earth, one that is belied by our dependence on Earth's nonhuman parts, our embeddedness in ecosystems, and the porous, networked character of our human selves and communities. It is estimated, for example, that at least half the cells making up a human body are not human cells at all but bacterial.[2] The oxygen that animates us, the calories that fuel us, the sun that warms and illuminates us, the physical forces that hold our parts together—all these more-than-human things are constitutive components of human beings. We are very much a part of nature, not outside it. Indeed, the whole idea of nature as a separate entity has been more or less repudiated over the last generation. In our era of anthropogenic climate change, all ecosystems now bear a human imprint, so the old notion of nature as untouched wilderness is obsolete.[3] Yet while human beings are a part of nature, we are not the whole of it. The material world we inhabit contains many beings and things that exceed the *merely* human. For this reason, William Connolly has warned against overly "sociocentric" views that ignore how human agency always interacts with "deeply nonhuman" beings, things, and "planetary forces with degrees of autonomy of their own."[4] The environmental domain manifests a "socionatural hybridity" in which human beings are constitutively entwined with nonhuman beings and things, with no one part being simply reducible to any other.[5]

In this book I refer to more-than-human beings and things under the rubric of nature, including both nonhuman animals and the Earth systems that we commonly think of as the natural environment. In using the language of nature, I never mean to mark out a domain that is fully cut off from human influence, or to deny the deep and important fact of human dependence on Earth others and embeddedness in ecosystems. Human beings are natural phenomena. At the same time, the scale of the destructive impact that human power has had on the Earth, and the fact that this power can be guided by deliberation and choice, do make the human species distinctive. We do not stand outside nature, but there are certain things that only we can do within it, such as take responsibility for the environmental harms we have caused, consciously cultivate new ways of thinking and new sensibilities, coordinate our action with others to alter the trajectories of our power, and create more sustainable, inclusive political communities going forward. To make progress on our environmental problems, we need to acknowledge both our embeddedness and our distinctiveness. Both are central to how we got into the environmental mess we are currently in, and both are necessary to find our way out.

The notion of the human domination of nature also may seem to overstate the extent and efficacy of human power. There is much in nature that we do not control, after all, including many of our own environmental effects, as climate change and superbugs and mass extinctions demonstrate. Yet domination has never been a matter of perfect control. Think of the despots depicted by Plato or Montesquieu, whose anxious efforts to master their subjects leave the despots themselves desperate and dispirited because perfect control perpetually eludes their grasp.[6] Domination is about power that lacks effective institutional constraints, not about perfect control. The purposes to which power is put also are relevant. Domination is self-serving and indifferent to the well-being of those it subordinates, instrumentalizing them to satisfy the superior's desires rather than showing them consideration in their own right. This feature of domination makes it intrinsically unstable as a form of political order, as both Plato and Montesquieu knew. Domination uses up the sources of its own life by eviscerating its subjects and the conditions of their common existence. It is not sustainable. This should sound familiar to us; it is a fitting description of how most of us relate to the nonhuman world. The power that human beings are permitted to exercise in relation to nonhuman nature is a form of domination both in its structure and in its ends, even though it is far from perfect control.

The use of nature for human purposes is not in itself domination, of course. Use is a necessary condition of existence, one that holds for all living things. To live on the Earth is inevitably to consume, transform, and destroy. Life entails violence. What makes our relationship to nonhuman nature one of domination is not the fact of our use but the insufficiently constrained structure of our power, and the unabashedly exploitative ends this power is permitted to serve. True, states routinely regulate the use of nonhuman beings and things by people, but the vast majority of animal and environmental regulation today is self-serving rather than principled. It is formulated to protect human interests, and when human interests are deemed to change, the regulations change too. Moreover, institutional protections for nature are for the most part only weakly entrenched and easily obviated, as the Trump administration's rapid retraction of many environmental regulations showed. While efforts by some countries to protect ecosystems and nonhuman animals through constitutionally established rights gesture toward more fundamental structural constraints on human power, at this point they remain mostly aspirational in character and are not widespread.[7] So the domination of nature is not the same thing as the use of nature for human purposes. Domination is a specific condition, the condition of systematic vulnerability to power that is insufficiently constrained and exploitative.

Domination so conceived is harmful and illegitimate. To some, the domination of nature will seem to be a misnomer in this regard. Nothing is more common in the Western canon of philosophy than the twinned ideas (1) that nature is composed of inert matter and thus impervious to harm, or at least impervious to harm that is of moral and political concern; and (2) that human beings, as the only morally significant things on Earth by virtue of their unique capacity for rational agency, are entitled to make use of nature however they like. From the biblical assertion that God gave human beings "dominion over all the earth,"[8] to Aristotle's idea that plants and animals "exist for the sake of human beings" as "instruments" to be used for human purposes,[9] to Locke's assumption that "the inferior ranks of creatures" are "made for human use,"[10] to Marx's depiction of nature as "man's inorganic body" and "the instrument of his life-activity,"[11] the Western tradition has tended overwhelmingly to legitimate the exercise of relatively unchecked, instrumentalizing human power in relation to nature, and to disavow the harm it brings to nonhuman beings and things. Political theories that agree on virtually nothing else agree with striking unanimity on this much.

The purpose of *Eco-Emancipation* is not to prove that the human domination of nature is harmful and illegitimate but rather to diagnose the dynamics that sustain domination and envision alternatives to them. There are multiple reasonable considerations that can be brought to bear in explaining the wrongness of domination in relation to nature, and we need not agree on all the particulars. As in the overlapping consensus that Rawls envisioned to sustain a pluralistic people's commitment to justice, we can make sense of the wrongness of environmental domination from within a range of different perspectives. My own view is that just as the domination of people is wrong because it imposes harm on subordinates that superiors have no right to impose, so nothing has endowed human beings with a legitimate title to exercise power over nonhuman parts of nature in this way. In the absence of a title to unconstrained, merely exploitative use, such use can only constitute a usurpation, a violation of the basic condition of nonhuman beings and things as existing in and for themselves, for their own diverse purposes and according to their own logics of being, within Earth's interdependent webs of life.

It is true that the wrongness of domination among people seems self-evident to us today in a way that does not hold for the human domination of nature. Yet historically the wrongness of domination among people was far from self-evident to many human beings—perhaps most—until relatively recently. The growing recognition of its wrongness has been the result of inventiveness in modern moral and political theory, along with activist struggle over centuries to establish the idea in practice, struggle that continues (unfinished) today. Think of Locke's inventive assertion that human beings are by nature free and equal in the sense that no person has a natural title to rule over others, or Kant's inventive assertion that the rationality of noumenal beings confers moral dignity on them and makes them ends in themselves. These inventive assertions have become our deepest moral intuitions in modern democracies, and they have made human societies better in some very important respects, despite the fact they are more like articles of faith than actual proofs.

For us to see and feel the wrongness of human domination in relation to nature with the force we now feel about prohibitions on domination among people, we do not need proof of the intrinsic worth of nonhuman beings and things any more than we need proof of the intrinsic worth of people. We do not have proof of the intrinsic worth of people. What we have in the case of people is a series of inventive assertions and articles of faith that over time, and with the help of activist struggle, have been internalized by enough of us in enough places to become common intuitions, and that have tended on the whole to make human lives go better. The new and inventive intuition we must now internalize is that nonhuman beings and things, like other people, are not *for us* in any constitutive or morally meaningful way, that no legitimate title exists granting authority to human beings to exercise unchecked power over nonhuman parts of nature, or to make use of them in merely instrumentalizing, exploitative ways. If internalized by enough people over time, this intuition has the potential to make it as self-evident to us that the human domination of nature is wrong as it is now self-evident that domination among people is wrong. This perspective on the wrongness of domination in relation to nature is woven into the chapters that follow, but one need not accept this perspective to learn from the analysis of domination and the vision of emancipation that are the focus of the book. The analysis of domination and the vision of emancipation offered here are compatible with a range of different perspectives in this regard.

The belief that people do have a legitimate title to rule nature has been tremendously durable and destructive. It not only excuses but also occludes the damage we do to Earth others, to one another, and to ourselves by means of insufficiently constrained power and exploitation, making it difficult for us to see that we are complicit in a usurpation *and* that we ourselves are subjugated by it.[12] The first objective of *Eco-Emancipation* is to make this unseen usurpation and subjugation visible, to awaken us to the multiple strands of domination that are with us everywhere, and that currently set the terms of human life on the Earth. One might be forgiven for thinking that this awakening is already under way. Environmental consciousness is clearly on the rise around the world. Recycling is now a major global industry, alternative energy use is expanding, workplaces and college campuses are going green, the language of sustainable development is everywhere, even large oil companies build advertising campaigns around their putative commitments to the Earth, and as a result of the 2015 Paris climate accord, 196 countries have agreed to limit their carbon emissions. Valuable as they are, however, these developments do not alter the fundamental structure of human power in relation to nature, and hence they do not change the basic conditions of environmental domination. Consequently, industrialized agriculture and factory farming are extending their reach worldwide while deforestation, species extinctions, toxic dumping, the proliferation of drug-resistant superbugs, the growth of greenhouse gas emissions, and the acidification of the seas continue apace. We may worry about our environmental problems today more than we did in the past, but we are not doing much to change the basic structure of human power that drives these problems, partly because we still do not see the domination it entails.

Historically, domination has had two sides: *dominium*, the exercise of insufficiently constrained power by particular persons, groups, and economic entities in the private sphere; and *imperium*, the exercise of insufficiently constrained power by public authorities or the state. Domination as dominium and imperium was associated with slavery, whether as personal servitude to a master or as political servitude to a despot.[13] Both dominium and imperium are evident today in how human power is exercised in relation to nature. In the private sphere, the power that individual people and groups exercise in their interactions with nonhuman beings and things is insufficiently constrained such that, for example, farmers and corporate agricultural operations are free to deplete the land and water supply and to impose unconscionable suffering on animals for the purpose of increasing their profit margins. In the public domain, the power of states to extract resources, dump waste, and permit carbon emissions within their borders likewise lacks constraints that are principled and reliably enforced.

The fact that environmental domination is a function of the structure of human power makes it relatively independent of individual human intentions in these contexts. Insofar as I *can* poison the soil with pesticides, the land I farm and the nonhuman populations that live there are vulnerable to me in a way that does not change simply because as an individual farmer I choose to go organic. Likewise, one US administration opting not to open the Arctic National Wildlife Refuge to oil drilling in no way mitigates the basic status condition of that land relative to the imperium of American public power as long as the next administration is free to do so. The structure of human power in relation to nonhuman beings and things, both individual human power and collective human power, puts nonhuman nature into a position of systematic vulnerability to people and treats nature as if it were primarily a resource for the satisfaction of human desires. The status condition of nature in this regard is separate from the intentions that particular human beings may have as individuals. Whoever we are and whatever we do, if we live in democratic societies that do not adequately constrain human power relative to nature or protect nonhuman beings and things from exploitation, we play a part in the domination of nature.

This is not to say that we all play the *same* part. As Naomi Klein aptly puts it, "You, me and Exxon (Mobile) are not all in it together" in the sense of being equally responsible for environmental degradation, or responsible in the same ways.[14] Similarly, wealthy Americans who opt to commute in gas-guzzling SUVs play a different role, given their relative privilege and political power, than local peoples of the Amazon who have been driven by poverty and political oppression into jobs that violently extract resources from their land. The large-scale structural forces through which the domination of nature mostly transpires are human inventions and are driven by human agency. Yet the human agency that drives them is compromised in varying degrees by prevailing relations of power.[15] Consequently, a core feature of domination in this form is that many of us contribute to the damage it effects without intending to do so, sometimes very much against our wishes.

Moreover, even as we participate in the degradation of the Earth, we ourselves, including both poor people and privileged ones, are confined and exploited by the forces through which the domination of nature transpires. We are confined and exploited when we are led to believe that the only path to job creation is to allow industries to extract, emit, and dump with abandon, compromising our own health and well-being alongside that of the nonhuman beings and things that live among us. We are confined and exploited by a production culture of planned obsolescence, in which we must purchase even the most basic tools of a modern existence again and again, filling our dumps with toxic, unnecessary refuse and our waterways with mountains of plastic because everything is made to be disposable. We are confined and exploited whenever the only goods available for purchase are toxic to us but profitable for the seller, and when our land, water, air, and bodies are polluted by commercial enterprises. We are confined and exploited by food industries that fill our grocery stores with products that fail to nourish us or actively sicken us while depleting and destroying the ecosystems we depend on. In all these contexts, we are treated not as ends in ourselves but as the means for generating profits for corporations and power for the political officials who serve them. Because human beings are a part of nature not separate from it, the shape-shifting specter that is the human domination of nature circles back to subjugate people too, albeit in different ways and to different degrees depending on how we are positioned in human hierarchies.

The effects that the domination of nature has on people compromise our ability to envision and enact the deeper changes required to solve our environmental problems. Activities such as dumping and extractivist modes of production are frequently carried out by means of exploitation and violence against people who are already poor and politically marginalized. This exploitation and violence further undercut their ability to resist the pressures of large multinationals and to hold their governments accountable for the damage they do. To be sure, the environmentalism of the poor has shown itself to be a formidable force in many places around the world. Still, the disabling effects on people that accompany the human domination of nature are real. They affect privileged people too, although in different ways. For example, many privileged people living in prosperous societies feel, not unreasonably, that today's big environmental problems are simply beyond their ability to influence. They may wish to live sustainably, they may even make a respectable effort to do so, but they know that the effects of their individual efforts are negligible, and that truly opting out of practices that degrade the Earth is not a live option for anyone living in modern societies, whether poor and politically marginalized or prosperous and privileged.[16] Whatever we do or eat or buy, in work and in leisure, in birth and in death, we inevitably find ourselves contributing to the despoiling of the Earth. We are at once complicit and entrapped. The domination of nature has been inscribed so deeply in the basic structures that organize our lives—political, economic, cultural—that we cannot really do otherwise; there is no viable way out for us as individuals.

In view of the multiple, interacting ways that the domination of nonhuman nature by people circles back to subjugate human beings too, it makes sense to understand these dynamics in terms of a broader concept of *environmental domination*. As the idea is developed here, environmental domination is a multifaceted phenomenon that includes the political, economic, and cultural forces through which human beings (1) *dominate nature*, understood as Earth's more-than-human parts; and (2) *are themselves dominated* in terms of both (a) the special burdens placed on poor and marginalized people with respect to environmental harms, and (b) the ways that virtually all of us—even privileged people in the world's most affluent societies—are confined and exploited by forces that degrade the Earth, often in our names and with our (not always willing) participation. Whoever we are, and whether we know it or not, we are in need of ecological emancipation, meaning the liberation of the Earth from human domination, and the liberation of human beings from a way of life that is at once exploitative and exploited, complicit and entrapped.[17]

The key to this emancipation is a new kind of political order, one that institutionalizes principled constraints on human power in relation to nonhuman beings and things, and that prevents the exploitation of nature and people. Ethical orientations emphasizing our interdependence with nonhuman nature and personal efforts at sustainable living are valuable, but they are radically insufficient because they are no match for the structural conditions that constitute environmental domination. To reverse this domination, real politics are needed. This means more than simply expanding state-based environmental regulations; it requires changing the basic structure of human power by means of new political institutions and forms of political incorporation for nonhuman nature, new practices of political economy, and new constellations of collective action.

All this goes beyond mere stewardship. In fact, it points up the insufficiency of the stewardship model. Environmental stewardship, as an ethical practice of ecological care, leaves human power unreconstructed, and it makes nonhuman beings and things essentially dependent on the kindness of strangers in their interactions with us. It does not solve the fundamental problem, which is nature's condition of systematic vulnerability to human power that is insufficiently constrained and exploitative. This problem cannot be solved without establishing robust limitations on human power, limitations that are supported through political institutions and collective action, and that can be coercively enforced by the state. Such limitations on power are not by themselves enough to reverse environmental domination, but they are necessary. Their necessity makes ecological emancipation a political project, not something that can be achieved through ethics alone.

It may seem strange to talk about the relationship between human beings and the natural world as a political one. We do not see ourselves as being in political relationship with nature at all. Yet nonhuman beings and things are everywhere subject to the coercive force of states and other political bodies, and to the political will of democratic majorities. Political power regulates how the nonhuman things we think of as natural resources are extracted and distributed and disposed of, how the animals that live among us are produced and slaughtered and studied, and how the Earth itself is divided up, populated, and protected (or not) by human beings. Our relationship to Earth's nonhuman parts is thoroughly infused with political power; it reflects our political values and is constitutive of our political communities. We may prefer not to see this relationship in political terms, but this preference is mainly a matter of bad faith. Given how we treat the Earth, acknowledging the political character of our relationship with it quite rightly makes us uneasy.[18]

A better life is possible, one that is freed of bad faith and liberated from insufficiently checked power and exploitation, but it will require inventing new kinds of political community. The political communities we need to cultivate will incorporate nonhuman nature through institutions of representation and regimes of rights that reliably constrain the use of human power and force nonhuman well-being to count with human decision makers. They will treat nonhuman beings and things as members, rather than as things whose sole function is to be used by members. Because politics is in part a domain of shared decision making for the purpose of guiding the collective use of power, human beings will have a distinctive place in these communities. Our abilities to deliberate, communicate, and coordinate with one another, and our capacity for norm-responsive choices, enable us to take on certain political responsibilities that are not feasible for other kinds of beings and things. Still, the fact that only people can deliberate with others in the ways required for a political assembly to make decisions about the collective use of power does not make it right for only human well-being to count in this deliberation. Political inclusion for, say, cows and rainforests need not entail asking cows and rainforests to vote or run for office. It just means setting things up institutionally so that people must consider cows and rainforests when making decisions about animal agriculture or gold mining. We can make sense of political membership without insisting on political equality in the form of the same set of rights and responsibilities for all members. We do need to support political equality for persons, albeit in the difference-respecting forms that many feminists, disability theorists, and Indigenous peoples have called for. Yet we can incorporate nonhuman beings and things through a range of institutional mechanisms that accommodate their variety while forcing their well-being to count. In the chapters to come we shall explore what this kind of political incorporation and more-than-human political community could look like.

Eco-emancipation will involve certain limitations on us as people, including limits on consumption, limits on population growth, and limits on our uses of nonhuman nature. It will also require active efforts on our part to respect Earth others, to take responsibility for our impact, to create new economic arrangements, and to carry out political change. Like any kind of emancipation, eco-emancipation is an activity rather than a gift, and it is demanding. Still, the limits and the demands it involves are not about ascetic self-denial or the sacrifice of all pleasure and prosperity. We can live well, meaning with pleasure and prosperity, by living better, meaning more sustainably and with more respect and responsibility. Likewise, eco-emancipation does not ask us to reject modernity or turn back the clock on human development. It is very much a forward-looking, world-expanding project for human beings, one that promises to make our lives better and, crucially, *freer*. It is of a piece with postcolonial efforts aimed at generating alternative modernities that bring into being more freedom, in diverse forms, for distinctive populations.

Freedom is certainly not the only illuminating lens for theorizing solutions to our environmental problems. Important recent work has focused on environmental justice, for instance, or on eco-virtue and the human Good, or on the shared human interest in species survival.[19] The freedom lens offers an especially important perspective, however. The specter of domination that haunts so many environmental problems today not only plays a role in creating the problems but also tends to occlude the dynamics that drive them, and to undermine effective responses. Until we properly diagnose this domination and address it as such, our remedies will remain weak and ineffectual, and we will never make much progress in solving the problems. In this sense, eco-emancipation is a necessary condition for achieving other valuable outcomes in the environmental domain from environmental justice to eco-virtue to species survival.

The domination of nature is a familiar trope in environmental ethics and environmental political theory. Its history is tied more broadly to the rise of modern science, philosophy, and politics.[20] The effort to understand the causal relations that govern the physical world so as to intervene in these relations in ways that could, as Francis Bacon put it, "ameliorate the human condition," marked the beginning of modernity in the West.[21] For a long time, the "domination of nature" referred to this effort to understand and control the nonhuman environment, and it was seen as an unambiguously good thing. This effort made possible new technologies and rising economic prosperity, promised an end to many forms of human suffering, and demonstrated the triumph of reason over ignorance and superstition. Its costs began to be visible with industrialization in the nineteenth century, which generated obvious environmental damage and engendered among many people a sense of alienation from the land and the more-than-human communities composing it. One sees a growing unease about these costs in novels of the era such as Mary Shelley's *Frankenstein* (1818), in poems like Wordsworth's "Michael" (1800) and later Whitman's *Leaves of Grass* (1855), and in the early nature writing of Thoreau's *Walden* (1854).[22] Yet systematic, critical analysis of the domination of nature as a problem came into its own only with the environmental studies movement in the 1970s. Since then, the trope has come to have a broadly negative valence, with the domination of nature being viewed as harmful and illegitimate, as well as dangerous to human interests.

Too often, however, the domination of nature has been identified simply with human damage to nonhuman species and ecosystems. Indeed, the term is commonly used today in a generic way to refer to all bad things that result from human interventions in the natural world. Yet this generic usage confuses more than it illuminates. It runs together different kinds of human impact, some of which are inevitable and unobjectionable, and it may seem to imply that the only way to avoid the domination of nature is for people to stop interacting with their environments entirely. Domination is not every bad thing; domination means being subject to insufficiently checked power and exploitation. Treating the domination of nature as all bad things muddies the waters of analysis and impedes us from finding a freer path forward. This freer path is not to withdraw from nonhuman nature (as if we could do so) but to change the conditions of our interaction that constitute environmental domination.

And we cannot make the requisite changes without first understanding the dynamics that drive this domination.

To grasp these dynamics in their full complexity we must include in our analysis the multiple ways that the domination of nature by people circles back to entrap and exploit human beings too. The last generation has seen important advances in this connection by scholars working in environmental political theory and critical theory. Murray Bookchin's *The Ecology of Freedom* offers an incisive account of how the exploitation of nonhuman nature, culminating in the rise of industrial capitalism, proceeded hand in hand with the exploitation of human labor. On his view, the environmentally damaging extractivism, pollution, and waste that he associates with the domination of nature was made possible by social hierarchies and the exploitation of the laboring classes by more powerful groups.[23] In a similar way, Val Plumwood's *Feminism and the Mastery of Nature* makes the case that the cultural orientation of mastery characteristic of human approaches to nature in the Western tradition is replicated in male/female relationships as well as other instances of social inequality along lines of race, class, colonization, and the like.[24] The now expansive literature on environmental justice also demonstrates that environmentally damaging practices play out in especially detrimental ways for people who are poor and marginalized, thus calling attention to the interaction between the domination of nature and the domination of particular groups of people.

A different strand of literature, this one growing out of Horkheimer and Adorno's *Dialectic of Enlightenment*, looks at how the domination of nature, understood as the mastery of a technological apparatus that enables the exploitation of the natural world for human profit, has been utilized in modern capitalist societies by a few human beings to exploit the many.[25] The domination of nature in this sense coincides with the domination of the masses as a whole, rather than particular groups of people who are poor or marginalized. And while it involves exploitation, domination in this context has a gentler hand, working (and concealing) its effects through the manipulation and satisfaction of consumer desires. Developed by figures such as Herbert Marcuse, William Leiss, Timothy Luke, and more recently Andrew Biro, the critical theory approach to environmental politics emphasizes the idea that the domination of nature always proceeds in conjunction with the domination of human beings.

Crucial as these different strands of literature are, each one has been limited by its focus on a particular category of people, whether on the laboring class, on women and other subordinate groups, on the poor and the marginalized, or on the privileged masses. Part of understanding how human beings are affected by environmental domination is to see the ways that these different forms of domination among people interact with one another, and to grasp the multiple, sometimes cross-cutting roles that people play in these dynamics. Then, too, work that explores the relationship between the domination of nature and the domination of human beings has tended to privilege the domination of people in its analysis and its focus of normative concern. Nowhere is this truer than in the work of Leiss, whose book *The Domination of Nature* offers a seminal account of domination as applied to the natural world but ultimately concludes that the true meaning of "the domination of nature" is only "that by such means . . . some men attempt to dominate and control other men."[26] For Leiss, the domination of nature is reducible in the final analysis to the domination of people, and the domination of people is the real problem. Although this conviction is not always articulated in such an explicit way, the literatures that explore interactions between the domination of nature and the domination of people do tend to focus on the people. There are good reasons for this focus. The human suffering and injustices that result from environmental domination are often extreme, and they should be of pressing concern to us. Also, addressing this suffering and injustice is a necessary step in remediating the human domination of nonhuman beings and things. Still, by decentering or even occluding the domination of nonhuman nature, the work remains partial and incomplete.

We need a new way of thinking about environmental domination, one that allows us to hold in view all at once the different forms, dimensions, subjects, and sources of this domination and their interactions with one another. Part of what makes environmental progress so difficult is precisely the fact that the tentacles of environmental domination reach so widely across the different domains of our lives, and across different human lives in different ways. Our analysis of environmental problems must be alive to this complexity, and our responses must reach as widely as the tentacles of domination do. Such an analysis is the purpose of this book. The holistic and intersectional framework developed here is new in how it connects an account of the ways that environmental domination compounds the harms of historical and continuing global power inequities among people to an account of how domination also cuts across these inequities, confining and exploiting all of us in significant respects even as it formally constitutes the political status of nonhuman nature as subordinate to human beings as a whole in law and public policy. The analysis is also distinctive in the close linkage it establishes between (the different forms of) environmental domination among people and the domination of nature per se, incorporating nonhuman beings and things at the center of the analysis and treating their domination as a normative concern in its own right, rather than sidelining it or viewing it as derivative of domination among people.

In addition to the holism of its approach, *Eco-Emancipation* offers a novel account of what environmental domination is. By emphasizing the idea that environmental domination involves vulnerability to power that is insufficiently constrained and exploitative, and that this vulnerability is a function of political, institutional arrangements and not only cultural orientations and personal values, it enables us to distinguish the domination of nature from the more general phenomena of human use and impact, and also from human control. This conceptual clarity offers activists and others engaged in shaping environmental policy and practices a more well-defined target. The target is not too broad, as when environmental domination is defined as any human use or impact, or as all bad things caused by human hands, thus implying that the only way to avoid environmental domination is by disengaging from the nonhuman world, or seeking to restore some mythical wilderness free from human influence. Nor is the target too narrow, as in demands to eliminate particular consumer goods or to promote certain sustainable technologies, which might make marginal improvements in some areas but still leave intact the larger, institutional apparatus of insufficiently constrained human power and exploitation. The account also makes sense of how human beings can exercise domination in relation to nonhuman beings and things (and one another), even though we quite obviously do not control them.

By clarifying what the domination of nature entails and how it operates, this account helps us to better understand the underlying causes of our environmental problems, and it points us to the changes needed to make a real difference, changes that focus on reconstructing how power flows between human beings and nonhuman nature, and among people. These changes involve establishing robust, institutional constraints on human power in relation to nonhuman beings and things, and protections against exploitation for both nature and people. And they combine new institutional arrangements with extra-institutional forms of political activism as well as civic ethos and cultural transformation, including a new sensibility of political respect for nature and new public practices of eco-responsibility. The promise of emancipation they offer is not a promise of perfect harmony between the human and more-than-human parts of nature, or among persons. Perfect harmony is not the goal; nondomination is the goal. Or better yet, the goal is a way of living that pursues

liberation from environmental domination for people and nature through political communities that constrain human power in new ways and formally
incorporate Earth's more-than-human parts so as to allow a freer life for all of
us over time.

The book begins by taking aim at a linchpin of environmental domination:
the old human exceptionalism thought to justify it. This exceptionalism rests
on an ideal of human agency as rational autonomy, even personal sovereignty,
that is rooted in individual reason and will and that putatively enables us to
exercise rational control over our actions. Agency so conceived is thought to
set human beings apart from and above the rest of nature. It purportedly frees
us from the mechanistic determinism said to characterize the natural world,
and it gives us both the capacity and the right to govern ourselves and everything else. Agency in this form is often seen as the sole source of moral value
and political standing; it makes human beings (and only human beings) ends
in themselves. The ideal of agency as personal sovereignty sets the boundaries
of moral and political belonging in a way that calls for limitations on the exercise of power over people but justifies human beings in exercising relatively
unconstrained power in relation to nature.

Chapter 2, "A New Exceptionalism," argues that this ideal of agency is deeply
misleading. It neglects human agency's nonsovereign, distributed character, the
fact that agency cannot be located exclusively within the individual, in inner
faculties such as reason and will. Agency does involve inner faculties, but it also
extends beyond the individual to include social and material exchanges as well,
meaning exchanges with other people and with nonhuman nature. Agency has
what David Abram refers to as a "porosity" that makes each agent like "an open
circuit that completes itself only in things, in others, in the surrounding earth."[27]
This porosity and dependence on both human and nonhuman others means
that action is never fully subject to the agent's rational control or even contained
within the boundaries of the self. Agency is a robust but *nonsovereign* experience, to invoke language introduced by Hannah Arendt.

The nonsovereignty of agency disrupts the strict, hierarchical divide between human beings and the rest of nature. If agency arises through circuits
of vitality that include and depend on nonhuman aspects of the material environment, then human agents can hardly claim to stand apart from and above
this environment. Human beings do have some distinctive capacities not
shared by most other parts of nature, and this distinctiveness is significant
insofar as it makes us subject to ethical and political accountability in special
ways. But to acknowledge this distinctiveness is a far cry from insisting on a

strict, hierarchical divide between human beings and everything else on Earth, one that could justify unchecked human power and exploitation in relation to nature. The truth is that we depend on the Earth as we depend on one another, and we depend on it to provide more than just a field of opportunity for the exercise of our agency. We depend on it as a vital, contributing source in the composition of agency, the very thing that supposedly sets us apart.

If human beings are not agentic in exactly the ways we have often thought, it is also the case that many nonhuman beings are more agentic than we have typically assumed. The last generation has seen an explosion in animal studies research documenting a range of agentic capacities, including reflective choice, social coordination, and norm responsiveness, among not just higher primates but many mammals and birds. Agency exists on a continuum and admits of significant diversity, and many beings other than human ones manifest agency in some form and to some degree. The distribution of agentic capacities across species further unsettles the old exceptionalism thought to justify the human domination of nature. At the same time, however, there are ways in which human agents do stand out, at least when it comes to accountability for environmental domination and efforts to generate eco-emancipation. We are distinctive both in the quality and scale of the damage we have done and in the potential we have to do things better going forward. This distinctiveness cannot sustain the old human exceptionalism with its claim to moral superiority and its justification of domination. Instead, it points to a new kind of exceptionalism, one that acknowledges that only human agents can rightly be held accountable for the abuse of human power, including the political institutions, social systems, and cultural values that effectuate environmental domination, and that human agents have a special role to play in correcting this abuse.

This new exceptionalism rests on an understanding of human agency as a nonsovereign, more-than-human phenomenon. It does not set people apart from and above the rest of nature. It will not support the illusion of human control over nature, and it does not invite human beings to instrumentalize nature solely for our own purposes. On the contrary, it gives us reason for humility and gratitude toward nonhuman beings and things, and sometimes awe and fear as well. The new exceptionalism of nonsovereign agency orients us to communities of interdependence marked by respect and responsibility toward nonhuman nature, rather than mastery and exploitation. It is a nonsovereign exceptionalism both in the sense that it is rooted in a distinctive but nonsovereign faculty of human agency and in the sense that the orientation to nature it recommends is one of respectful interdependence, rather than of aspirations to sovereign control. Yet it insists that overcoming environmental domination will require engaging what is distinctive in human beings alongside what we share with other parts of nature.

Chapter 2's account of agency draws on work by Arendt, who helps us see the social distribution of agency, and by new materialists such as Jane Bennett, who turn us to the material aspects of human agency and to the agentic capacities of some nonhuman parts of nature. Yet the theory of agency developed here integrates the social and corporeal dimensions of agency in ways that neither Arendt nor the new materialists have done, and it attends more carefully to the ways that power differentials figure in the social and corporeal assemblages that compose agency. It also departs from previous work in showing the need for a new, nonsovereign exceptionalism in relation to nature and in demonstrating the importance of the new exceptionalism for eco-emancipation. The chapter lays groundwork for the larger argument of the book, setting up the discussion of environmental domination in chapter 3, and providing background for the new frameworks of political respect for nature and eco-responsibility developed in chapters 4 and 5. Above all, it underlies the deep relationality of the freedom envisioned in chapter 6 as eco-emancipation, a freedom that is rooted in the intersubjective, interspecies, ecosystemic assemblages that compose us all.

Chapter 3, "Environmental Domination," develops the book's holistic understanding of domination, which includes the interacting dynamics involved in the human domination of nature and the variegated forms of domination among people that figure in the environmental context. This view draws on contemporary republican theory in arguing that domination involves a status condition that is fundamentally political, rooted in a particular way of situating subjects relative to human power within the field of political institutions, law, and public policy. This status condition is one of systematic vulnerability to insufficiently constrained power and exploitation. To be sure, environmental domination is also tied to cultures of instrumentalization and political economies of extractivism. We shall have plenty to say about culture and political economy as the project unfolds. Yet the political status-condition aspect is crucial, both for understanding how the domination of nature differs from the simple use of it, and for identifying more emancipatory alternatives. It also helps us see the distinction between domination and perfect control, thus making it possible to understand how human beings can be said to dominate nature even as phenomena such as climate change and superbugs demonstrate the limits of human control.

Although the account draws on republican theory in its emphasis on the status-condition aspect of domination and its focus on insufficiently constrained power, it departs from conventional republican views in significant respects. Above all, it extends the political-institutional view of domination to cover the exercise of power by human beings in relation to nonhuman nature. This departure forces modifications to the republican concept of domination and, by extension, to its idea of freedom. In particular, it decenters the role of reflective choice. Domination among people compromises freedom by hindering them in the exercise of their choices, but many parts of nature lack the capacity for reflective choice. For them, being subject to insufficiently constrained human power jeopardizes not freedom as choice but a more general liberty to live on their own terms, meaning to manifest the logics of their diverse existences and to fulfill the purposes (however unreflective) that are distinctive to their kinds, without having their existence distorted or their well-being obstructed by insufficiently constrained, exploitative human power. The capacity for reflective choice is indeed a necessary condition of exercising domination; without it, no institutional framework of insufficiently constrained power nor systems of exploitation could exist. But the capacity for reflective choice is not a necessary condition of being subject to domination.

Another departure from (at least some) republicanism is that the account of environmental domination developed here rejects the model of personal control as the defining dynamic of domination. It holds that domination can be effected through impersonal structural forces through which the well-being of subordinates may be compromised by insufficiently checked power and exploitation, even absent relations of personal control on the traditional models of slavery and despotism, or the personal relations of husband and wife under patriarchy, or employer and worker under unreconstructed capitalism. It also denies that any agent, including those who occupy positions of superiority within human hierarchies, ever has full control over subordinates, given the nonsovereign nature of human agency and the degree to which we are all embedded in prevailing relations of power that shape and constrain our action. Often the dynamics of environmental domination involve people participating in large-scale structural forces that entrap and exploit nature, other people, and themselves, although as individuals they do not control any of it; and they sometimes participate without being aware of their impact.

The integral role that exploitation plays in the meaning of environmental domination as it is developed in these pages also distinguishes the view from at least some republican theory. Exploitation has sometimes been seen as the concern of a very different tradition of political thought, in fact, namely Marx-ism.[28] Although we typically associate exploitation, as Marx did, with the labor sector, where it refers to treating employees "unfairly in order to benefit from their work," the word has a wider life.[29] I mean to use it in a broad sense to include benefiting in a general way at others' expense, or extracting value from others in a way that brings harm to them. To be exploited is to be treated as a mere instrument for the profit or power of another, without regard to one's own well-being. Taken together, these departures are sufficiently deep that it would be a mistake to regard the concept of environmental domination devel-oped here as a republican one, strictly speaking. It draws from republican per-spectives on domination but ultimately reconstructs the concept for new purposes.

Chapter 3 also builds on work in the environmental justice and critical theory literatures to elaborate key aspects of domination among people that arise in the environmental context. Yet it moves beyond that prior work to develop an intersectional approach, one that acknowledges the sometimes cross-cutting ways that environmental domination affects people, and intro-ducing a plural, differentiated account of responsibility that responds to this complexity. The intersectional approach is important because it illuminates not only environmental domination's distinctive effects on people who are poor and marginalized but also the ways it cuts across human hierarchies to confine and exploit all of us, often without our awareness. To the extent that we associate environmental domination exclusively with people who are poor and marginalized, we perpetuate the blind domination of the more privileged populations diagnosed by Horkheimer and Adorno. The reality is that we are all in need of emancipation, even if the precise dynamics of our environmental domination differ. To see this, we must hold multiple realities in view simul-taneously; we must learn to recognize what is common and what is distinctive about how environmental domination affects different human populations, and how it affects nonhuman ones.

Understanding the varied and intersecting dynamics of environmental domination is a necessary step toward emancipation, but understanding alone is not nearly enough, as we shall see in chapter 4, "Political Respect for Na-ture." At the structural level, political respect for nature supplements political respect for persons with institutional mechanisms that formally constrain how human power may be exercised in relation to nonhuman beings and things, and that require us to use our power in ways that are attentive to nature's well-being along with our own, thus interrupting exploitation. And much as respect for persons, when internalized by citizens as part of their shared public ethos, protects against the abuse of power over other people, so a public ethos of respect for nature promises to motivate greater self-restraint and responsiveness in our interpersonal relations with Earth's nonhuman parts. Political respect for nature means acknowledging that nonhuman beings and things count, that they deserve to be treated according to standards of right, that there are principled limitations on how human power may be exercised in relation to them. It means formalizing these limitations in the basic structure of society, and fostering a public sensibility of self-restraint and responsiveness.

Chapter 4 explores what the meaning, experience, and practice of respect in this form could be, drawing inspiration from two very different sources: Kant's normative theory of respect for persons and Levinas's phenomenology of response to the other, which I approach through Jacques Derrida. I take Kant and Levinas as points of departure, but I develop the notion of respect in ways that go beyond both. First, I take up the meaning of respect as involving the Kantian idea that others should count with us always also as ends in themselves, but I reconstruct this idea so as to eschew Kant's focus on the putatively autonomous individual, and to cover nonhuman beings and things as well as people. Next, I examine the experiential dimensions of respect for nature, including the deep existential challenge it poses to us as human beings, given existing conceptual frameworks of human superiority and entitlement. For insight here I draw on Derrida's notion of "abyssal rupture,"[30] along with the Levinasian concepts of alterity and asymmetrical response across difference. Finally, I explore some concrete practices of political respect for nature that combine self-restraint with responsiveness to the well-being of nonhuman others.

As we shall see, respectful interactions are not always harmonious ones. Ecosystems are often violent places, and our relationships with Earth others regularly entail conflict. Respect for nature does not mean the end of this conflict. Nor does it preclude the defense of basic human interests when conflicts arise. It allows for us to defend ourselves against pests and predators, and to provide for our own well-being, even when this requires damage to nonhuman nature. What it rules out is the unreflective degradation of nature for the purpose of satisfying endless consumerist desires and the boundless pursuit of profit, or in thoughtless reaction to the inconveniences that life in a biotic community inevitably imposes on all its members. Respect asks us to bring a more discriminating sensibility to the pursuit of human well-being, and to pair it with attunement and responsiveness to the well-being of Earth others. There will be plenty of conflicts and competing needs here, some of them irreducible. Respect for nature is not a solution to these conflicts but a political approach to navigating them. It asks us to treat human needs and interests as parts of a larger whole that has value, rather than as the only things that have value. To interrupt the destructive dynamics of our environmental domination, we need to establish respect for nature in the political institutions that govern our collective life with one another and with nonhuman beings and things, and to affirm it as a public ethos that is authoritative for us, even imperative for us, as democratic citizens of more-than-human polities.

Along with political respect for nature, moving beyond environmental domination will require new ways of thinking about and practicing responsibility. Our current conceptions of responsibility not only are ill suited to many environmental problems but can be positively disabling insofar as they treat individual intentionality and control as preconditions of responsibility. This way of thinking about responsibility is at odds with the structure of many environmental problems, in which people often contribute to damage without intending to do so or controlling their effects. It also conflicts with the nonsovereign character of human agency itself, and it is inattentive to the differential effects of power on differently placed persons. Chapter 5, "Eco-Responsibility," develops a pluralist approach that enables us to distinguish among types and degrees of responsibility for environmental damage, acknowledging the interacting dynamics of domination, the structural complexity of environmental problems, the nonsovereignty of human agency, and the differential effects of power. It draws on recent work in political theory that seeks more capacious ways to understand responsibility in the context of structural injustice, and it elaborates a new repertoire of responsibility that distinguishes responsibility as *culpability* from responsibility as *accountability* and *responsiveness*, arguing that all three must have a role in the environmental domain.

In addition to changing how we think about responsibility, we need to generate new cultures and practices of responsibility, including networks of what Brooke Ackerly calls "connected activism" in which people purposefully cultivate their ability to respond to environmental domination together with others.[31] Moreover, because existing social epistemologies shape what we think we are responsible for, including what we even regard as a problem requiring a response, we will need to shake up some of our core assumptions about the world and our place(s) in it. Disruptive politics can be an important resource for changing existing cultures of responsibility by forcing us to confront forms of environmental damage and creaturely suffering that have been masked by prevailing epistemologies of ignorance.[32] Disruptive politics can generate social and cognitive crises that open the door to more reflective thinking and to behavioral change.

In this respect, the cultivation of eco-responsibility must build on the diagnostic work undertaken in chapter 3, which makes the dynamics of environmental domination visible and helps us to see and feel the violations it entails. Eco-responsibility also draws support from the analysis pursued in chapter 2, which shines light on the nonsovereignty of agency and illuminates the limitations of traditional views of responsibility, with their emphasis on intentionality and control. Eco-responsibility is nonsovereign responsibility, and it is alive to how power differentials impact agency, but it also has the potential to be empowering for people across the whole spectrum of human hierarchies. It relies as well on efforts to cultivate political respect for nature as described in chapter 4, which reorient our sensibilities toward nonhuman beings and things, shifting us away from the mere instrumentalization of Earth others toward forms of use and engagement that incorporate greater responsiveness to their well-being. Yet even as eco-responsibility builds on ideas developed in other parts of the book, it also supports them; these different dimensions of ecological emancipation are reciprocally reinforcing. The practice of eco-responsibility generates learning about nonhuman nature and the human place in nature, and it cultivates capacity for change on the part of nonsovereign human individuals and more-than-human communities. In doing so, it makes us better able to respond with respect to the needs of Earth others, human and nonhuman, to resist domination in its various guises, and to create more emancipatory forms of political relationship.

Chapter 6, "Ecological Emancipation," explores what these more emancipatory forms of relationship might look like, and how the freedom they generate might feel. I use the language of emancipation to characterize this freedom because of the conceptual and historical associations between emancipation and domination. To experience emancipation is to gain release from the dynamics of insufficiently checked power and exploitation that constitute domination. The language is familiar to us from the historical struggles of American slaves before abolition, of the working class under industrial capitalism, and of women subjected under patriarchy to the tutelage of husbands and fathers. I do not mean to equate these different forms of domination with one another or with the environmental domination of nature and people. Each one entails its own unique violations and forms of suffering. Still, they share a structural similarity insofar as all are marked by a status condition of systematic vulnerability to insufficiently checked power and exploitation. In each of these contexts, emancipation was conceived as a release from domination based on a change in the structural conditions of life, such as the systems of property law, economic production, and the patriarchal family. To be sure, people who struggled for emancipation in all these contexts knew, or came to understand, that the formal change in status that constituted abolition or the collectivization of property or women's enfranchisement was not by itself sufficient to release them from domination. Emancipation includes not only a change in formal status but a transformation of selves and a shift in the wider interpersonal relations that constitute culture and society. To speak of *ecological* emancipation is to focus on how the liberation of people from environmental domination is inextricably entwined with the liberation of nonhuman beings and things and the networks of interdependence that make up ecosystems.

It is true that the ideal of freedom, at least in certain guises, has often been invoked by people to justify or excuse many forms of environmental damage as well as practices that impose great suffering on nonhuman animals, even to sustain environmental domination. When freedom is equated with unfettered property rights, for example, or limitless consumer choice, it tends to end in the exploitation of Earth others. Still, not every form of freedom ends in domination, and some of them are very much worth having. We are not wrong to care about freedom; in fact, caring about it is crucial to remediating our environmental problems. Yet we need to understand it differently. Freedom as eco-emancipation consists in continuing practices of worldmaking in tandem with human and nonhuman others, practices that embody new institutional constraints and extra-institutional mobilizations. These constraints and mobilizations are geared toward limiting how human power may be exercised over nature and people, and toward more inclusive incorporation for all. Emancipation also includes political respect for nature and persons along with a culture of responsibility that makes us accountable and responsive to a wide range of others, both human and nonhuman. And even as it orients us in new ways to the more-than-human world, it avoids resting the emancipation of nature on the domination of certain groups of people. Once again, eco-emancipation does not promise perfect harmony, either among persons or between people and nature. What it promises is release from the entrapment and exploitation that constitute environmental domination; it prevents us as human beings both from exercising domination in this form and from suffering it.

Eco-emancipation will affect differently positioned people in different ways, and it will affect human beings differently from other parts of nature. It is a plural, diversified phenomenon in this sense. Moreover, the freedom it entails is a nonsovereign kind of freedom. Instead of individual or collective mastery, eco-emancipation unfolds through relations of interdependence across individuals, communities, and types of being. And while it does involve greater influence over the human forces that shape our lives and affect the Earth, this influence is far from an experience of perfect control. Emancipation always coexists with uncertainty and precarity (our own and that of others), and it is marked by continuing contestation among the members of the more-than-human communities it sustains. Then too, emancipation is never complete because domination is a permanent possibility of power. We live on a continuum in which domination and emancipation are perpetually in play, which means that there is always work to be done and that we regularly face irresolvable remainders, but also that there is ever a reasonable hope of progress toward greater liberation. Envisioning what this liberation could be—its meaning, its mobilizations, its institutions—can help us make good on that hope. Chapter 6 lays out the meaning of ecological emancipation as combining a status condition of nondomination with political respect for nature and a culture of eco-responsibility, and it explores the plural, nonsovereign character of emancipation in this form. The chapter then takes up techniques for mobilizing eco-emancipation and examines some political, economic, and cultural mechanisms for institutionalizing it.

Each of the book's chapters engages a concept that has been fundamental to political theory in the modern West—agency, domination, respect, responsibility, emancipation—and reconfigures it in ways that serve the goal of theorizing freer forms of more-than-human political community. I draw on existing work for this purpose, sometimes on work that has been highly influential in the field, such as Kant and Levinas on respect, Philip Pettit on domination, Hannah Arendt and Jane Bennett on agency, Iris Young on responsibility, Hardt and Negri on emancipation. Yet in each instance I develop the concept in ways not envisioned by the people I draw from, often in ways that they might reject. I also rework the concepts to apply to our relationships with nonhuman beings and things, and this reworking frequently requires of the reader a certain exercise of imagination, sometimes even a leap of faith. I have found this combination of invoking the familiar, on the one hand, and calling for imagination and leaps of faith, on the other, to be unavoidable in theorizing novel types of human/more-than-human relations. Nothing runs deeper in the social epistemologies of the modern West than the subordination of the nonhuman to the human. This subordination is so pervasive in our conceptual frameworks that it saturates the very language we have for talking about it. This makes it a real challenge to articulate in ways that are legible within our current terms of reference a genuinely different vision of human/nonhuman relationship. The method I have adopted is to begin with something familiar and then work it, like clay, to see what shape it might take when extended beyond our human-dominant frames.[33] In being worked this way, the concepts have all come out in the end meaning something different from what they meant at the beginning.

I hope that the novel ways of thinking about agency, domination, respect, responsibility, and emancipation that are introduced here will have a life beyond the environmental context. They seem to me to offer promise for understanding other important problems in political theory, including structural injustice, oppression, sovereignty, and irresolvable conflict, among other things. Perhaps the concept whose reconstruction here has the widest significance is the concept of political community itself. *Eco-Emancipation* challenges an assumption that has been constitutive of the field since its inception in ancient Greece, namely that the political domain is an exclusively human one. The book joins with other recent work in environmental political theory to contest this constitutive assumption by imagining more-than-human forms of political order, and by helping us to see them as genuine possibilities—and emancipatory ones.

The aim of *Eco-Emancipation* is partly critical in the critical-theory sense of excavating and unmasking hidden realities. It means to uncover the deep dynamics of domination that currently undergird human relationships with nonhuman beings and things, dynamics that saturate and define the structure of human power in most contemporary democratic societies. It means to reveal the illegitimacy of these dynamics, to help us see that the emperor has no clothes on, that our naked assertion of power in relation to nonhuman nature is nothing more than a naked assertion of power. It is intended to awaken us, as Socrates put it, from a dogmatic slumber that makes us oblivious to the true character of our way of life and to the harms it effects. The book also means to sting those of us who are relatively privileged and prosperous into an awareness of our own subjugation, to make us feel our confinement and exploitation at the hands of the same forces that ravage the Earth for profit and power, often in our names and with our support. It means to generate an awareness in us that environmental domination affects us too, that it is not only the poor and the marginalized whose bodies, minds, and futures are being instrumentalized by the toxic products, production processes, and waste that are the basic, inescapable conditions of modern human existence today. In this sense, the book aims to provoke not only a certain shame about our usurpations but even more an indignation at our subjugation. It also means to illuminate the roles we play, often unwittingly or unwillingly, in perpetuating these dynamics. Its objective is less to blame people for what human beings have done to the Earth than to awaken us, as human beings, to how what we do figures in the forces that now sustain environmental domination, including our own.

In addition to this critical aim, *Eco-Emancipation* has an aspirational one. It points us to new ways of structuring (and contesting) human power, and to new forms of political community that could help reverse environmental domination and enable freer ways of life. It is true that the forces sustaining environmental domination are large and powerful, and the environmental problems they generate are tremendously complex. There is nothing surprising about how helpless so many of us feel in the face of these forces. Still, part of the emancipatory promise of the project is to remind us that our complicity in these forces is also their vulnerability. Because the political, economic, and cultural systems that sustain environmental domination depend in the end on participation by all of us, they are ultimately subject to our influence. This influence is not the same thing as sovereign control, and it can be exercised only through coordinated action and sustained effort. The fact of our influence should not be taken to imply that making change is easy; nothing could be further from the truth, as the persistence and acceleration of our environmental problems demonstrate. Yet *Eco-Emancipation* means to inspire us to take up the challenge by making the case that the current terms of our existence are not as intractable as they seem.

Admittedly, the project is also aspirational in the further sense that it cannot promise us success. In fact, because we can begin to make change only from within the context of our current condition, which is a condition of pervasive domination, even our best efforts, taken separately, are bound to be limited in how much impact they have. Struggles for liberation typically unfold over the course of a *longue durée*, and they usually include losses and periods of retrenchment. Liberation is an iterative and uncertain process, and no single effort or initiative could ever take us all the way to the finish line. In truth, there is no finish line when it comes to getting free of environmental domination. The impulse to subordinate and exploit, to take from the Earth and from other people without being responsive to their well-being, is likely to be with us indefinitely. If the dream of fully eradicating these impulses is unrealistic, however, we can reasonably hope to contain and redress them with the right institutional arrangements and forms of civic engagement, and by nurturing a political ethos of respect and new cultures of responsibility.

Eco-Emancipation is aspirational as well as critical, then, because in addition to awakening us it means to activate us—for the long, precarious, and always-unfinished business of making better, freer political communities. And although the freer way of life it aims for cannot be guaranteed, the approach it offers is firmly rooted in reality. Rather than asking us to disengage from nature, it helps us to rethink and reconstruct the interactions that we cannot help but have with the other members of our Earthly home. And instead of focusing narrowly on piecemeal efforts at greater sustainability—carbon cap-and-trade schemes, for instance, or geo-engineering, or personal recycling—*Eco-Emancipation* puts us in touch with the deeper, broader dynamics that generate environmental domination in all its forms, and guides us to the kinds of comprehensive changes that could make a real difference. In this sense, the project of eco-emancipation points us to a radical reconstruction of selves and societies. Yet however aspirational it may be, the project rests on a clear-eyed assessment of our situation and a realistic understanding of what is actually needed to transform it: a politics of nondomination for people and the Earth, an Earthly politics of freedom.

2

A New Exceptionalism

THE DOMINATION OF NONHUMAN beings and things by people has long been underwritten by a form of exceptionalism grounded in a particular ideal of human agency, a way of understanding agency that sets us apart from and above the rest of nature. This ideal locates agency within the individual subject, in the inner faculties of reason and will. It identifies agency with the exercise of intentional choice, rational control over action, and self-determination. Agency so conceived is a kind of personal sovereignty in which the meaning and impact of one's action is determined by the content of one's will rather than by instinct, circumstance, or the wills of others. As such, agency purportedly frees us from the mechanistic determinism often said to characterize the natural world, and it gives us both the capacity and the right to govern ourselves—and everything else. It makes us (and only us) ends in ourselves, uniquely entitled to moral consideration and political standing. This familiar ideal of agency as personal sovereignty sets the boundaries of moral and political belonging in a way that requires constraints on power over people but justifies human beings in exercising relatively unconstrained power in relation to nature.

However familiar, this ideal is deeply misleading. It neglects human agency's distributed, intersubjective character, the fact that agency cannot be located exclusively within the individual, in inner faculties such as reason and will, nor reduced to personal control over action. Agency does involve inner faculties, but it also extends beyond these faculties to include the social and material exchanges that bring our willed initiatives to fruition in the world, meaning exchanges with other people and with nonhuman parts of the material world. Agency has what David Abram calls a "porosity" that makes each agent like "an open circuit that completes itself only in things, in others, in the surrounding earth."[1] This porosity and dependence on others, both human and nonhuman, means that action is never reducible to the agent's willed intentions or even contained within the boundaries of the self. Agency exceeds the individual will and eludes individual control. It is a robust but, as Hannah Arendt said, nonsovereign experience.[2]

The porosity of agency disrupts the old exceptionalism with its strict, hierarchical divide between human beings and the rest of nature. If agency arises through circuits of vitality that include and depend on nonhuman aspects of the material environment, then human agents can hardly claim to stand apart from and above this environment. Human beings do have some distinctive capacities not shared by many other parts of nature, and this distinctiveness is significant insofar as it makes us subject to ethical and political accountability in special ways. But to acknowledge this distinctiveness is a far cry from insisting on a strict, hierarchical divide between human beings and everything else on Earth. We depend on the Earth to provide more than just a field of opportunity for the exercise of our agency. We depend on it as a vital, contributing source in the composition of agency, the very thing that supposedly sets us apart. Understanding the nonsovereignty of human agency thus dispels the illusion that we stand outside and above the natural world, and it is an important step in moving beyond the old exceptionalism that has justified environmental domination.

The old exceptionalism is also troubled by the fact that many nonhuman beings have agentic capacities in some measure. Not all things are agents, of course. Agency involves intentionality and a sense of self, even if it is not reducible to the exercise of will. It also includes norm responsiveness, the ability not only to act but to orient one's action with reference to norms, which may include standards of right and conceptions of the good. Intentionality, the sense of self, and norm responsiveness require consciousness and reflexivity. These capabilities exist in varying degrees across multiple species, or so the literature on animal studies suggests. Current research documents a spectrum of agentic capacities among higher primates, for instance, as well as many other mammals and birds.[3] Consequently, it makes sense to see agency as existing on a continuum that includes different levels of complexity, varying degrees of consciousness and reflexivity, and diverse forms of expression.

The point of recognizing the nonsovereignty of human agency and the agency of some nonhuman beings is not to deny that there are real differences between human and more-than-human parts of nature, including differences that are relevant in certain ways to moral status and political standing. Nor is the objective to seek moral and political inclusion for nonhuman nature by attributing agency to it. I do mean to extend moral and political inclusion to nonhuman nature, but not (or not only) by insisting that it has agency. Agency is not the only basis for being entitled to respect, to responsible treatment, and to emancipation from human-generated domination. We should treat nature with respect and responsibility, and we should seek its emancipation, not because all nature is agentic—or not solely on the condition that it manifests agency—but because the being of nature's nonhuman parts exceeds their use value to people. Nature is not *for us* in any morally or politically meaningful sense; it just is. Nonhuman parts of nature are ends in themselves in this regard even when they are not agents. We shall have more to say about this in chapter 4.

My point for now is that the realities of human and more-than-human agency cannot support the old exceptionalism once thought to justify the human domination of nature. At the same time, however, these realities do require us to acknowledge some differences between people and other parts of nature, even point us to a new kind of human exceptionalism. This new exceptionalism resists the moral disregard and political exclusion of nonhuman beings and things, but it also refuses to treat all things as if they were the same. In particular, the new exceptionalism envisioned here acknowledges the distinctive ways that human agency has fostered environmental domination and insists on the special role that human agency must play in overcoming it.

The chapter begins by exploring the link between the sovereigntist ideal of agency and the old exceptionalism, as a claim to the moral superiority of human beings over Earth others and a justification for their political exclusion. I draw on recent work by George Kateb to illustrate the old exceptionalism, in part because Kateb's account offers an unusually sophisticated version of that exceptionalism, and also because, despite his defense of human superiority, Kateb means to foster greater care for the Earth. Yet the conventional conception of human agency on which Kateb's view rests is blind to the nonsovereignty of agency—its socially and materially distributed character—and to the agentic capacities of many nonhuman animals. The second part of the chapter diagnoses the difficulties inherent in the sovereigntist way of understanding agency and lays out an alternative, nonsovereign, and more-than-human account, one that takes seriously the porosity of agency and situates it within the broader context of human and nonhuman assemblages. The third part shows how the right understanding of nonsovereign agency opens up a new, more widely liberatory human exceptionalism, one that is both necessary and perilous for eco-emancipation. The chapter concludes with brief reflections on how best to proceed in the face of these necessary perils. The new exceptionalism and the nonsovereign account of agency on which it rests are important presuppositions of the larger argument of *Eco-Emancipation*. Going forward, they will help us to make sense of the entwined but distinct meanings that environmental domination holds for people and for nature; to think in productive new ways about the respect and responsibility we owe to nonhuman others; and to see why the freedom promised by eco-emancipation is so deeply relational, meaning rooted in the overlapping constellations of intersubjective, interspecies, ecosystemic assemblages that enable us all, human and nonhuman, to be who we are and do what we do.

The Old Exceptionalism and the Limits of Sovereignty

George Kateb's *Human Dignity* is a powerful example of how agency has been mobilized to justify moral hierarchy between human beings and the rest of nature, and to explain the political exclusion of nonhuman beings and things. The book is intended to fortify practices of human rights by shoring up their theoretical foundations, and the heart of the project is the very reasonable aspiration to defend decency among people. Yet Kateb is convinced that the only way to achieve this aspiration is to tie the equal *status* of persons relative to one another to what he calls the high *stature* of human beings relative to everything else on Earth. Decency among persons, in other words, requires the subordination of nonhuman nature. The idea of human dignity itself entails this subordination, according to Kateb. The "core idea of human dignity," he says, is that "humanity is the greatest type of beings" on Earth and that every human being "deserves to be treated in a manner consonant with the high worth of the species."[4] In other words, "all [human] individuals are equal; no other species is equal to humanity. These are the two basic propositions that make up the concept of human dignity."[5] Importantly, the two propositions are not themselves equal. The second is foundational to the first in the sense that "conceptually, human stature precedes individual status; the greatness of humanity precedes the equality of the species."[6] This precedence means that the two propositions cannot be prized apart. To support human equality, on Kateb's view, is necessarily to assert human superiority.

The basis of human superiority, according to Kateb, is human agency.[7] Agency involves individual creativity, "the will to break with what has gone before, to try what has not been tried before, . . . to start on a different path altogether."[8] Kateb connects this creativity, following Rousseau, to "the ability either to succumb to or to resist nature's command, which a human being experiences as a resistible pressure."[9] By contrast, "all other animals succumb without choice to whatever nature commands; they can resist no pressure, no urge that comes from within them in the course of coping with what is outside them."[10] This capacity for creative resistance to instinct is very much an individual phenomenon, according to Kateb, grounded in the "inwardness" of the individuated human self with its capacities for reason, self-consciousness, and will.[11] Agency so conceived establishes "humanity's partial discontinuity with nature," meaning that humanity is "significantly not natural."[12] This break with nature makes humanity "the highest species on earth."[13] In view of their agency, then, human beings "matter existentially more than members of all other species" because "in being partly and commendably non-natural, a human being has an incomparably higher status than any animal."[14]

Although Kateb thinks that human beings stand (partly) outside nature and are superior to it, the final section of the book makes the case that we should serve nature as its stewards.[15] We must abandon "the human prejudice that animals and the rest of nature exist solely for human use" and instead seek their "preservation" by "drastically controlling the growth in human population, and practicing radically new forms of human abstemiousness."[16] Moreover, we should cultivate "sympathy and fellow feeling" for nature, qualities that sublimate our "species snobbery" and "ease the way to appreciation and admiration" for the nonhuman.[17] Kateb acknowledges that stewardship of nature "may necessitate restrictions on doing what one wants and living as one likes," and that restrictions such as population control may put pressure on certain human rights.[18] Yet if such restraints may sometimes compromise the human rights that instantiate dignity as equal status among persons, they help to sustain dignity as the high stature of the human species as a whole. For "preserving nature is the greatest achievement" that humanity can attain, "the purest and also most urgent expression of human stature."[19]

However welcome the effort to elicit greater concern for nature may be, the idea that human beings stand apart from and above nature in the way that Kateb insists on is little more than a wishful desire. He acknowledges as much when he says of human agency that "I would like to see it as a tremendous break with animal consciousness, as a tremendous break with nature altogether, perhaps the greatest one."[20] Yet throughout the book this wishful desire is treated as fact. It also reflects a lack of information about other species, as when Kateb asserts that "instincts, impulses, and reflexes together with appetites and drives seem to define exhaustively . . . all other creaturely species but humanity," ignoring reams of research on nonhuman animals reported over the last generation.[21] Above all, Kateb's exceptionalism rests on a misunderstanding of human agency, one that is widespread in philosophy and political theory.[22] It assumes that agency is an inner faculty of the individual, located in the exercise of reason and will, and associates agency with intentional choice and control over action. This way of conceiving agency misses agency's fundamentally distributed structure, meaning the ways it is composed through social and material processes that exceed not only the inner faculty of will but the very boundaries of the individual self.[23] Agency does require the exercise of will in the form of individual initiative, but it does not end there because agency involves actually doing things, making things happen, with real impact and effect. The efficacy aspect of agency distinguishes it from mere willing, and it makes the social and material processes that sustain efficacy as much a part of agency as individual initiatives are.

The dual character of agency as involving both initiative and efficacy means that agency cannot be reduced to an inner faculty. Our effects depend as much on how the world receives and responds to our initiatives as they do on our personal will and intentions. This is not to say that agency exists *only* in its reception, as distinct from the intentions and initiatives of the individual. The point is rather to locate agency in the interaction between individual initiative and the forms of uptake that shape how this initiative affects the world. Our deeds are always a function of how our intentions and initiatives interact with the responses they provoke. Agency is a dynamic, interactive phenomenon with widely extended sources that include but are not limited to the individual subject. It involves intersubjective and intercorporeal exchanges, not solely faculties such as the will that are internal to a particular individual, or what Kateb calls an individual's "inwardness."[24]

The stakes involved in how we understand agency are high. For one thing, when we equate agency narrowly with intentional choice and control over action, we make it difficult to establish accountability for social dynamics to which individuals contribute without intending to do so and without controlling the outcomes. This applies to dynamics such as systemic oppression, implicit bias, and the frequently impersonal exploitation involved in globalized production processes. It also applies to outcomes such as climate change and other forms of environmental degradation. In all these cases, outcomes exceed the control of any particular individual, and they often result from effects that are unintentional and even unconscious at the individual level. If we did not consciously intend to discriminate or exploit or pollute, we think, and if we did not have personal control over these outcomes, then they could not be a product of our agency, and so they could not be our fault.

Yet dynamics such as these persist only because many people contribute to sustaining them, however partially or unintentionally, and these contributions embody agency in varying degrees and forms. Nowhere are these dynamics more evident than in the context of environmental domination, as we shall see in chapter 3. They will not change unless we hold ourselves and one another accountable for acting differently, and in particular for creating more emancipatory political relationships and institutional forms. We cannot do this so long as we believe that our agency, which is the source of our accountability, lies solely in activity that we intended and controlled. So in addition to justifying a form of human exceptionalism that promotes the domination of nature, our sovereigntist ways of thinking about agency tend to undercut the accountability needed to uphold standards of right and to generate effective political change in the face of violations, including the violations involved in environmental domination.

Another consequence of the sovereigntist ideal, somewhat ironically, is to undermine our sense of possibility, our confidence in being able to make things happen, our faith that we can affect the conditions of our own coexistence. Because we do not appreciate the socially and materially distributed character of agency, we do not recognize the importance of nurturing the social and material formations that help compose it. Even as the forces governing our lives have grown larger, more complex, and more impersonal, we have neglected the infrastructure of associational life, social movements, and mutuality with more-than-human beings and things that human agency needs to flourish. The result is a widespread sense of disempowerment. In the environmental context, this means that however much we may wish to live more sustainably or to opt out of environmental domination, many of us feel impotent in the face of forces that so clearly dwarf us and exceed our control. Whatever we do or eat or buy, we find ourselves simultaneously participating in the despoiling of nature and suffering its effects—in superbugs and rising seas, or tapped-out water sources and air that is too polluted to safely breathe. We know that our individual efforts to resist these forces—through recycling, for example, or alternative energy use, or animal advocacy—have negligible effects and sometimes generate additional, unintended damage. We feel weak and ineffectual because we *are* weak and ineffectual in the face of forces such as global capitalism and increasingly nondemocratic states. And we are weak and ineffectual as individuals because the social and material conditions needed to sustain our agency have been eroded concurrently with the immense growth in the scale and power of impersonal economic and political forces.

Because we think of agency in terms of personal sovereignty, we have failed to protect the sources that nourish it, and a result is the growing sense of impotence pervading so many democratic peoples today, a lost confidence in our own efficacy. This loss goes together with our impaired capacity for accountability. They are twin casualties of our sovereigntist assumptions about agency. Eco-emancipation, like a healthy democracy, depends on citizens who have both a robust sense of accountability and confidence in their own political efficacy, but neither one can flourish without the right conditions. Creating the right conditions begins with understanding the nonsovereign structure of human (and other) agency. And when we understand the nonsovereignty of agency, the old exceptionalism begins to crumble.

Nonsovereign Agency

Agency as a socially distributed phenomenon. The notion of nonsovereign agency was first introduced by Hannah Arendt.[25] As she puts it in *The Human Condition*, there are "two parts" to any action, "the beginning made by a single person and the achievement in which many join by 'bearing' and 'finishing' the enterprise, by seeing it through."[26] Action begins with individual initiative, an effort to start something new through which the agent reveals his or her distinctive identity. Yet personal initiative is not the whole of action because action "needs the surrounding presence of others" to have an impact; and impact on the world is a defining feature of action.[27] Other people therefore contribute to an individual's action as "co-actors" who help bring "the actual achievement" of this individual's "enterprise" to fruition.[28] In the same way that a leader's initiatives depend for their impact on the responses of his or her followers, so the efforts of any individual rely on a community of "bearers" to sustain their efficacy. Arendt insists for this reason that an agent "is never merely a 'doer' but always and at the same time a sufferer," for "the story that an act starts is composed of its consequent deeds and sufferings," meaning the way that the initiative is interpreted and taken up by others to determine its actual impact on the world.[29] The responses that other people have to our initiatives powerfully affect the impacts we have on the world, and consequently they shape what it is that we have actually done. They help to transform our initiatives into actual outcomes and thus to compose our action.[30]

The social uptake that helps constitute agency is subject to the "wills and intentions" of other people, and hence it is never fully within the control of the individual agent nor always consistent with the agent's intentions.[31] In view of agency's dependence on social uptake that eludes the control and may exceed the intentions of the agent, Arendt characterized agency as an aspect of "human non-sovereignty,"[32] meaning that it cannot be captured by the idea of sovereignty as control, or "uncompromising self-sufficiency and mastership."[33] Because agency is more than mere willing, because it involves real action and impact on the world, which makes it dependent on the interpretations and responses of other people, agency can never be reduced to a particular individual's willed intentions, or even contained within the boundaries of the individual self. Agency is a socially distributed phenomenon in this sense.

Much of the time, agency's dependence on social uptake is invisible to us because uptake is normally forthcoming, at least for those whose identities and initiatives are recognizable within prevailing norms of discourse and relations of power. That is, we regularly function as the bearers for one another's agency in Arendt's sense, meaning that we respond to one another's initiatives in ways that help to establish their impact on the world. When I step up to the lectern on the first day of class, my students recognize this initiative as an effort to begin the course, and they (generally) respond accordingly. In the absence of their enabling response, my effort to begin the course could not come to fruition, and my agency would be frustrated. Likewise, when I approach the counter to swipe my credit card at the grocery store, the clerk knows exactly what I am trying to accomplish and responds in a way that facilitates it. Societies are set up to provide just this kind of uptake, at least for those who are privileged. Agency thus arises through the complex interaction of personal intentions with the communicative exchanges, background meanings, and social responses through which one's initiatives come to be manifest in one's effects.

The deep relationality of agency means that our deeds do not always track the intentions that motivated our initiatives; agency often reverberates in ways that take it beyond the initiatives of the agent and elude the agent's personal control.[34] Consequently, the nonsovereignty of agency tends to extend the breadth of our accountability. Consider Oedipus, for example, whose tragic misery consists in the fact that he holds himself accountable for deeds that were, in an important sense, unintended. He did not mean to have sex with his mother and murder his father, and yet the reason for his misery is that he understands these actions as his own, however unintended they may have been. He recognizes that his agency extends beyond his will, and beyond the impacts that he intended and controlled. In a similar way, we commonly acknowledge the fact of implicit bias in which people perpetuate norms of racism and sexism without meaning to do so: a woman who unconsciously grasps her handbag more firmly as a young Black man approaches her on the sidewalk; or the male colleague who hears the good idea in a group discussion as having come from another man instead of from the woman who actually voiced it. People are regularly the agents of racism and sexism without meaning to discriminate, given the ways that our individual initiatives and the uptake they generate interact with background meanings and relations of power.

We can identify with Oedipus and unwitting racists and sexists because we see, as Bernard Williams once said, "that in the story of one's life there is an authority exercised by what one has done, and not merely by what one has intentionally done."[35] The nonsovereignty of human agency extends the bounds of personal accountability beyond the will, and beyond outcomes that we intend and control. In this sense, agency has a wider reach than we often realize, or reaches more widely than we may wish to admit.[36] Accepting the enlarged scope of accountability that nonsovereign agency entails is a necessary condition of decent democratic politics and emancipatory political change, including emancipation from environmental domination.[37]

At the same time, agency's nonsovereignty also makes it more precarious than we often assume, especially in relation to social inequality. If agency's socially distributed character is often invisible to those who are privileged, this aspect of agency is keenly felt by people who are marginalized. Indeed, agency's dependence on social uptake may be clearest in cases where uptake is missing. Systematic inequality disrupts the social interpretation of individual initiatives on the part of marginalized people, undermining the community of bearers required to sustain effective action and generating widespread failures of agency.[38] James Baldwin's "Notes of a Native Son" vividly illustrates the precarity of agency in contexts of social inequality. "To be a negro," Baldwin writes, "meant that one was never looked at but was simply at the mercy of the reflexes [that] the color of one's skin caused in other people."[39] Describing his experience one year working and living in New Jersey "among southerners," he says that "I acted in New Jersey as I had always acted, that is as though I thought a great deal of myself . . . with results that were, simply, unbelievable."[40] Because his demeanor was so much at odds with social expectations for Black men, he immediately "earned the enmity . . . of all my superiors and co-workers."[41] They really believed, he says, "that I was mad."[42] He was eventually fired and run out of town. The result of having his initiatives interpreted through the lens of racial stigma and stereotypes was that Baldwin consistently found himself "doing" things that he never intended and could not identify with: "I simply did not know what was happening. I did not know what I had done."[43]

Racism frustrated his agency by distorting the background of social meanings against which his initiatives were read and taken up by others, thus making it impossible for these initiatives to come to fruition in his deeds, and attributing deeds to him that were at odds with the actions he initiated and with his own sense of himself. Likewise, women whose demeanors fail to conform to conventional norms of feminine deference frequently find themselves provoking effects, such as hostility and resistance, that at are odds with their initiatives and that impede their efficacy, generating similar failures of agency. Experiences like these are well known to people who are marginalized or members of subordinate groups. In view of agency's nonsovereignty, subtle dynamics of social uptake and non-uptake affect agency in ways that are extremely powerful, however invisible (to the privileged) and difficult to articulate they may be.

It is important to see that the failures of agency arising under conditions of social inequality are not simply a function of an agent's intentions being out of step with his or her effects. As the examples of Oedipus and the unwitting racist and sexist demonstrate, our effects can exceed our intentions without necessarily undoing our agency. The failures of agency that we see in people like Baldwin and nondeferential women involve a background of systematic and unjust social inequality that makes it impossible for others to see them in their initiatives and to respond to the actions they begin in ways that could help sustain their efficacy. In such cases, the responses of others distort or impede the impact of the agents' efforts, and consequently what they are thought by others to have done is not anything that affirms their actual initiatives or discloses their identities. They cannot see themselves in their impact because this impact is shaped by a background of stigma and bias that obstructs and distorts who they actually are and what they are trying to do. Oedipus, by contrast, did see himself in his unintended deeds, hence his misery; his agency was never in question. Against a background of systematic inequality, however, agency is often troubled.[44] This explains why the sovereigntist injunction to pull yourself up by your bootstraps is a losing proposition. It locates agency solely in the individual will, ignoring agency's socially distributed character. It fails to acknowledge that empowering individuals means changing the background conditions that undo their agency and creating new communities of bearers who can help bring it to fruition.

Thus even as our impact on the world can sometimes exceed our intentions, thereby extending our efficacy in ways we may not expect, so our impact also can fall short when our actions fail to manifest our initiatives and identities, thus disabling agency. These are among the dynamics that the Black Lives Matter movement has tried to illuminate. The backgrounds of racialized social meaning against which the actions of Black men and women are interpreted in police encounters in the United States have a powerful impact on their efficacy, on how they actually affect the world. These backgrounds and the forms of social uptake they foster interact with individual initiative in ways that too often turn deadly. As a college student, I did door-to-door fund-raising for a Naderesque nonprofit. One night when we were working in an affluent, white suburb of Boston, one of the other fund-raisers (a young Black man I'll call David) was late for his pickup. When he finally arrived, sauntering casually up to the car, the field manager said to him, "David, if you're going to be late and keep us all waiting you could at least hustle a little and run to the car." David replied, "If I run in this neighborhood people will think I just stole their TV, and you'll be picking me up at the police station." David knew that for him to run in that neighborhood was not simply to move quickly but to arouse suspicion and invite incarceration. Arousing suspicion and inviting incarceration were not separate from the act of running, in his mind, but part of it. He understood that his agency was a function of the interaction between his initiatives and the social uptake they generated. In this case, that uptake was not only at odds with his intentions but blind to who he really was as an individual because it was based on racial stigma and bias.

Black Lives Matter shines light on these dynamics. The resistance that the movement has generated is in part a function of how much we misunderstand the nature of human agency, how deep our sovereigntist assumptions run. To insist, with opponents of the movement, that "all lives matter" is to obfuscate the fact that the interaction of individual initiative with social uptake has differential effects on agency in contexts of entrenched inequality. If agency were sovereign, we would not need to worry about what actually happens to it in the presence of stigma and bias. Because we assume it *is* sovereign, we resist the transformative work that Black Lives Matter is asking us to do. A nonsovereign approach helps us see the ways that agency can be both more potent and more precarious than we often assume, and it presses us to attend to the broader context of intersubjective dynamics needed to sustain agency.

Agency as a materially distributed phenomenon. The nonsovereignty of agency also includes the ways in which agency is materially or corporeally distributed, meaning that our efficacy results in part from how our initiatives interact with the material world and the many vitalities of nonhuman beings and things. In exploring this dimension of agency we must move beyond Arendt, who did not theorize the role of nonhuman nature in the composition of human action. For her, the nonsovereignty of agency was a (human) social phenomenon, not an intercorporeal one.[45] The literatures on new materialism in political theory and philosophy offer valuable resources here, although we shall see that there are reasons to be selective in what we appropriate from them. The new materialisms help us see that what we typically experience as individual agency is in fact composed of an "assemblage" that includes not only other people but also what Jane Bennett calls material "actants."[46] As Bennett puts it, "the productive power behind effects is always a collectivity," and the collectivities that help compose agency encompass more than just human beings.[47]

In one sense, the materially distributed character of agency is obvious. When I speak, the formation of sound that I initiate with my vocal chords, my breath, and my lips can have an impact only because of the vibration of molecules in the media (liquids, solids, gasses) through which the sound waves I generate move. Without the movement of molecules through media, my agency in this instance could not come to fruition. Likewise, when I sit down to eat breakfast, the chair at the kitchen table holds me up while gravity holds me down. The verb "holds" expresses something real here, which is that there are physical forces doing things in and around us all the time, things that interact with our initiatives in ways that can either support or obstruct them. Matter is not inert but full of vitality, and its vitalities interact with our initiatives to constitute our agency in ways that we do not fully control or always understand.[48]

Ecologist Aldo Leopold's "land ethic" was alive to this interaction. As he puts it, "many historical events, hitherto explained solely in terms of human enterprise, were actually biotic interactions between people and the land."[49] He cites as an example the settling of the American South and Midwest. Whereas historians debate about the relative influence of American pioneers, French and English traders, and Native Americans, Leopold draws our attention to the contributions of the soil. Specifically, he wants us

to ponder the fact that the cane-lands, when subjected to the particular mixture of forces represented by the cow, plow, fire, and axe of the pioneer, became bluegrass. What if the plant succession inherent in this dark and bloody ground had, under the impact of these forces, given us some worthless sedge, shrub, or weed? Would Boone and Kenton have held out? Would there have been any overflow into Ohio, Indiana, Illinois, and Missouri? Any Louisiana Purchase? Any transcontinental union of new states? Any Civil War?[50]

In short, he says, "the plant succession steered the course of history" as much as the initiatives of human beings did.[51] Or more precisely, "what the human actors in this drama tried to do" depended for its efficacy "in large degree on the reaction of particular soils to the impact of the particular forces exerted by their occupancy."[52] What the people did—and hence their agency—was a product of this interaction. Their agency exceeded their wills and transgressed the boundaries of their persons, even the boundaries of their species. When Leopold speaks of "land as a community," he is pushing us to acknowledge that our agency is an assemblage and that the Earth provides some of its most important bearers.[53]

Similarly, Steven Vogel emphasizes that the human ability to have an impact on the world depends on nonhuman material things and forces that always retain an element of "wildness" insofar as they exceed our full understanding and control. One cannot "hammer without the force of gravity," for example, or bake bread "without relying on complex biochemical processes taking place within millions of yeast cells."[54] These natural forces and processes are constitutive components of our agency. While it is true that the material world also "comes to be what it is through our actions ... at the same time, our actions are absolutely *of the world,*" meaning that our agency is partly composed through "the operation of forces that [we] are ... unable to master, to predict, or even fully to understand."[55]

Some of these forces and nonhuman organisms operate within us as well, as in the microbiota that "help compose the body and cultivate its agency," as Elizabeth Anker puts it.[56] The human microbiome "refers to the trillions of nonhuman microorganisms living inside and around the human body, forming distinct ecosystems in the gut" and other parts of us from the nose to the toes.[57] Different compositions of microbiota have been shown to "dispose hosts to particular affective states," influencing feelings, thoughts, and subjective sensibilities.[58] They are "unpredictable, unmasterable ... complex ecosystems" that transgress at once the human/nonhuman divide and the boundaries of the self. Anker rightly insists that acknowledging their role in the composition of human agency divests agency of sovereignty "since actions interpreted as individual will and desire are here often powered by imperceptible and unknown forces" that operate both within and outside us.[59] Individual agency is not located exclusively in the individual, not reducible to intentional choice or personal control; it is a materially distributed phenomenon, an assemblage of the human and more-than-human beings, things, and forces through which our initiatives come to fruition in our deeds.

We tend to be oblivious to matter's role in composing agency in part because we are so focused on the aspects of agency that do happen inside us—the willing, thinking, and desiring. Then too, as adults we have extensive experience in learning how to act in ways that are upheld rather than undercut by the material world, and we have adapted our initiatives to the matter we regularly encounter. Moreover, the material fields through which agency emerges tend to be relatively stable and predictable. Once adapted to them, we interact with them in ways that support our agency with a fair amount of consistency. Likewise, we construct our built environment in ways that are specifically tailored to sustain human agency. This adaptation and tailoring make the role of material forces in constituting agency recede from view, and they allow us to feel far more sovereign than we actually are.

To be sure, the habitual feeling of sovereignty is limited to those whose bodies conform to conventional standards of "normal." As disability theorists point out, for those whose bodies depart from these standards, agency's constitutive dependence on the vitalities of the material world never recedes from view. They regularly experience the differential effects that the material environment has on the agency of differently abled individuals. The stairs that invisibly (to me) support my agency as I effortlessly make my way to the front door of the campus library actually impede the agency of those who need wheelchairs to ambulate. The disability literature thus shines light on the often dark recesses of agency's material assemblages.[60] This literature also brings out the ways in which failures of social uptake and failures of material uptake can interact in thwarting the agency of people who are marginalized. Our built environment is constructed in ways that regularly undermine the agency of people with disabilities because historically the social uptake for their agency has been highly compromised. Others have seen them through a lens of stigma and stereotype that tends to deny their individual identities and shut down their initiatives. The fact that the built environment makes it difficult or impossible for people with certain disabilities to get around in public spaces then reinforces their invisibility and deepens the absence of social uptake. This vicious circle itself recedes from view when we think about agency as an exclusively inner faculty and fail to acknowledge its distributed character.

In this connection, we might also think about how the destruction of natural habitats through extractivist enterprises and climate change can undercut the agency of their human inhabitants, whose relations with their more-than-human compatriots have been a vital force in the composition of their agency. For example, Kyle Whyte's work on the forced displacement of Native peoples under settler colonialism in North America demonstrates the destructive impact on human agency that results from disrupting the more-than-human communities of bearers that help to sustain it. He compares the catastrophe of displacement in this regard to catastrophes of climate change, especially those experienced by people who are poor and marginalized, which similarly rupture the more-than-human assemblages that help compose human agency.[61] Because human agency is not only adapted to but partly composed through the material assemblages that constitute a particular people's environment, a radical change in the environment, whether from forced displacement or climate change, can powerfully undermine the vitality of their agency, leading to a host of personal and social difficulties.

So agency is an intercorporeal phenomenon as well as an intersubjective one, meaning that it is characterized by a constitutive dependence on the material world, including both the built environment and more-than-human nature. This dependence is what Abram has in mind in when he refers to the "porosity" that makes each agent like "an open circuit that completes itself only in things, in others, in the surrounding earth."[62] The material circuitry of agency further undermines the ideal of agency as personal sovereignty and disrupts the strict divide between human beings and the rest of nature, undercutting the old human exceptionalism.[63] Still, human beings do have some distinctive capacities that are not shared by most other material entities. To acknowledge this distinctiveness is quite different from defending the moral disregard and political exclusion that underwrite the old exceptionalism and the human domination of nature it authorized, but it does suggest that as human beings we are subject to ethical and political accountability in special ways. Understanding both our embeddedness and our distinctiveness is crucial to nourishing emancipatory forms of agency and reversing environmental domination. These considerations suggest the need for a new kind of exceptionalism, one that is alive to the nonsovereignty of agency and to our embeddedness in more-than-human assemblages, but that enables us to mobilize what is distinctive about us for eco-emancipatory purposes.

Toward a New Exceptionalism

The materially distributed character of agency is sometimes thought to imply that everything in the world is agentic. Indigenous scholar Vanessa Watts, for example, insists that "all elements of nature possess agency."[64] This view is also evident in some of the new-materialist and posthumanist literatures.[65] Bennett herself takes a somewhat more nuanced view but still attributes agency very widely. She holds that "there are various sources or sites of agency, including the intentionality of a human animal, the temperament of a brain's chemistry, the momentum of a social movement, the mood of an architectural form, the propensity of a family, the style of a corporation, the drive of a sound-field, and the decisions of molecules at far-from-equilibrium states."[66] Attributing agency exclusively to human beings, she thinks, understates this "ontological diversity of actants."[67] She uses the term "actants" to suggest "agentic capacities" in the form of "the ability to make a difference, to produce effects, or even to initiate action,"[68] but to distinguish such capacities from "figurations of agency centered around the rational, intentional human subject."[69] Actants so conceived can include "electrons, trees, wind, [and] electromagnetic fields" as well as other parts of nonhuman nature or putatively inanimate objects.[70]

Bennett's effort to broaden the scope of agency beyond the human domain is intended to undercut the hierarchical divide between human beings and nonhuman nature, to "horizontalize" the relations among us.[71] Her purpose in this regard is one I share. Yet there are good reasons to distinguish agency from material vitality or activity per se. It is true that the vitality of matter frequently manifests in certain kinds of responsiveness, as when Leopold's soil responds to the plow, or your eardrum responds to the sound waves generated by my voice. Earth's ecosystems are intricate webs of responsiveness in this sense, and this responsiveness is what enables the material world to be an effective "bearer" of agency. Yet if the responsiveness of the material world helps compose agency, responsiveness alone is not sufficient for something to count as agentic. Agents are able to be responsive in a distinctive way, namely responsive to norms, or standards of right, or ideas about how the world should be.[72]

The concept of agency has a normative function in this regard. It allows us to distinguish sources of activity that are properly subject to ethical and political accountability from those that are impervious to accountability. Hurricane Katrina caused a great deal of misery in New Orleans in 2005, but although we recognize the causal force of the hurricane in this connection, no one attributes ethical or political accountability for its impact to the hurricane itself.

We reserve accountability for sources of activity that are more than simply the causes of outcomes, sources that are also agents. Agents are sources of activity that can be responsive to notions of what ought to be—to principles of justice and conceptions of the good, to the needs of others, to their own dreams and aspirations. The normative dimension of political agency is crucial for democratic politics because by making accountability possible it enables a collective life that answers to standards of right, and it allows for things like political respect, the rule of law, principled contestation, and reciprocity.

In acknowledging the importance to agency of norm responsiveness, we need not limit agency to human beings. As noted at the outset of this chapter, research on animal behavior increasingly finds agentic capacities in varying degrees in a range of nonhuman animals, including capacities for a sense of self and for norm responsiveness. As Sue Donaldson and Will Kymlicka point out, "social animals adhere to norms governing many aspects of their lives, such as mating, playing, and grooming." Although people "tend to dismiss a lot of this behavior as blind instinct," recent studies have shown that much of it "in fact reflects a process of conscious learning, negotiating, and developing social norms."[73] Such norms facilitate, for example, "cooperative hunting and other activities" among wolves, killer whales, and "countless other animals."[74] Similarly, capuchin monkeys have been shown to "carefully monitor equity and fair treatment among peers" in the context of food sharing.[75] Wolves, coyotes, and dogs regularly engage "systems of rules and expectations, and sanctions for violations, in social play."[76] Canids "invite one another to play by bowing, indicating that play is under way, with its special set of rules," including the expectation that "during play it is okay to transgress rules that apply outside of the play context" but that "you have to control your power and the strength of your bite so that others aren't hurt."[77] These animals, in other words, "have the capacity for understanding and negotiating social rules, and for observing and responding to the expectations of others in the social group."[78]

Dogs are responsive to canine norms in their interactions with one another, as anyone who has ever taken a puppy to a dog park will have observed, but they also can be responsive to certain human norms in their interactions with us.[79] Well-socialized adult dogs have learned not to grab the food from their people's dinner plates or lunge at visitors, and they will temper their movements around those who are feeble or very young. Dogs are admittedly distinctive in their responsiveness to human norms, in part because their "repertoire of skills for social cooperation . . . has evolved in a dog-human community."[80]

Yet the fact that canine behavior manifests norm responsiveness in some form is not so distinctive, if we acknowledge the emerging literature on animals from birds to apes to whales and beyond. The content of norms and the mechanisms for communicating and enforcing them vary immensely, but norm responsiveness in different degrees and diverse forms is found among a much wider range of animals than just human beings.

It is difficult at present to know for sure how many animals have agentic capacities, in part because, as Donaldson and Kymlicka point out, "we've only just begun to ask" this question in a serious way, and hence "there is enormous uncharted territory here."[81] Moreover, many animals are hindered in the development and exercise of their agentic capacities by human beings, whether indirectly through human impact on habitats that constrain the social development of nonhuman species, or directly through enclosure and exploitation, as in the case of many domesticated animals and animals in zoos. Because all agency is nonsovereign, animal agency, like human agency, needs communities of bearers if it is to come to fruition in the world. Animal laboratories, factory farms, and traditional zoos interfere in very concrete ways with the flourishing of such communities, and hence with the development of agentic capacities among nonhuman animals. We can learn more about the full extent and forms of nonhuman agency by attending with greater care to the lives of other animals, and by restructuring our interactions with them so as to enable both them and us to be bearers of whatever agency is possible for them.[82]

Agency as a source of accountable activity exists on a continuum, then, and many beings exercise agency in one degree or another. Yet not all material entities that manifest vitality are also capable of agency. And even among beings with agentic capacities, human agents stand out in some important ways, at least when it comes to addressing problems of environmental domination and trying to generate eco-emancipation. Only people can rightly be held accountable for the abuse of human power, including the institutions, social systems, and cultural values that effectuate environmental domination, and people have a special role to play in changing this abuse. Both our distinctive accountability and our particular role in making change derive from aspects of human agency that, while not necessarily exclusive to human beings, are at least developed in us in unusual ways. These capacities enable large-scale, complex coordination of action through institutions and social systems that have wide impact on the Earth and that answer to (or can answer to) standards of right. These capacities are implicated in environmental domination and the damage it has caused, but they also make it possible for us to be responsive to the

demands of justice and the needs of others, human and nonhuman, in transformative ways. We are distinctive kinds of agents, then, both in the quality
and scale of the damage we have done and in the potential we have to do things
better going forward.

The catch is that to achieve our agency and the political possibilities it
opens up—including emancipation from environmental domination—we
must begin to think of human agency in nonsovereign, more-than-human
terms. This means acknowledging our dependence, as Abram puts it, on
things, on others, on the surrounding Earth for the composition of our agency.
And it means cultivating the kinds of relationships with others, human and
nonhuman, that could nourish our ability to make things happen together,
things that are liberatory and nourishing rather than confining and exploitative. So long as we continue to equate agency narrowly with intentional
choice and control over action, we are likely to neglect the actual sources of
our agency, including the nonhuman parts of nature that are constitutive
members of our own agentic assemblages. This neglect can only perpetuate
the lack of accountability and the sense of entrapment and impotence that
plague so many people today in confronting environmental domination.

What all this suggests is that dealing effectively with our environmental
problems will require us to acknowledge that human agency is always embedded in more-than-human assemblages and that it is not the only agency out
there, but also that human agency is indeed distinctive as a source of environmental domination and as a resource for eco-emancipation. These considerations point us to a new kind of human exceptionalism. This new exceptionalism
rests on human agency as a nonsovereign, more-than-human phenomenon. It
does not set people apart from and above the rest of nature, or assert our moral
superiority, or justify the political exclusion of Earth others.[83] It will not sustain the illusion of human control over nature, and it does not invite human
beings to instrumentalize nature solely for our own purposes. On the contrary,
it gives us reason for humility and gratitude toward nonhuman beings and
things, and sometimes awe and fear as well. The new exceptionalism of nonsovereign agency points us to communities of interdependence marked by
respect and responsibility toward nonhuman nature, rather than mastery and
exploitation.

It is a nonsovereign exceptionalism both in the sense that it is rooted in a
distinctive but nonsovereign faculty of agency and in the sense that the relationship to nature it recommends is one of respectful interdependence rather
than aspirations of sovereign control or domination. It facilitates the

reorientation to nature that Bennett and other new materialists and posthumanists seek, but without ascribing agency to everything under the sun. Ironically, the effort to elevate the moral and political status of nature relative to human beings by ascribing agency to all of it recapitulates the old, false assumption that agency is the sole basis for moral and political standing, the only reason that things should matter. We must abandon this assumption and acknowledge instead that there are many ways to count, both morally and politically; agency is one way to matter, but it is not the only way.

Understanding the nonsovereignty of agency in the ways developed here thus collapses the strict, hierarchical divide between people and the rest of nature, even as the new exceptionalism reveals a distinctive place for people within nature. In exploring the dynamics of environmental domination and eco-emancipation in the chapters that follow, I highlight human agents because of their special role in these dynamics. Then too, only human agents (at least as far as we now know) can be moved by books like this one to act on the obligation to reverse the domination they have helped to effect. And only human beings are so obligated, or so I shall argue. At the same time, nonhuman agents and nonagentic material vitalities will have roles to play in eco-emancipation, both as the beneficiaries of certain human actions and as participants, meaning participants in the assemblages that compose human agency and participants in the more-than-human forms of political community that eco-emancipation must entail. We shall have more to say about all this as we move forward. One thing to bear in mind is that the new, more emancipatory communities envisioned here, which incorporate intersubjective, intercorporeal types of relationality across species and other material forms, may reasonably be expected to support greater flourishing of agency among more kinds of beings than what we find today under present conditions of environmental domination. As we shall see in chapter 6, we cannot know in advance all or exactly what eco-emancipation will open up for Earth others, and for ourselves. And even though people have a distinctive role to play in pursuing emancipation, we cannot do this (or anything) alone, either as individuals or as a species.

The new exceptionalism is a necessary step on the path to eco-emancipation, but it is also a perilous one. Given the background of existing social epistemologies and the long history of human domination in relation to nature, any assertion of human distinctiveness is ripe for abuse; it may easily be reappropriated to justify the status quo, meaning the old exceptionalism that promotes environmental domination. Yet however perilous, this is a path we must walk if we mean to pursue emancipation. The best approach, it seems to me, is to walk the path with our eyes wide open to its dangers, to be cognizant of our tendency to turn distinctiveness into superiority in our own minds—and to resist this tendency wherever it arises. We can practice this resistance by focusing on our interdependence with human and nonhuman others, by cultivating curiosity and learning as well as responsiveness and respect in our relations with them, and by reminding ourselves at every turn that human agency is not the only basis of value, and that we are not the only things that count.

Conclusions

Agency is not what we thought it was—or what many of us thought it was. It is not a strictly internal property of the person, and not reducible to intentional choice or control over action. In the exercise of agency we are dependent on how our initiatives interact with dynamics in the social and material worlds that we can never fully master. In addition to eluding our control, agency also regularly outruns our intentions because it is a distributed phenomenon that arises through intersubjective, intercorporeal exchanges. Agency is more than mere causality because it involves activity that is responsive to norms. It places us in special relations of accountability that are not open to nonagentic beings and things, and it gives rise to a sense of possibility that has uniquely liberatory potential for politics. Moreover, although human agents are distinctive in certain ways, this distinctiveness is not the same thing as superiority. Human agents are not the measure of all things; we are particular kinds of things with our own kind of value and dignity, which is not the *only* kind of value and dignity. And even as agency is nonsovereign, it is nevertheless robust and full of life. Its sources are found in the initiatives of individuals, the affirming communities that sustain social uptake, and the vitalities of the more-than-human world around and within us.

Our old ideas about agency are deeply implicated in the environmental domination that everywhere haunts us today. We can do better. The dream of mastery is an illusion, but the special responsibility we bear for emancipation is real. Emancipation—of human and other creatures, of the Earth itself—is possible, but it requires new ways of conceiving agency and new ways of being human. Understanding the nonsovereign yet distinctive nature of human agency opens the door to this emancipation. It helps us make sense of the different meanings that environmental domination has for people and for nonhuman nature, and it explains why they are inextricably entwined such that the human domination of nature circles back to confine and exploit us too. It sets the stage for the cultivation of a new kind of political respect for nature and for more ecologically sustainable ways of conceiving responsibility, and it helps us to identify the types of institutions and mobilizations that could bring Earth others into freer kinds of political community with people. Before we can pursue this freer path forward, however, we need to understand more fully the dynamics of the environmental domination that currently confines us.

3

Environmental Domination

THE NOTION THAT human beings dominate nature is in one sense quite familiar. Since Francis Bacon first championed his new method for understanding the physical world and "remaking the earth and its natural resources as objects for human use," as the historian Carolyn Merchant puts it, the language of domination that he introduced in relation to nature has been regularly recapitulated.[1] Bacon spoke of ruling nature as a despot does and making it the "slave" of human beings.[2] More generally, his work helped foster what Merchant has called "a larger mainstream narrative of Western culture that has propelled science, technology, and capitalism's efforts to 'master' nature—a narrative into which most Westerners have unconsciously been socialized and within which we ourselves have become actors in a storyline of upward progress."[3] In this sense, then, the human domination of nature is a well-known trope, one that has been invoked often in environmental philosophy and political theory.[4]

As familiar as it is, however, the notion that nature is subject to human domination is also contestable. In the face of intractable problems such as climate change, global pandemics, escalating species extinctions, and the countless ways that Earth systems continually evade human efforts to predict and manage them, the idea that people dominate nature may seem not only misplaced but laughable. Then too, the concept of domination could appear to be ill suited to nonhuman beings and things. In mainstream philosophy and political theory, after all, domination is most often conceived as threatening the exercise of freedom as reflective choice. From this perspective, much of nature is not the kind of stuff that can be dominated at all; hence the domination of nature is a misnomer, or so one might think. Another way that the language of domination is used in the environmental context has to do with the forms of domination among people that arise in connection with anthropogenic damage to nonhuman nature. This use of the term is less controversial, but it is often understood too narrowly to fully illuminate the dynamics driving many environmental problems today. Specifically, discussion of environmental domination among people has overwhelmingly focused on the special burdens of ecological damage borne by people who are poor and marginalized. These burdens do often manifest domination, as we shall see, but they are not the only ways that environmental domination affects human beings. Privileged people too are regularly subject to environmental domination, often in ways that they fail to see and are unwittingly complicit in, even as they also participate in the domination of nature and other people, sometimes without realizing it.

For all these reasons—because the idea of the domination of nature is more contestable than it seems, because environmental domination among people is more multidimensional that typically acknowledged, and because the domination of nature and the domination of people interact in constitutive but not always visible ways—the idea of domination as it figures in the environmental context calls for careful interrogation and new thinking. The present approach disentangles the domination of nature from control over it, decenters the role of choice, and argues for an intersectional understanding of the multiple ways that environmental domination affects people and interacts with the human domination of nature.[5]

As the idea is developed here, domination means being subject in a systematic way to insufficiently constrained power and exploitation. I borrow from republican theory the notion that domination involves a status condition that is fundamentally political, rooted in a particular way of situating subjects relative to human power within the field of political institutions, law, and public policy, a condition of systematic vulnerability to the power of others.[6] To be sure, domination in the environmental domain is also tied to cultures of instrumentalization and political economies of extractivism. Yet the political status-condition aspect is crucial, even if it does need to be understood in ways that take us beyond most republican views, as we shall see. The status-condition dimension, if properly conceived, helps us distinguish domination from control, thus clarifying how human beings can be said to dominate nature and one another despite phenomena, from rising seas to superbugs, that demonstrate the limits of human control. As reconstructed in the pages that follow, the concept of domination also helps us see how parts of nature that lack the capacity for choice may still be subject to domination, and how the domination of nature differs from the simple use of it, which is unavoidable and not in itself objectionable. Finally, because a status-condition approach makes environ-mental domination a function of human power and institutions, it also ex-plains the special role that human agency plays in generating environmental domination and the distinctive obligation that human beings have to undo it.

As noted in the introduction, I treat environmental domination as a multi-faceted phenomenon that includes the political, economic, and cultural forces through which human beings (1) dominate nature, understood as Earth's more-than-human parts; and (2) are themselves dominated in terms of both (a) the special burdens placed on poor and marginalized people with respect to environmental harms, and (b) the ways that virtually all of us—even privi-leged people in the world's most affluent societies—are confined and ex-ploited by forces that degrade the Earth, often in our names and with our unwitting (or unwilling) participation. Understanding environmental domi-nation through this multifaceted lens enables us to take a nuanced view of the human in relation to nonhuman beings and things. On the one hand, environ-mental domination reproduces and compounds the harms of historical and continuing global power inequities from colonialism to slavery to patriarchy, as work in environmental justice, eco-feminism, and critical political ecology has demonstrated.[7] On the other hand, environmental domination also cuts across these inequities, both because it confines and exploits virtually all of us in significant respects, and because of how it formally constitutes the political status of a generic "nonhuman" as subordinate to a generic "human" in law and public policy. The framework developed here asks us to simultaneously hold in view these diverse and in some ways conflicting aspects of the human rela-tionship to the Earth, insisting that a holistic approach illuminates dynamics of domination that are otherwise occluded but that are crucial for effectively redressing contemporary environmental problems.

This approach also makes the domination of nonhuman beings and things central to the analysis. Because the domination of people in the environmental context often imposes terrible harms on them—violence, displacement, im-poverishment, illness—work that focuses on the interhuman dimensions of environmental domination has tended to emphasize human experiences and to sideline the domination of nonhuman beings and things, or even to reduce it to relations of domination among people. Then too, many influential ways of conceiving domination, including most republican views, construe it in terms that limit its distinctive harms to human beings, as noted above. The present account insists that many nonhuman beings and things can be domi-nated in the sense of being subject to insufficiently constrained human power and exploitation, that domination in this form can compromise the well-being of nonhuman parts of nature (albeit not always in the same ways that it compromises the well-being of people), and that when it does compromise nonhuman well-being, environmental domination is wrong. This chapter therefore links the discussion of the environmental domination of human beings to an account of what it means for (different groups of) human beings to dominate nature, and it treats the domination of nature as irreducible, meaning not subsumable under the harms of domination among people.

The first part of the chapter begins with a preliminary definition of domination, to be deepened and developed in the course of the argument. It then draws on work in environmental justice and critical theory to elaborate key aspects of domination among people that arise in the environmental context, arguing for an intersectional approach that acknowledges the sometimes cross-cutting ways that environmental domination affects people, and introducing a plural, differentiated account of responsibility that responds to this complexity. This pluralist account of responsibility, although introduced here, will be developed in more detail in chapter 5. After exploring environmental domination among people, we turn to human domination in relation to nonhuman nature, engaging the critical environmental philosophy of William Leiss along with Philip Pettit's republican political theory. The two views offer some important resources but also define domination in ways that limit it to human beings. My account moves beyond them in reconstructing the idea of domination to include nonhuman parts of nature and specifying how the domination of nature figures in environmental domination more broadly. I mean to press the point that we cannot make fundamental progress on environmental problems without emancipating both people and nonhuman nature from human domination. By the same token, when we do take up environmental action we are not simply doing justice to nature, or helping people who are disadvantaged, or creating a better future for our children. Environmental action does serve these purposes, but it is also about liberation—and liberation for all of us, human and nonhuman both, a politics of nondomination for people and the Earth.

Environmental Domination in Interhuman Relations

Although domination varies in ways that we shall explore, its core features include: (1) being subject to unchecked or *insufficiently constrained power*; and (2) being subject to *exploitation*. Power is insufficiently constrained when it can operate without institutionally established checks that make it responsive in a robust, reliable way to the well-being and, where relevant, the influence of those subject to it. To be exploited means to be treated as a mere instrument for the profit or power of another without regard to one's own well-being. We associate exploitation most commonly with the labor sector where it refers to treating employees "unfairly in order to benefit from their work."[8] Yet the word has a wider life, and I mean to use it in a broad sense to include benefiting at others' expense, or extracting value from others in a way that brings harm to them. We speak of predatory lending schemes and the predatory promotion of pharmaceuticals as exploitative in this way. Modern food systems are rife with exploitation, as well, in the form of corporate profiteering from "foods" that fail to nourish us or actively sicken us while enriching the coffers of their industrial producers. When basic aspects of human well-being are sacrificed to enhance the profits and power of others, people are treated in a merely instrumental way, and exploitation is in play.

Domination is associated with slavery and despotism because they manifest in a striking way this combination of insufficiently constrained power and exploitation.[9] Yet slavery and despotism do not exhaust the possible forms that domination can take. Both presuppose a clearly identifiable individual in the position of superior who exercises a form of personal control over clearly identifiable subordinates. In this regard, the classic examples neglect the phenomenon of structural or systemic domination made visible by a range of literatures from critical theory to feminist theory, critical race theory, and queer theory.[10] These literatures demonstrate that domination can also be effected through impersonal forces such as racial majorities, cultures of patriarchy and heteronormativity, and corporate entities and other large-scale, nonstate actors. The power of such forces, if insufficiently checked, may confine and exploit people without exercising personal control over them in the manner of a master over a slave or despots over their subjects. And just as the superior can be an impersonal, collective entity, so the subordinates may be social groups or even, as the Frankfurt school saw, the undifferentiated masses of "the common people" in modern capitalist societies.[11] Domination also admits of degrees. Power may be more or less unconstrained and exploitation more or less attenuated, depending on the institutional context and the broader background of power relations in play. Some instances of domination will be more extreme than others, then, and it is possible for domination in certain forms to coexist in some measure with social privilege and material prosperity.

Environmental domination refers to forms of domination that transpire in and through human interactions with more-than-human parts of nature. One familiar example in the context of interhuman relations is the fact that poor and marginalized people disproportionately bear the brunt of environmental damage that brings profit to or enhances the power of other people. In the United States, for instance, racial and socioeconomic disparities are known to correlate with the placement of waste disposal sites and hazardous industrial operations.[12] Companies can dump their toxic waste or emit noxious fumes more easily in low-income, racially stigmatized neighborhoods, where companies' power to impose their wills on local residents is not sufficiently checked by zoning commissions and other political agencies, and where the companies are freer to exploit people who carry less weight with decision makers and the general public.[13] Similar dynamics operate at the global level as well, with wealthy countries farming out their poisonous waste and many of their most polluting industries to impoverished (and often less democratic) ones, while the global poor disproportionately suffer the effects of climate change created mainly by others.[14]

These differential practices and disproportionate impacts reflect histories of racial, ethnic, and gender-based domination, as well as the legacy and continuing life of capitalist-colonial extractivism. The damage they do to the Earth is entwined with the distinctive damage they do to politically vulnerable human populations, including damage to health, to livelihoods, and to cultural life and community vitality. Where people are displaced, the damage includes loss of homeland; where they are drawn into jobs in extractivist industries, it often includes the exploitation of their labor. Human life itself is regularly at stake, not only from the "slow violence" of pollution and climate change,[15] but from the immediate and direct use of force targeting people who mobilize for eco-activism.[16] Environmental domination in this sense is a function of insufficiently checked power on the part of states and corporations in relation to vulnerable people and their environments, together with the exploitation of such people and environments for profit and power. It both reflects and reinforces domination in other forms.

Such dynamics can be deeply disempowering, as the resources that people might otherwise bring to bear in resisting environmental domination are compromised by racial oppression, economic privation, and other forms of disadvantage. To be sure, environmental justice movements around the world have shown themselves to be a force to contend with, as poor and marginalized people mobilize for political action that at once contests their own domination and interrupts human domination in relation to nature.[17] Still, the interactive effects of domination in these different forms are powerful; they regularly inhibit meaningful environmental change.

Another aspect of environmental domination among people, illuminated by work in critical theory and critical political ecology, involves the ways in which the technologies associated with the human domination of nature are used by some people for the purpose of gaining power or profit over others. As Horkheimer and Adorno argued in *Dialectic of Enlightenment,* the "technical apparatus" that enables human beings to harness natural processes and tap natural resources for more efficient means of production also endows "the social groups which administer it [with] a disproportionate superiority."[18] Marcuse later elaborated this point, saying that "the technical apparatus of production and destruction which sustains and improves the life of [human] individuals" also subordinates them "to the masters of the apparatus," with the result that "the domination of nature" is intrinsically "linked to the domination of man."[19]

In contrast to the forms of domination that are most often discussed in the environmental justice literature, which specifically target people who are poor and marginalized, the domination that figures in the critical theory tradition (at least its original iterations) is a mass phenomenon. When Horkheimer and Adorno said that the technical apparatus gives those who administer it "disproportionate superiority," they meant disproportionate "to the rest of the population" as a whole, not to specific groups within it.[20] Their critique was addressed to "the masses" or "common people" who constitute the majority in modern democracies, whom they saw as subject to insufficiently checked, exploitative power on the part of capitalist forces aligned with the state. Despite their numbers, their relative economic prosperity, and their formal political inclusion, the modern masses are subject to domination in the form of insufficiently constrained power and exploitation, and this domination is inextricably bound up with the domination of nature.

In addition to it being a mass phenomenon, Horkheimer and Adorno characterized the domination they diagnosed as "blind," meaning that the masses are mostly unaware of it.[21] Its presence is concealed by the gratification of material desires that the productive apparatus makes possible, and by the fact that it involves little outright force. Instead of force, it works through a capitalist system of nominally free labor and consumer choice, together with a "culture industry" that generates "mass deception" about human needs and interests, with the result that the "deceived masses" are "captivated by the myth of

success even more than the successful are."[22] Their subjection to the productive apparatus is deepened by the insatiable consumerism that feeds the apparatus; and their "impotence and pliability . . . grow with the quantitative
increase in commodities allowed them," until finally they "insist on the very
ideology which enslaves them."[23] Marcuse refers to this dynamic as "domination in gratification" and "enslaving contentment."[24] This aspect, too, differs
markedly from the domination that figures in the environmental justice literature, which typically involves painful, even disastrous, losses—of health, of
resources, of homeland, of traditional lifeways and community, of nonhuman
companions—and in a way that makes people acutely aware of their subordination and lack of standing. Moreover, in the environmental justice context,
whatever impotence and pliability may arise among subordinates results less
from material prosperity and the satisfaction of consumerist desires than
because of outright coercion, sometimes violent, by states and corporations.

Then too, the domination of the masses regularly transpires through institutional and structural forces, rather than through personal relations of mastery.[25]
As Marcuse puts it, "the society that projects and undertakes the technological
transformation of nature alters the base of domination by gradually replacing
personal dependence (of the slave on the master, the serf on the lord of the
manor, the lord on the donor of the fief, etc.) with dependence on the 'objective
order of things' (on economic laws, the market, etc.)."[26] Structural or institutional domination involves insufficiently checked power and exploitation, but
not always a discrete, clearly identifiable "master" who exercises personal control over subordinates. Marcuse insists that the productive apparatus comes
to assume the life of a "machine" in which even "the capitalist bosses and
owners" lose "their identity as responsible agents" and become mere "bureau-
crats," or cogs in the machine.[27] In fact, the "organizers and administrators
themselves become increasingly dependent on the machinery which they organize and administer" in such a way that their relationship to the masses "is
no longer the dialectical relationship between Master and Servant," but "rather
a vicious circle which encloses both the Master and the Servant" and absorbs
all in a "web of domination."[28]

Domination in this form can be deeply disabling. In the contemporary
environmental context, the privileged masses of prosperous societies overwhelmingly "know they ought to 'do something'" about environmental degradation, but they are often "paralyzed by the disproportionate gap between
what they are capable of and what is needed."[29] Partly this paralysis reflects the
complexity of many environmental problems, a complexity that is truly

immense in cases such as climate change. Yet it also follows from the fact that the context of human action in which we all move now, with its global networks of interlocking forces and structures, includes forms of domination that inhibit our ability to respond effectively to environmental problems, forms of domination that affect all of us, not simply those on the lower rungs of human hierarchies.[30] And while they tend to inhibit effective environmental action, these forms of domination are not limited to the environmental domain; they permeate our lives across multiple registers. They help explain the more generalized feeling of disempowerment on view in many democratic societies at present, what Wendy Brown refers to as our sense of "impotence" in the face of the seemingly "unharnessable" political and economic powers of our time.[31]

Taken together, the environmental justice and critical theory literatures make it clear that to speak of the human domination of nature in a universalizing way is not only incorrect but also unfair. When we understand how the domination of different groups of people interacts with human domination in relation to nonhuman beings and things, it no longer makes sense to say that "it is simply humanity as a species that is to blame" for our environmental problems.[32] Instead, as Val Plumwood puts it, "the forces directing the destruction of nature and the wealth produced from it are owned and controlled overwhelmingly by an unaccountable, mainly white, mainly male, elite."[33] At the same time, however, the differences between the environmental justice literature and critical theory reveal the multidimensionality of environmental domination as it affects human beings across the full spectrum of human hierarchies, meaning the plurality of techniques, experiences, and forms of subjugation it entails. This is important. The environmental justice movement has raised public awareness of how environmental domination affects the poor and the marginalized, which is an immensely important achievement. Yet if this focus leads more privileged people to assume that environmental domination is something that happens only to others, it may abet their blindness to their own subjection and its connection to ecological damage. To be sure, on the continuum that constitutes domination, the experience of the privileged masses is at considerable remove from the environmental domination of the poor and the marginalized, and even more distant from domination as slavery and despotism. Yet insufficiently checked power and exploitation are common to all these contexts, and they always compromise freedom.

Consider the iron-like inescapability of the environmentally damaging practices that sustain daily life for everyone in modern societies, from energy and transportation systems dependent on fossil fuels, to the industrialized food supply, to the ubiquitous presence of pharmaceuticals, plastics, and toxic chemicals. Opting out of these practices and their effects is simply not a live option for most individuals in any modern society. People do attempt it— contemporary homesteaders, for example, living off the grid—but they never fully escape. However self-sufficient homesteaders may be, they cannot prevent their water wells from being polluted by fracking in the next county, or their crops from being infected by GMOs from a neighboring field, not to mention the effects of climate change. The entrapment of the masses in environmentally damaging practices affects virtually all of us living in modern societies. It reflects the fact that life today is structured by forms of power that are insufficiently checked and not adequately responsive to the influence of those they affect. This insufficiently checked power is compounded by exploitation insofar as the systems we cannot escape and do not control regularly instrumentalize us by compromising the land, air, water, and ecosystems on which our well-being depends for the purpose of generating profits for corporations and power for the political officials who serve them.

Moreover, as much as the masses in affluent societies are subject to domination, the critical theory perspective emphasizes that they also help to perpetuate it, however blindly. The insistence of the masses "on the very ideology that enslaves them" is depicted by Horkheimer and Adorno as a powerful force. In fact, they say, the common people's "misplaced love . . . for the wrong which is done them is a greater force than the cunning of the authorities."[34] The masses qua consumers are the "totality" that sustains "the technical apparatus" and that keeps capitalism and the culture industry afloat—and profiting—in its sea of deception.[35] Along these lines, Murray Bookchin has argued that while "the industrial machine seems to have taken off on its own without the driver (to rephrase Horkheimer)," in fact "this metaphor . . . impute[s] too much autonomy to the machine. The driver is still there."[36] According to Bookchin, the driver is *us*, meaning "we who have created this machine" and whose consumerism and complacency sustain it. He goes on to say that if we are to have any hope of changing the course of the machine, we "must be awakened from our own slumber."[37]

The "we" is striking, given that Bookchin was very much aware of the role of social inequalities in environmental domination and the inadequacy of blanket references to "humanity" in this connection. He criticized the tendency of some environmentalists "to speak of the ecological crises that 'we' or 'people' or 'humanity' have created," characterizing it as a ruse that blames "the human victims of an exploitative society for the social and ecological ills of our time," instead of acknowledging the "hierarchical and class divisions" that he saw as the true engines of environmental damage.[38] Bookchin was right, both to criticize the blanket blaming of humanity and to insist on the role that people often play in their own domination. Moreover, the "misplaced love" that at once encloses and motivates the masses, thus contributing to their domination, also helps sustain the exploitation of nonhuman nature. And the extractive industries that supply the consumerism of the relatively privileged masses impose disproportionate and unjust environmental burdens on poor and marginalized people. In this sense, then, the domination the masses so blindly help perpetuate is not solely their own.

Along these lines, Timothy Luke remarks on the ways that many people in contemporary capitalist democracies "enthusiastically volunteer in the rape of Nature to enjoy corporate consumerism."[39] He goes on to qualify this critique by acknowledging that while people do "choose to live this way" their choices are typically "made from a very narrow array of alternatives presented to them as rigidly structured, prepackaged menus of very limited options." He emphasizes that these options have been structured by "corporate imperatives to stimulate mass consumption" and to obfuscate their environmental impact.[40] We should remember, too, that these "enthusiastic volunteers" are themselves being exploited for profit and power in the very practices through which they participate in the exploitation of nature and other people. There is a measure of complicity here, but it is a forced complicity, rooted in manipulation and in systems that entrap and exploit.

The idea of forced complicity may seem like an oxymoron because it both denies and asserts the condition of control that lies at the heart of liberal conceptions of responsibility.[41] Yet this mixed dynamic is a common feature of contemporary life in modern societies. As Jamieson and Di Paola note, "The second I flip on a light switch I am forced into a global network of eco-altering financial and economic interests, political agreements, and avenues of cultural reinforcement whose solid yet ever-changing configuration is largely unknown to me, but which I am at no liberty to side-step and which I suddenly find myself sponsoring with my behavior."[42] The fact that I contribute to systems that damage the environment when I turn on a light is, of course, due to domination exercised over me by companies in the global energy domain and by governments who abet the insufficiently checked power and exploitative practices of these companies. The point here is not to make us all equally responsible for environmental harms or responsible in an undifferentiated way; that would be to occlude important power differentials, both among individual human agents and between individual agents and large-scale social actors.[43] Yet part of the power of the critical theory analysis is to illuminate the ways in which domination by large-scale social actors may draw force and efficacy from the participation of many of the people it subjugates. Such participation entails some kind of responsibility, even if it is not the same as the responsibility of large corporations and governments.

One way to make sense of these dynamics is to disaggregate attributions of responsibility that entail blame and justify punishment from attributions of responsibility that simply acknowledge an agent's participation in an outcome and potential to contribute to change going forward. It is not true that "we" as all humanity are equally blameworthy for environmental problems and the domination of people and nonhuman nature, but it *is* true that many of us participate in these dynamics and that all of us have some capacity— albeit of varying types and to different degrees—to help shape how things unfold for the future. Some of us are positioned to have more influence than others, and these differences are relevant to the differentiated types and degrees of responsibility we bear. Thinking again about the light-switch example, we might say that my forced complicity in this context entails a measure of responsibility for the environmental domination in play but not as *blame* for climate change, or environmental injustice, or my own exploitation. Instead, the responsibility I bear makes me accountable for (1) awakening to my mixed role(s) in environmental domination; (2) working with others to make visible the most powerful contributors and hold them culpable for their damage; and (3) working (again collectively) to exert pressure for the kinds of institutional changes that would resolve the problem of forced complicity from the ground up by reconstructing the systemic conditions of environmental domination.

This differentiated conception of responsibility responds to the tensions inherent in environmental domination as it affects people across the spectrum of human hierarchies, tensions that become visible when we adopt a holistic approach that integrates environmental justice and critical theory perspectives. It allows us to attribute blame in the places and measures warranted, but it does not stop there; it also calls us in a forward-looking and potentially empowering way to work with others, using whatever resources and influence our particular positions in life allow, to create the conditions for more emancipatory ways of living with other people and with nonhuman beings and things. It is of a piece with recent efforts to refigure conventional conceptions of responsibility to address complex structural problems such as global inequality, institutional racism, and patriarchy.[44] We shall pursue this pluralized approach to eco-responsibility in chapter 5.

So environmental domination as it bears on human beings includes the disproportionate harm and the often violent exploitation experienced by the poor and the marginalized in the context of extractivism, pollution, climate change, and the like, but it also covers the "blind domination" of the masses in affluent societies, who are captivated as much as coerced into a system that gratifies many of their desires even as it subjects them to insufficiently checked power and exploitation. Their participation makes them complicit in their own domination as well as the domination of nature and other people, but it is often a forced complicity that attenuates the type and degree of responsibility they bear. Environmental domination thus admits of multiple forms, it has diverse perpetrators, its victims are not always entirely innocent, and it is frequently invisible even to those it subjugates. All these features make it difficult to diagnose and to reverse. As we shall see, the most promising approach to liberation is a multifaceted one that combines the cultural awakening targeted by critical theory with the collective mobilization emphasis of the environmental justice movement, and joins them to an account of political institutions that support nondomination for people and the Earth. We shall pursue these different aspects of eco-emancipation in the coming chapters. Still, the domination of people is only one side of environmental domination. Before we can take up possibilities for liberation, we need a fuller picture of what environmental domination entails. Specifically, we need to consider what it means for (different groups of) people to exercise domination in relation to nature.

Environmental Domination in Human-Nature Relations

Perhaps the most comprehensive account of the idea of domination as it applies to the relationship between human beings and the nonhuman world is William Leiss's *The Domination of Nature*, and the book offers valuable resources for conceptualizing domination in this form.[45] Leiss defines the "domination of nature" as "the extraction of resources from the natural environment to turn them into commodities for the satisfaction of needs, without apparent limit."[46] Domination in this context means "to get what we want . . . by transforming the planet into nothing but a supplier of our wants."[47] This way of understanding domination resonates with the classic republican examples of domination as despotism and slavery. Indeed, Leiss attributes to Bacon, whom he credits with having made "the concept of the human mastery of nature" prominent among human concerns, the ambition to rule the "kingdom of nature" on the model "of despotism" and to make nature the "slave" of human beings.[48] It is worth emphasizing here that to notice the structural similarity among types of domination—the common vulnerability to insufficiently checked power and exploitation—is not to assert their moral equivalence. Above all, the actual enslavement of human beings is sui generis in terms of the distinctive horrors it entails. The point is to understand the basic structure of domination, not to assert the moral equivalence of its different instantiations, which may involve different types and degrees of harm.

Importantly, Leiss emphasizes that the domination of nature is not the same thing as the mere use of it for human purposes, even destructive use. "Quite obviously," he points out, "humans *must* destroy other entities and their habitats in order to survive and develop."[49] Nor is domination to be equated with perfect control. Partly this distinction reflects the fact that "external nature appears as a reluctant and recalcitrant host; she does not willingly yield all her most precious fruits."[50] Instead, nature regularly responds to human interventions in ways that elude, exceed, or counteract human intentions. The distinction between domination and perfect control also reflects the fact that the efforts of "the ruling strata" to master nature are vulnerable to "struggles among men" for "control of nature's resources," and consequently any particular group's mastery can be "neither complete nor permanent."[51] Domination of nature, then, goes beyond mere use and never achieves full control.

Along these lines, one recent commentator has distinguished between the *appropriation* of nature, the *destruction* of nature, and the *mastery* of nature.[52] The first two are inescapable conditions of all life, including human life. Mastery—or domination—is different, not simply because it is avoidable but because it involves a particular way of seeing nature and valuing it. Domination entails "a total subsumption of nature under societal aims . . . without respecting that nature has its own meaning."[53] It means treating nature as if its existence were exhausted by its use value to human beings. Marcuse is again helpful here. He describes being dominated as "to exist as an instrument, as a thing," which he refers to as "the pure form of servitude."[54] It calls to mind the exploitation we have seen as part of the environmental domination of people— instrumentalizing others for power or profit without regard to their well-being.[55] It also suggests unlimited power, not in the sense of perfect control or power that always achieves its objectives, but in the sense of power that is not reliably checked by principled constraints.

As important as Leiss's account is, however, it tends to recapitulate the dominating perspective on nature that it ostensibly means to contest. In fact, it turns out that on Leiss's view there is in truth no such thing as the human domination of nature. The reason, he says, is not only that "the putative subject of this enterprise [humanity] does not exist," given the divisions produced by social inequality and conflict, but that nature is not the kind of thing that can be dominated, properly speaking.[56] Leiss cites Hegel in support of the idea that "an essential feature of domination is the struggle for recognition of the master's authority," meaning that "the necessary correlate of domination is the consciousness of subordination in those who must obey the will of another."[57] He therefore concludes that "only other men can be the objects of domination."[58] Consequently, "if the idea of the domination of nature has any meaning at all, it is [only] that by such means . . . some men attempt to dominate and control other men."[59]

As we have seen, however, domination among persons is commonly "blind" in Horkheimer and Adorno's sense, as in the domination of the masses in modern capitalist societies who are oblivious to their subjugation.[60] Likewise, when Marcuse defined domination as "to exist as an instrument, as a thing," he went on to emphasize that "this mode of existence is not abrogated if the thing . . . does not feel its being-a-thing," if it is not aware of itself as dominated.[61] Insofar as domination among people is possible without consciousness of subjugation, the absence of such consciousness among nonhuman beings and things cannot be grounds for denying that they can be dominated. If we are serious about exploring domination in relation to nonhuman nature, we will need to move beyond Leiss.

A resource in this regard is the work of Philip Pettit. Although Pettit himself theorizes domination exclusively in the context of human society, some of his insights can be creatively extended in ways that illuminate the domination of nature.[62] For our purposes, the most significant aspect of Pettit's account is his notion of domination as a status condition with its focus on institutional context. As Pettit characterizes it in *Republicanism*, domination describes any relationship in which a person or public authority is in a position "(1) to interfere; (2) on an arbitrary basis; (3) in certain choices that the other is in a position to make."[63] Power is arbitrary, for Pettit, when it fails to track the interests of those subject to it or eludes their control.[64] To be in a position to interfere on an arbitrary basis is a function of institutional arrangements involving the absence of external checks on the power of the superior and the lack of formal entitlements to consideration on the part of subordinates.

The institutional status-condition aspect of domination means that the dominant party need not actually interfere with the subordinate in order for a condition of domination to be in play; the dearth of institutional constraints and entitlements is enough. It also makes domination independent in principle of the consciousness of subordinates and explains why domination can be present even when subordinates are unaware of their subjection.[65] Additionally, it implies that the intentions of a dominant party relative to his subordinate are irrelevant; he need not be bent on conquest and control in order for domination to exist. Indeed, he may regret his position of superiority. As Pettit puts it, "unwilled domination" is possible in "relationships of inalienable asymmetric power" because the general status condition that constitutes domination is independent of the particular will of any given individual.[66] In view of its status-condition character, domination "can only be contained by external checks" in the form of an institutional apparatus that takes the possibility of arbitrary power off the table in a reliable way.[67]

Insofar as domination on Pettit's account involves the capacity to interfere in the choices of others, it may seem to be orthogonal to many nonhuman beings and things, and Pettit's own conception of domination clearly limits its harm to people. True, some nonhuman animals do make choices. Yet much of nature is not in a position to do so, as far as we know, whether it is subject to the arbitrary power of people or not. Arbitrary human power does pose a threat to nature, but this threat is different from the one that Pettit emphasizes. Domination undermines well-being by compromising freedom, and freedom for Pettit consists in having the ability, the opportunity, and the resources to make one's own reflective choices and act on them. Yet we need not follow him in defining freedom and domination so narrowly in terms of reflective choice. A more capacious understanding is suggested by an eighteenth-century republican tract that Pettit himself quotes approvingly, which defines liberty as "to live upon one's own terms" and domination as "to live at the mere mercy of another."[68] The notion of living on one's own terms *could* mean living on terms that one reflectively chooses for oneself, but it need not be interpreted this way. One's own terms could simply refer to the conditions that support the fullness of one's distinctive existence, whatever that may be. Individual choice making is important for the fullness of human existence (although it is not the only important thing), and consequently one aspect of the domination of people is hindering them in the exercise of their choices. Interference in choice making may play a role in the domination of certain nonhuman animals as well, but insofar as individual choice making has no place in the existence of many other parts of nonhuman nature, violations of choice will not be central to domination as it affects them. For them, domination compromises freedom by making them "live at the mere mercy" of human power instead of according to the unfolding logics of their own distinctive being. In this way, it undercuts the fullness of their existence, their well-being.

It is worth emphasizing that for all living things, including people, well-being as the fullness of existence depends on innumerable interdependencies. All living things need other things to thrive. In this sense, living on one's own terms is always an intersubjective phenomenon that emerges through webs of relationality.[69] Still, all living things do have terms of existence that are unique to them, conditions that make possible the functioning and capabilities specific to their kind.[70] Their lives can be lived out on these terms, or, alternatively, they can be lived out in a way that systematically puts them at the mercy of people, in a position to be subjected to insufficiently constrained power and exploitation, whether by individual human beings or by large-scale social actors and human systems. An account of domination that covers nonhuman beings and things as well as people thus decenters individual choice, focusing instead on a capaciously conceived notion of liberty as living on one's own terms, while acknowledging the diverse terms of existence that attach to nature's different parts and the relational embeddedness of them all.[71]

These considerations reflect a substantial reconstruction of the concept of domination relative to Pettit's account. Another necessary departure concerns the meaning of arbitrary power. Pettit defines arbitrary power in terms of power that is insufficiently responsive to the interests or control of those subject to it.[72] Like his emphasis on choice, these criteria are an awkward fit for many nonhuman beings and things. Interests are often thought to imply conscious concerns on the part of a rational subject; likewise, sharing in political control over power requires not only complex reasoning but sophisticated linguistic capacities. Insofar as many nonhuman beings and things do not have interests in the relevant sense and cannot share in political control, Pettit's theory of domination leaves them out. Yet many nonhuman beings and things clearly suffer harm from the exercise of human power that is, if not arbitrary in Pettit's specific sense, then at least insufficiently constrained, meaning not subject to institutionalized checks that force it to be responsive to the well-being of those it affects, and, where relevant, to their influence. Influence is relevant where subjects have the capacities needed to share in shaping the trajectories of political power. This way of thinking about domination, which replaces interests and control with well-being and influence in the definition of arbitrary power, covers the domination of human beings but also enables us to make sense of how human beings can be said to exercise domination in relation to many parts of nature. Anything that has a well-being can be subject to domination so conceived, as a condition of vulnerability to insufficiently constrained human power and exploitation.

Nature is therefore subject to domination to the extent that the power people exercise in relation to it is insufficiently limited in an institutional sense, meaning that there are few if any principled constraints on this power, no division and balance of human power in relation to nature, little in the way of a formal apparatus of legal rights or mechanisms of redress and representation that would force human power to track the well-being of nonhuman animals and ecosystems. Environmental regulations do exist, of course, but the vast majority of them are not so much principled as self-serving. Their purpose is typically to protect human interests rather than nonhuman nature itself, and when human interests are deemed to change, the regulations change too. And far from being fixed and fundamental, effectively removing the option to exercise arbitrary power, most protections for nature exist mainly at the level of administrative rules and public policy rather than fundamental law. For this reason, they can often be reversed with the stroke of a pen, as the Trump administration's rapid retraction of many environmental protections demonstrated.

It is worth emphasizing, as Leiss points out, that human domination in relation to nature is not equivalent to control over it. Domination is about power that lacks principled, institutional constraints and protections against exploitation, not about perfect control. It is also important to see that any society that lacks such constraints and protections in regard to how human power can be exercised in relation to nonhuman nature positions nature as subordinate relative to people in general. Even though there are real differences of privilege and power among persons in connection with environmental damage, as we have seen, the absence of robust institutional constraints and protections for nature makes Earth others systematically vulnerable to all of us, however we are positioned relative to one another. In a structurally similar way, Jim Crow made Black people as a group systematically vulnerable to white people as a group—poor and politically disempowered whites as well as wealthy, influential ones—because, as differently positioned as whites were relative to one another, the law constituted them all as a privileged class relative to African Americans. Once again, the point here is not to equate the harms of Jim Crow with the harms involved in the human domination of nature; the violations involved are not equivalent. The point is rather to note the structural similarities across these different types of domination with respect to how domination renders subordinates systematically vulnerable to the insufficiently checked power and exploitation of those whom the law constitutes in a generic way as members of a dominant class.

One of the harms that comes to people from the human domination of nature is precisely that it encloses all of us as human beings, whoever we are, within a status position relative to nature that many people abhor. Think of the people from Indigenous tribes in Amazonia whose only way to put food on the table in recent years has come to be working for mining operations that lay waste to an ecosystem they regard as *family*. Or consider average members of the American masses whose daily lives are totally automobile dependent because no reliable public transportation is available in their area but who deeply regret their carbon emissions and their effect on the Earth. Although certainly not equivalent, the two cases share something important. If the status condition of nonhuman nature were not constituted in law and public policy as subordinate relative to human beings in general, then rapacious mining operations and fossil-fuel-based, single-driver transportation systems would be off the table, and these particular human beings would not be forced into a general status position—and a complicity—they regret. This entrapment and the exploitation that accompanies it is part of how human beings are subjugated by environmental domination. The environmental domination of specific people in this sense is made possible by the generic human domination of nature; the different forms of environmental domination interact. Undoing environmental domination across both dimensions will require changing the basic status condition of nature relative to people in political institutions, laws, and public policies.

The political status-condition account also further clarifies the distinction between the domination of nature and mere use of it. Domination involves insufficient constraints on use and a lack of entitlements that prevent exploitative use. When we operate against an institutional background that does establish principled constraints on our use, constraints that track nature's well-being for its own sake and not simply for ours, we can make use of it without dominating it. Thus the concept of domination allows for human needs to be met; what it disallows is insufficiently checked power and exploitation. We must eat, for example, but we can feed ourselves without the profit-driven animal suffering of factory farms or the ecological damage of large-scale monocultural crop production. Nondomination directs us to principled, ecologically sustainable, respectful use. True, such use will regularly generate conflicts between human beings and nonhuman parts of nature. Many of these conflicts will involve violence: we cannot eat without killing other organisms, for instance. As we shall see in chapter 4, respectful use does not ensure an easy harmony, but the conflicts that inevitably accompany it differ from domination. While we cannot live without generating conflicts deriving from the use of nonhuman nature, we *can* live without dominating it if we organize things institutionally to prevent people from exercising arbitrary power and exploitation in relation to Earth others.

In a related vein, nonhuman beings and things make use of one another all the time—for food, for shelter, for all the resources that sustain their various terms of existence—and this use can be violently destructive of others, including other species and even whole ecosystems. Yet however destructive it may be, this use will not constitute domination if it does not reflect norm-responsive choices embedded in the institutional regulation of power. The structures that constitute domination are established by legal-institutional frameworks that embody collective human choices consolidated over time, choices that have the potential to be responsive to principles of right. In this sense, domination presupposes both institutions and a capacity for norm-responsive choice making. Some nonhuman beings may be capable of dominating others in this way (I leave this open for present purposes), but many are not. Still, nonhuman beings and things can be subject to domination even when they cannot be agents of domination. They can be subject to domination simply insofar as they are in a position of systematic vulnerability to the insufficiently constrained and exploitative power of people, a vulnerability that compromises their freedom to live on their own terms and undercuts their well-being in an unnecessary and illegitimate way.[73] The domination of nature is unnecessary because human beings can meet their needs through forms of use that incorporate principled constraints on power and protections against exploitation; it is illegitimate because nothing has endowed human beings with a right to sacrifice the well-being of others, human or otherwise, to their own unfettered desires.

The diverse characters and capacities of nature's different parts means that domination can be experienced in multiple ways, generating varying effects and diverse harms. The harms that come to people from insufficiently checked, exploitative human power differ depending on where people are placed in human hierarchies. These harms are different in significant respects from the effects of such power on cows or rivers or rainforests, although there are surely commonalities too, and we should not underestimate the potential suffering of nonhuman others. Diagnosing these diverse harms and preventing (or mitigating) them will require substantial understanding of other species and Earth systems, a requirement that presents real challenges given the limited extent of our ecological knowledge. Still, perfect knowledge is not needed in order to begin to contain and reverse human domination in relation to nature. Provided that we remain open to new information as it arises and build reflexivity into our decision-making processes so that we can respond accordingly, we can reasonably hope to make progress over time.

To make good on this reasonable hope of progress, however, we will also need to address the forms of domination explored earlier that affect people. These different dimensions of environmental domination interact in powerful, reciprocally reinforcing ways. For example, the more products we purchase and discard and purchase again as the result of planned obsolescence, which exploits us as tools of corporate profiteering, the more damage we do to the Earth through resource extraction, toxic production processes, and waste. If there were limits on what human beings were entitled to take from and impose on nature, it would be far more difficult for corporations to exploit people in this way. Likewise, the rhetoric of "jobs versus the environment" so prevalent in public discourse today, which justifies the exploitation of nonhuman beings and things, also holds people hostage to the power of corporations by undercutting the public will to constrain their power and to hold them accountable for the human costs of their environmental impact. To counter these forces, we need a politics of emancipation that is as multifaceted as environmental domination itself. Each of the next chapters explores one aspect of this multifaceted politics, from political respect for nature, to a public culture of eco-responsibility, to the institutions and mobilizations of more-than-human political communities.

Conclusions

Many environmental problems today embody a logic of domination, not contingently or tangentially but in a constitutive way. We cannot make progress in resolving the problems unless we undo the domination. Marcuse once said that "all liberation depends on the consciousness of servitude."[74] In pressing the multiple ways that environmental domination affects people across the spectrum of human hierarchies, the holistic approach offered here means to prompt liberation by raising consciousness across the board. We need to hold in view simultaneously what we know about the different ways that environmental domination subordinates and disempowers people *and* the fact that the domination of nature as a status condition interpellates all persons into a generic position of dominance relative to nonhuman beings and things. Acknowledging this complexity is crucial to a full understanding of how environmental domination works. There is resonance here with the literature on intersectionality in race and gender studies that demonstrates how people are often multiply positioned relative to others, meaning that any particular individual may be simultaneously privileged and marginalized with reference to different constellations of power.

The reality is that we are all in need of emancipation, even if the precise dynamics of our environmental domination differ. To see this, we must learn to recognize what is common and what is distinctive about how environmental domination affects different human populations, and how it affects nonhuman ones. Consciousness-raising is not enough, of course. The cultural shift envisioned by critical theory very much needs to be paired with institutional changes that reconstruct how power can be exercised over nonhuman nature, as well as over people. This reconstruction also depends on active citizens who contest subjugation on behalf of themselves and others. Civic activism gives life to the institutional constraints and entitlements of nondomination, communicates relevant interests and forms of well-being, and contributes to the collective influence of self-government. It is more than supplemental to democratic institutions; it is essential to their proper functioning.

The challenges of meaningful transformation are enormous, but understanding the dynamics of environmental domination in the holistic way articulated here can help. For one thing, it illuminates the multiplicity and depth of the harms that environmental domination imposes on human beings. These harms are not limited to damaged health, livelihoods, and communities but also include co-opting people, sometimes forcibly, into participating in systems that destroy their relationships with Earth others, systems they may abhor but cannot escape. It makes visible a form of domination that implicates virtually all of us (albeit in different ways), one that almost every aspect of modern life at once enforces and obfuscates. The domination frame also pushes us to think differently about our reasons to work for environmental change. Insofar as the environmental problems we face today are driven by domination—our own as well as nature's, and our own whoever we are—to work for environmental change is to work for a liberation that includes us. It is also about doing right by nature and future generations of people, but environmental action is fundamentally a matter of living *freer*—all of us, human and nonhuman—here and now.

4

Political Respect for Nature

UNDERSTANDING THE DYNAMICS of environmental domination and the roles we play in it, sometimes as perpetrators, sometimes as victims, is a crucial first step. To move beyond domination, however, we will need to do more. Among other things, we must begin to cultivate a new, political respect for nature. The "political" in political respect for nature is crucial. Ethical respect for nature is important, but it is not sufficient. Ethical injunctions have never been a reliable check on domination in any form. Nondomination requires a political apparatus that institutionally limits the exercise of power and is backed up by the coercive force of law.[1] In the absence of enforceable constraints, nonhuman beings and things are more or less dependent on the kindness of strangers in their interactions with us. Moreover, individuals acting alone are no match for the large-scale structural forces that contribute to environmental domination. Reconstructing these forces for more sustainable and emancipatory living requires collective action, legal and institutional change, and a new public ethos. For all these reasons, the respect for nature we need to cultivate must be political.[2]

Political respect for *persons* is a familiar feature of contemporary democracies. As a political principle, respect for persons provides a justification for the structural limitation of power through mechanisms such as political representation and rights, and it says that political power is legitimate only when it answers to the well-being of the people subject to it. As a public ethos, it also orients citizens in their relations with one another, generating both self-restraint and responsiveness to others. A principle of political respect for nature, properly conceived, must do similar work. At the structural level, it supplements political respect for persons with institutional mechanisms that formally constrain how human power may be exercised in relation to nonhuman beings and things, and that require us to use our power in ways that are attentive to nature's well-being along with our own. And much like respect for persons—when internalized by citizens as part of their shared public ethos—protects against the abuse of power over other people, so a political ethos of respect for nature motivates greater self-restraint and responsiveness in our interpersonal relations with Earth's nonhuman parts. Political respect for nature means acknowledging that nonhuman beings and things count, that they deserve to be treated according to standards of right, that there are principled limitations on how human power may be exercised in relation to them. It means formalizing these limitations in the basic structure of society and fostering a public ethos of self-restraint and responsiveness.

In what follows, I explore what the meaning, experience, and practice of respect in this form could be, drawing inspiration from two very different sources: Kant's normative theory of respect for persons and Levinas's phenomenology of response to the other, which I approach through Jacques Derrida. I take Kant and Levinas as points of departure, but I develop the notion of respect in ways that go beyond both. The first part of the chapter takes up the meaning of respect as involving the Kantian idea that others should count with us always also as ends in themselves and never merely as the means to our own ends, but it reconstructs this idea so as to eschew Kant's focus on the putatively autonomous individual and to cover nonhuman beings and things as well. The second part examines the experiential dimensions of respect for nature, including the deep existential challenge it poses to us as human beings, given existing conceptual frameworks of human superiority and entitlement. For insight here I draw on Derrida's notion of "abyssal rupture," along with the Levinasian concepts of alterity and asymmetrical response across difference. In the third part, I explore some concrete practices of political respect for nature that combine self-restraint with responsiveness to the well-being of nonhuman others, and that point us to new human/nonhuman forms of relationality.

The Meaning of Respect: Always Also as Ends

Respect carries multiple meanings in common parlance, including the special esteem we feel for those we admire, and the deference sometimes required toward people who have authority over us, such as parents, teachers, or employers. We also use the language of respect to acknowledge the force of something impressive, even potentially threatening; in this sense, respect can convey awe, intimidation, and sometimes fear. In the political context of democratic citizenship, respect is a more impersonal phenomenon than the esteem or deference we may feel for particular others. It does have an affective valence, but it does not derive from the particularities of our personal relationships or from special attributes unique to any specific individuals. And while respect for persons should not normally entail fear, it does involve an awareness that in a democratic society the legal framework of rights and representation gives other people standing in their own right, as opposed to their being mere vehicles for the satisfaction of one's own purposes, and so it makes other people forces to contend with. To exercise political respect for persons is to acknowledge the normative force of others' independent standing, their being-for-themselves, the irreducibility of their existence as exceeding their use value to us. Above all, political respect for persons involves a habit of self-restraint. It means limiting our inclination to subject others to the unbounded force of our own desires and perspectives. The practice of political respect also involves responsiveness to the well-being of others, as we shall see, and it often results in the enlargement and enrichment of the self through new forms of relationality as well. It makes life with others freer and more rewarding over the long term, but it begins in a kind of self-restraint.

Kant's principle of respect for persons is one way to conceptualize this restraint. The principle holds that human beings are to be regarded always also as ends in themselves and never merely as the means to the ends of others.[3] In healthy democracies, this principle forms an essential part of the structural framework of society and is internalized as part of the shared public ethos of citizens. Kant grounded respect for persons in rational autonomy, of course. In his view, the capacity to formulate ends *for* themselves makes rational beings ends *in* themselves.[4] As such, they are entitled to be protected from the unconstrained, instrumentalizing power of others. Indeed, given their more-than-instrumental status, the exercise of unconstrained, merely instrumentalizing power over them is always illegitimate and a violation of political right. Thus while Kant formulated the principle of respect for persons as part of his moral theory, it also has a political life. Specifically, it calls for democratic political forms, including rights and political representation, intended to ensure that persons are treated as ends in themselves and thereby to prevent domination.[5]

I do not mean to endorse the Kantian conception of the person or Kant's notion of human agency. The Kantian view misconceives human agency by ascribing rational autonomy to what we have seen is a fundamentally nonsovereign phenomenon, and it fails to acknowledge the agentic capacities of many nonhuman animals.[6] Moreover, in making rational autonomy the basis of moral and political standing, this approach excludes many persons and all nature. Indeed, it is one source of human domination in relation to nature, as it has helped to fuel the notion that people stand apart from and above nonhuman beings and things, and to justify insufficiently constrained power and exploitation in relation to them. Yet despite these deficits, Kant's concept of respect is a powerful way to express the important idea that the being of others exceeds their use value to us. It also connects this moral orientation to a political framework that establishes institutional protections against insufficiently limited, merely instrumentalizing power. I mean to detach these aspects of Kantian respect from the other parts of Kant's philosophy, especially his sovereigntist conception of agency, and to reconstruct them as resources for resisting environmental domination and creating new kinds of political order.[7]

From a post-Kantian, ecological perspective, what entitles others—human and otherwise—to be respected as ends in themselves is not rational autonomy in particular but the more general fact that their existence unfolds according to logics that exceed the purposes of others. Earth's ecosystems and their more-than-human inhabitants are not *for us* in the sense of existing solely for the sake of satisfying human desires. Nor is their well-being defined or necessarily advanced by serving us. Nature just is; it unfolds for itself. Like people, Earth's nonhuman parts are ends in themselves in the sense that they are not in any constitutive sense *for* anything else, including us.

Some ecologists make this point by invoking the idea of "autopoiesis," meaning self-production or self-renewal. Autopoiesis is thought to be a feature of all life systems, including "populations, gene pools, ecosystems, and individual living organisms."[8] The activity of autopoietic entities, on this view, manifests an "internal telos" oriented toward the unfolding of their own potentials, although the unfolding life activity of nonhuman beings often transpires without conscious intentionality.[9] The internal telos of a thing is distinct from the notion of an external telos, the idea that the nature of a thing is realized by serving something else, and it need not entail an Aristotelian teleology writ large, conceived as a single, hierarchical order.[10] Nor does the idea of internal telos posit a fixed, unchanging essence for each thing. On the contrary, the ecological view assumes that living things evolve, and hence that their well-being can change. Yet because "the primary product of the operations of living systems . . . is themselves, not some goal or task external to themselves," as one commentator puts it, autopoietic entities are reasonably considered to be "ends in themselves," and hence "deserving of moral consideration in their own right."[11]

The language of autopoiesis is admittedly somewhat misleading, as Donna Haraway points out, in that no living organisms are entirely self-producing or self-renewing.[12] Scientific ecology demonstrates instead the deep interdependence of organisms and ecosystems. Haraway thus speaks of "sympoiesis" rather than autopoiesis as a way to characterize the vitality or life force of all beings. In a similar way, the nonsovereignty of agency makes all human action an intersubjective and intercorporeal phenomenon, as we saw in chapter 2. Indeed, Jane Bennett's vital materialism helps us understand in a more general way that what we conventionally think of as discretely bounded individual organisms are always assemblages comprising things and forces that exceed the individual, as in the bacteria that account for 50 percent of the cells in the average human body.[13] We could not be who we are, either as agents or as individuals more generally, without the many others, both around and within us, who participate in the assemblages that compose us.

In view of the distributed or sympoietic quality of all things, one might worry that the ideal of respect being developed here is too individualized. Bennett rejects Kant's idea of respect on just these grounds, saying that "to face up to the compound nature of the human self is to find it difficult even to make sense of the notion of a single end-in-itself."[14] Yet while the assemblage view of agency and subjectivity complicates what it means to be an individual and makes the boundary around the individual porous, it does not dissolve the individual entirely. On the contrary, interdependence presupposes individuation insofar as particular organisms look to distinctive others for the things they require but cannot provide for themselves. Likewise, the distinctiveness of the individual parts of any assemblage is what makes it an assemblage rather than a singular, undifferentiated mass.

Plants, animals, and people are simultaneously individuated and embedded in assemblages. I am composed of many things that are not reducible to me, including the bacteria in my microbiome, the physical forces that keep my parts together, and the social relations that help shape my consciousness and enable (or undercut) my agency. Yet my dog (like my people) can easily distinguish me from other human assemblages and from various nonhuman individuals. This kind of individuation is all we need in order to make sense of the notion of an end in itself, meaning something that should count with us in a way that is not reducible to its use value for us. Still, these considerations do suggest that respect for nature should increase our attunement and responsiveness not only to the individuated instances of sympoiesis that we recognize as individuals but also to the ecosystems, species, and other assemblages in which they are always embedded.[15]

Along these lines, Paul Taylor defends what he calls "a biocentric outlook on nature" according to which each organism "is seen to be a teleological (goal oriented) center of life, pursuing its own good in its own, unique way," albeit often in the absence of consciousness.[16] To count as an end in itself, on Taylor's view, an organism need only be a living, "unified system of organized activity, the constant tendency of which is to preserve its existence by protecting and promoting its well-being."[17] Anything that has a good of its own is covered.[18] Nonbiotic things are excluded because, as Taylor sees it, they "have no good of their own and so cannot be treated rightly or wrongly."[19] The latter grouping includes many parts of what we think of as nature, such as rocks, soil, water, and air, and they are to be "sharply separated from the animals and plants that depend" on them.[20]

Taylor acknowledges that insofar as animals and plants do depend on such things for their well-being, "it may still be the case that moral agents should treat [these things] in a certain way" in order to fulfill their moral duty.[21] Yet the sharp separation he insists on is misplaced. Many things that are widely seen as inanimate, such as rivers, mountains, and dirt, are actually composed of complex communities of living creatures interacting with nonbiotic matter. In practice, the line between biotic and nonbiotic parts of nature is more porous than Taylor allows, and respecting nature will regularly mean extending moral considerability to the simultaneously biotic/nonbiotic assemblages that typically compose organisms and ecosystems. We will also need to expand Taylor's analysis beyond the moral domain so that respect for nature covers political standing and not merely moral considerability. Yet Taylor's key insight (like Kant's) is an important one. Respect for nature orients us in a more than merely instrumental to a very wide range of nonhuman beings and things. It means regarding Earth's more-than-human parts as entitled to moral and political consideration, independently of "any instrumental . . . value" they may have for us; it means treating their well-being always also "as an end in itself" and never merely as the means to human ends.[22]

Respect for nature does differ from respect for persons in some ways. For one thing, the capacities on display in the sympoietic unfolding of human potential include forms of reasoning, reflective feeling, and communication that are shared among, and in some measure distinctive to, the human species, as we saw in chapter 2. Respect for persons is rooted in a recognition of these shared capacities; in exercising it we acknowledge capacities in other people that we experience in ourselves. In respecting nature, by contrast, while we may be aware of some similarities between people and certain nonhuman beings, the feeling of respect need not involve a sense of similarity, and it does not require likeness. It may instead elicit feelings triggered by an awareness of our differences, such as awe and admiration, but also perhaps unease, sometimes even intimidation or fear. We shall have more to say about this presently. In a related way, respect for nature is not necessarily reciprocal. Part of what we are respecting in the practice of respect for persons is other peoples' ability to exercise the same restraint and responsiveness toward us as we do toward them. This capacity is an element of what makes human beings ends in themselves because it is a constitutive feature of the sympoietic unfolding that is distinctive to beings of our kind. It is not a constitutive feature of the sympoietic unfolding of many other parts of nature, however, and consequently not something that human beings can rightly expect of them. Thus while respect for persons carries with it an expectation that one's respect will be returned in kind, respect for nature entails no such reciprocity.

To be sure, exercising respect for nature involves mutually responsive exchanges with nonhuman beings and things, as our exercise of respect shifts the ways that we affect and are affected by Earth others. Moreover, the political institutions that instantiate respect for nature, discussed in chapter 6, incorporate nonhuman beings and things into political community in ways that enhance their ability to help shape the trajectories of human (and other) action. The point is that political respect for nature does not carry the same expectation of direct reciprocity that respect for persons does. Respect as it is conceived here means acknowledging that other beings and things, human and otherwise, exist in and for themselves and not solely for the sake of serving our purposes. The being of different things unfolds according to different logics; some of these logics are similar to our own, and in these cases our respect may involve a sense of similarity and an expectation of reciprocity. Yet similarity and reciprocity are not required to acknowledge that other things are more than merely instruments for the satisfaction of our own purposes.

It is important to see that respecting others always *also* as ends and never *merely* as means is not the same thing as respecting them *only* as ends. The use of other beings and things is a necessary condition of all existence, including human existence, as we saw in chapter 3. Relationships that combine respect for the other with personal benefit are common among human beings and are unobjectionable in principle. If I employ you on genuinely fair terms and uphold these terms, I am treating you as an end in yourself even though I am also making use of you as a laborer. When we confide in our friends and lean on our family members—or simply enjoy their company—we are benefiting from them. Indeed, it is partly because we expect to benefit in this way that we seek out their company, which means that we are making use of them, although hopefully not in a merely instrumental way. A merely instrumental use would mean satisfying our own purposes without any consideration of their well-being for their own sake. Merely instrumental use is exploitation, as in a master's use of his slave. Slavery is use without respect. Friendship and love involve respectful use, which distinguishes them from exploitation, even if they also involve a noninstrumental form of appreciation, and sometimes unconditional giving as well. In a similar way, respect for nature is in principle compatible with the human use of it. We can exercise respect for nature while also making use of it to meet our needs, provided that we accept principled constraints on our power of use and that we attend as much as we can to nature's well-being alongside our own. There is no perfect harmony here, but perfect harmony is not the point of respect for nature any more than it is the objective of nondomination.

Respect for nature so conceived is a way of relating to nonhuman beings and things that is more than merely instrumental but that does not fetishize nature as untouchable.[23] Not only does human life depend on the use of nonhuman beings and things, but there is no longer any nature on this Earth that has not already been touched by human beings.[24] Even the most remote parts of the world, which may otherwise retain a pristine wildness, are now subject to human influence, given the ubiquitous effects of our greenhouse gas emissions. A good deal of the nonhuman world reflects much deeper human influence as well, from the crops and domesticated animals whose gene pools have been shaped by our selective breeding practices, to the directly cultivated nature in our urban parks and suburban gardens. The notion that nature should remain untouched, that respect for nature means simply disengaging from it, is antithetical to the human condition. It may be detrimental to nonhuman beings and things too. As William Cronon has observed, many of our "most serious environmental problems start right here, at home, and if we are to solve these problems, we need an environmental ethic that will tell us as much about *using* nature as about *not* using it."[25] This is not to say that wilderness conservation has no place in political respect for nature.[26] The point is that the principle of respect does not imply a strictly hands-off stance toward the nonhuman world or thorough disengagement from it.

Still, if nature, like other persons, is not fundamentally *for us* then the exercise of insufficiently constrained, exploitative human power over nonhuman beings and things will be as illegitimate as the exercise of insufficiently constrained, exploitative power over people. To be sure, the specific harms effected by such power will differ in the case of persons as compared with many other parts of nature. Yet the illegitimacy of power will be the same in the two cases. Nothing has endowed human beings with a legitimate title to dominate nature. We have seen that the agency-based justification collapses once we understand the nonsovereignty of human agency and the agency of some nonhuman animals. Even the Old Testament's book of Genesis, which is still sometimes invoked to depict the human domination of nature as being underwritten by the authority of God, falls short in this regard. According to Genesis, on the sixth day God created human beings and bestowed on them "dominion over the fish of the sea, and over the fowl of the air, and over the cattle, and over all the earth."[27] Yet Genesis envisions human power as subject to the watchful eye of God and answerable to God's command. Indeed, the "dominion" language has sometimes been read through a lens of responsible stewardship, even respect, rather than domination, and there are plenty of contemporary ecologists for whom biblical faith is a motivating source of environmental concern and care.[28] In any case, whatever inspiration the Bible may offer people in their moral lives, it is not an accepted source of political authority in modern democratic societies. In modern democracies, the use of public power cannot be authorized by invoking God's will, and this is true of the public power that people exercise in relation to nature. In the absence of a legitimate title to dominate nonhuman beings and things, such use can only constitute a usurpation. Yet this kind of use is the norm today. Nothing runs deeper in us (or in most people living in modern democratic societies) than the assumption that nature is for us. Consequently, political respect for nature requires a deep, even existential shift in how we understand both nature and ourselves.

The Experience of Respect:
Rupture, Epiphany, and Response

Jacques Derrida's extended meditation on the experience of being addressed by his cat forcefully captures the depth of this shift and the "abyssal rupture" it may entail.[29] One day while getting dressed Derrida notices his cat sitting in the corner of the room gazing at him. He realizes that the cat is watching him, and he sees her register the fact that he sees her watching. He becomes aware that he is being addressed by her, that he and the cat are interacting. Suddenly, he realizes that he is naked, and he finds himself flooded with shame. Why? Surely his nudity means nothing to the cat. As the meditation unfolds, we come to understand that this exchange has exploded the objectifying conceptual frame through which Derrida has always looked at nonhuman animals. The cat appears to him now not merely as an anonymous instance of the genus "cat," but as a distinctly individuated being, a particular embodied consciousness, an "unsubstitutable singularity."[30] He realizes that she is capable not only of movement but of purposeful action, and not only action but also the iterated address and response that constitutes interaction with another.

Moreover, her gaze makes him conscious of himself in a new way, aware of "the abyssal limit of the human."[31] Like most of us, his orientation to animals has been a largely instrumentalizing one, a way of looking at nonhuman others that projects the human self—its needs, desires, purposes—onto them, subsuming the other under this projection of self, and interpellating her/him/it as a mere thing available for human use. But "the animal that sees me see it seeing me" is clearly not reducible to me, and it is not a mere thing.[32] The radical alterity of the cat stops Derrida in his tracks. This alterity is not a denial of common ground or potentially shared experience between the cat and the man. Instead, it is an assertion of the cat's existence as "wholly other" in the sense of not being subsumable under the being of the man, not reducible to the man, not definable solely in terms of human consciousness and human purposes.[33] This "abyssal rupture" makes Derrida conscious of his limits, his boundedness, because he suddenly feels the force of the feline other as an independent being who exists in herself and for herself, rather than simply for him.[34]

The rupture shatters the illusion of the authority that Derrida has always assumed in his relations with animals. This is the source of his shame. It is an emperor-has-no-clothes moment in which he suddenly sees that there is no justification for the "subjection of the animal" to human domination.[35] The very term "animal," with its connotation of inferiority, of brutishness, of thingness available for human use, is nothing more than "an appellation that men have instituted, a name they have given themselves the right and the authority to give to the living other."[36] This authority has no objective ground; it is a naked assertion of power, devoid of legitimacy, a usurpation. Derrida's shame, which is the shattering of his human sense of entitlement, is an ethically transformative epiphany. As he puts it, "the animal looks at us, and we are naked before it. Thinking perhaps begins there."[37] This epiphany stimulates ethical consciousness and opens the door to a form of respect for animal others that was not previously possible.

It is true that Derrida himself does not exactly walk through the door that his epiphany opened. As Haraway points out, although Derrida "came to the edge of respect" in his exchange with the cat, he neither tells nor shows us what the practice of respect for nonhuman animals might involve.[38] The cat's gaze calls for a response that Derrida fails to provide. Haraway gives him credit for recognizing the "absolute alterity"[39] of the animal other, in the sense of acknowledging the cat's more-than-merely-instrumental standing, and for resisting the "facile and imperialist move of claiming to see from the point of view of the other," which may inadvertently subsume the other under the mantle of the self.[40] Yet she insists, rightly, that "shame is not an adequate response" to the denuding of human authority brought about by the cat's gaze.

Haraway herself speaks of respect for animal others as a form of responsiveness through work and play that is a practice of "becoming-with" them, a "co-constitutive naturalcultural dancing" among "those who look back reciprocally" at one another.[41] To respect is "to hold in regard," as Haraway puts it, to "notice, pay attention to," to be curious about the other's feelings, actions, and thoughts—and responsive to them.[42] She gives some examples of scientists who study animals in ways that manifest this respect, and her own work is replete with anecdotes that help to illustrate her vision.[43] Still, while respect involves "looking back at the other reciprocally" in the sense of registering and returning a gaze that contains an address, Haraway acknowledges that there is an irreducible asymmetry between people and nonhuman animals in view of their different ways of being and diverse capacities.[44] One implication is that it may be incumbent on people to respond to animals in ways that animals themselves cannot precisely reproduce with us, or with one another.

The alterity of the other and the asymmetry of response call to mind Emmanuel Levinas, whose phenomenology of "facing the other" inspired Derrida's meditation on being addressed by his cat. As Derrida notes, Levinas himself paid little attention to the animal gaze. His account of respect as attunement and response to the call of an other is limited to human beings. Still, the account is generative for thinking beyond the human.[45] For Levinas, ethical subjectivity is constituted in moments of epiphany like the one Derrida describes, in which one suddenly finds oneself called into question by the face of an other who makes an address. Levinas emphasizes both the alterity and the vulnerability of the other, which he associates with the "defenseless eyes" and the destitution and hunger[46] of "the poor, the stranger, the widow, the orphan."[47] The face of the other as a site of independent being and irreducible needs is a wake-up call to the previously unreflective subject. The other "disturbs the being at home with oneself" of the subject, the "I."[48] Levinas describes this being at home with oneself as a form of "egoism," a "spontaneous freedom" through which the subject projects itself onto the external world without limit, "negating or possessing the non-me."[49] This "imperialism" of the self is a "naïve," unself-conscious exercise of power.[50] Levinas calls it freedom, but it locks the subject into a self-referential "totality"[51] that is actually a kind of stultified containment, even captivity, one that contrasts with the "infinity" that opens to the subject by welcoming an other who exceeds the subject and who "brings me more than I contain."[52]

The face of the other impresses his or her being on our consciousness and "puts the spontaneous freedom within us into question," generating "a critical attitude" that challenges "the naïve right of my powers, my glorious spontaneity as a living being" to use, posses, and subsume all that is not me as if it were there *for* me.[53] It makes me aware of myself as a bounded, limited thing, and aware of the other as having an existence that cannot be reduced to me. This awareness evacuates of authority my unreflective assumption that the world is there solely for me, that I am entitled to make use of others simply for my own purposes. It generates ethical subjectivity in me because "morality begins when freedom, instead of being justified by itself, feels itself to be arbitrary and violent."[54] This "shame that freedom feels for itself"[55] is the shame that Derrida felt before his cat, whose gaze stripped him of his naïve imperialism of the self (and species), started him thinking, and made him acknowledge the emptiness of the presumed right by which people dominate animals.

Two aspects of this Levinasian response to the other are worth highlighting because they can help us fill out the notion of respect for nature. The first is the primordial quality of the response as grounded simply in the alterity of the other; the second is its asymmetry. The response is primordial in the sense that it rests on nothing more than the force of the other's irreducible alterity, meaning the unsubsumable nature of their existence. We are called to respond not necessarily because we identify with the other, not because we see ourselves in the other's needy eyes, not because we recognize some essentially shared experience or common quality between us.[56] This is not to deny the possibility of commonality, whether among persons or between people and nonhuman parts of nature. Instead, it is to emphasize what Levinas sees as the ethically generative quality of the response. As he puts it, "the welcoming of the other is the ultimate fact,"[57] meaning that my responsiveness is not dependent on any facts about the other, such as "attributes" that would "reduce him to what is common to him and other beings," including me.[58] Nor does the response presuppose an independent set of principles or standards of right; no system of ideas underlies the epiphany, according to Levinas. The address of the other simply presents him to me as "a nudity," meaning a being whose existence is irreducible. As Levinas says, in addressing me "the face has turned to me—and this is its very nudity. It *is* by itself, and not by reference to a system."[59]

It is true that Levinas emphasizes the neediness of the other, referring regularly to vulnerable groups of people, to their "defenseless eyes"[60] and to their "destitution and hunger."[61] Yet he insists that the epiphany is not dependent on anything in particular about the other aside from his alterity, meaning the independence of his existence as something that cannot be subsumed under my existence or merely instrumentalized for my purposes. By addressing me, the simple "presentation of being in the face" of the other, whatever its affective comportment may be, "introduces into me what was not in me" and "puts into question the brutal spontaneity" of my "egoism" as an "immanent destiny."[62] It makes me aware of the independence of the other as not reducible to me, and awakens me to my own tendency to project my will onto others and to treat them as if they *were* reducible in this way. It makes this tendency itself questionable to me. In this respect, Levinas's recurring references to the widow, the orphan, and the poor are somewhat misleading. The other need not be suffering in ways I can identify with to elicit in me the epiphany of self-awareness and to generate an ethical response.

Coming face to face with the suffering of others can be an arresting experience, to be sure. This is true as much for animal suffering as for human suffering. The lengths to which American society goes to hide from human view the animal suffering that transpires in factory farms, slaughterhouses, and animal laboratories is an indicator of just how potent the face of the suffering other can be. It is also an example of how disavowal can obstruct ethical epiphanies that we would rather avoid, and block responses that we do not wish to make. Earth others present themselves to us in ways that do not always involve suffering, however. Derrida's cat, after all, addressed him impassively and in no apparent distress. She disrupted his naïve imperialism of the self simply by making her distinctive being present to him. For those who are attuned to the "faces" of nonhuman others, a stand of trees or a mountain in repose against the evening sky may also generate an epiphany, making us feel the irreducible alterity of their being and of our "emprise" over them as nothing more than what Levinas calls a "usurpation."[63] The primordial quality of the response means that we need not assimilate nature's various parts to ourselves in order to feel the force of their presence; we need not make likeness a condition of respect.

To respect nature in a post-Levinasian way is therefore to acknowledge the existence of nonhuman beings and things as having significance that cannot be captured by their significance for us, but it does not require us to specify the content of this remainder. It eschews a merely instrumental orientation to nature, without insisting that nature has intrinsic value by virtue of some particular set of attributes or shared characteristics.[64] Consequently, we can have different interpretations of nature's ethical remainder and the basis of its more-than-merely-instrumental standing. Some of us may characterize this remainder in religious terms, as in the idea that creation embodies divine meaning and purpose. Others may see it in aesthetic terms, focusing on the grandeur or sublimity they find in nature. Still others may remain agnostic about the remainder, simply accepting that Earth's being exceeds its being-for-us without needing to say why. Like respect for persons, respect for nature can be affirmed from a variety of different perspectives much in the way of an overlapping consensus.[65] Although there are plenty of worldviews today that run counter to respect for nature, many others are compatible with it. The diverse breeds of environmentalists on the contemporary scene, from eco-feminists to conservative Christians to neo-Marxists to green capitalists to Indigenous spiritualists and beyond, are evidence of this diversity. The unspecified quality of the ethical remainder in the other is therefore an advantage rather than a deficit. It can help stabilize the principle of respect in the context of pluralistic societies, where substantial disagreement about ultimate values exists. It also gives the principle traveling power across societies, which is crucial given the global nature of so many environmental problems and the need for cooperation among otherwise diverse peoples.

The asymmetry of the response is also important. "What I permit myself to demand of myself" by way of response to the other, Levinas writes, "is not comparable with what I have the right to demand of the other."[66] There is no assumption that the other will—or even could—repay me in kind. To respond to the other is "to give" as one can, with no strings attached.[67] One gives simply because one is called and one is able. In extending a Levinasian ethos of respect beyond the human, this asymmetry matters in two ways. First, at the individual level the epiphany attunes my ethical sensibility to the being of the other, but it focuses my practical, action-guiding faculties solely on myself. It tells me nothing about what the other should do, and it gives me no grounds for expectations in this regard. Rather than generating a relation of reciprocity between us in which I could reasonably expect the other to return my respect in kind, it creates a relation of responsiveness that has the character, as Levinas puts it, of a gift. Even as a gift, however, responsiveness is very much an inter-subjective, relational experience. A gift is an intervention into an ongoing relationship, after all, intended to generate *some* kind of reaction on the part of the recipient. This reaction need not take the form of a gift in kind, or even a direct acknowledgment. A gift can elicit a reaction simply through the effects it has on the unfolding relationship between giver and receiver. In the environmental context, this means that although my expression of respect for my cat or the forest behind my house will not be exactly reproduced by them or returned to me in kind, it will nevertheless shape the continuing context of interactions between us over time, the quality of the relationships through which we affect one another. In this regard, while the asymmetry of respect distinguishes it from reciprocity, respect remains a deeply relational practice.

Asymmetry matters at the species level as well. The epiphany answers a distinctly human question: What should we do, and how should we live? The "we" here is a human one, and our answers to the question are intended to guide human action in particular. What other beings and things should do, or how Earth systems themselves should behave, is no part of the ideal of respect being developed here. It would be wrong to hold nonhuman beings and things to the same standards of behavior that we expect from people. Martha Nussbaum has written that nonhuman animals not only are entitled to be treated justly by human beings but should be made to act justly themselves through "the gradual formation of an interdependent world in which all species will enjoy cooperative and mutually supportive relations with one another." She acknowledges that "nature is not that way and never has been," but she insists that this fact "calls, in a very general way, for the gradual supplanting of the natural by the just."[68] Yet part of respecting nature is allowing nonhuman beings and things to be who and what they are, not trying to make them like us. In this sense, the asymmetry of the post-Levinasian approach makes it a human-centered view but not an anthropocentric one. The approach is not anthropocentric because it does not see the value of all things as being reducible to human use value. Nor does it assimilate all things to a human standard, expecting the same things from them all and insisting on likeness with the human as a condition of moral and political standing. It also asks us to be open to learning about—and learning from—other beings and things so as to make new forms of relationship with them and new ways of being human possible over time.

Yet if the practice of respect for nature is binding only on people, it enables us to be moved and affected by nonhuman beings and things in ways that are not otherwise available to us. In this sense, respect for nature is not exactly a one-way street. It makes us more alive to nature's many vitalities. It involves active listening, looking, communicating (in most cases nonlinguistically), and feeling-with Earth others, and it therefore puts us into more responsive relationships with them. So it would be wrong to see respect for nature as something that human beings bestow on a passive field of recipients. Nature is not passive but full of vitalities, and respect for nature means being in relationship with complex networks of *others*, not objects. In all these ways, respect for nature asks us to reach beyond the confines of our habitual self- and species-referentiality. A post-Levinasian respect for nature is therefore nonanthropocentric and fully embedded in more-than-human relationality even as it is also distinctively human.

One might wonder whether all nonhuman others have a "face" in the sense of being able to address us in ways that inspire epiphany and response, given that the communicative capacities required to make an address are not shared by all things.[69] Cats, who can form conscious purposes and communicate their intentions to us ("Let me out the door," "Feed me," "Let's play," etc.), address us in ways that a forest or a river cannot do. Cats also can experience suffering that is not open to things that lack sentience. Still, forests and rivers are assemblages of countless nonhuman beings and things that affect and are affected by us. Their existence can erupt into our consciousness in all kinds of ways, as when a breeze carries the scent of pine or the sound of birdsong from a nearby forest, or when the river behind us overspills its banks, flooding our homes and fields. These eruptions differ from a conscious, purposive address. Yet they do present the being of others to us in ways that convey their vitality and information about their condition, and this can be transformative for us if we are receptive. Indeed, they can function much like the address of a human or animal other, enlarging our own subjectivity by "introduc[ing] into me what was not in me" and "put[ting] into question the brutal spontaneity" of my "egoism" as an "immanent destiny."[70] So the face of a river or a forest can stimulate the epiphany that makes us mindful of others in their irreducible alterity, meaning their status as other-than-us, the fact that their existence cannot be fully captured by what they can do for us. In addition to animals, then, nonhuman things can be catalysts for the emergence of ethical epiphany, for self-consciousness about our limits and shame about our usurpations, and hence for respect for nature as self-restraint and responsiveness.

Eruptions of nature's vitality, animal and otherwise, can be extremely forceful and are not always welcome. They put is in touch with the humbling aspect of respect, which arises when the independent force of an other confronts us not simply as beauty or as vulnerability but as something threatening. Acknowledging the independent force of nature regularly involves a sense of unease, sometimes even fear, in the face of nonhuman vitalities: a volcanic eruption, a drought, a virus, a tick. A healthy humility about the limits of human capacity and the potential force of nonhuman beings and things is an important part of respect for nature. In this regard, respect means acknowledging not only that the being of Earth others exceeds their use value to us but also that it eludes our control and may pose a threat to our well-being.[71]

This is another way that political respect for nature differs from respect for persons. An institutional order that instantiates respect for persons secures them against one another through a system of rights and the coercive force of law. In this context, the fear and awe dimensions of respect are much diminished and do not play a significant part in the regular experience of respect. Although a political order that instantiates respect for nature reliably constrains human power in relation to nonhuman beings and things, it can never make the behavior of nature altogether predictable. Consequently, fear and awe may be more persistent features of political respect for nature than they are in the case of respect for persons. The unease that may accompany respect for nature reflects the fact that although nature can be subject to domination by human beings, with the many harms this generates, it cannot be fully mastered or controlled by us. Indeed, as destructive as people are in the environmental domain, we are also immensely vulnerable to nonhuman beings and things. Respect for nature involves accepting this fact, a humble attunement to the ultimately ineradicable wildness of Earth's more-than-human parts.

If nonhuman beings and things *can* be catalysts for the ethical epiphany that Derrida and Levinas depict, in practice they regularly fail to produce this response. Of course, the same is often true for the people who address us. Levinas formulated his account of the face, the epiphany, and the response in the aftermath of the Holocaust. As a European Jew who lived through World War II, he knew that the address of the other frequently fails to elicit a response, and he saw how destructive disavowal can be. Yet if he was alive to the limits of the face as a catalyst for ethical response, he offers few political resources for attenuating these limits. We very much need political resources today. Our current condition is one of overwhelming disavowal of nonhuman others.[72] We are so steeped in the mentality of the old human exceptionalism, with its sense of species superiority and the instrumentalization of nature, that we have made ourselves blind and deaf to the addresses of nonhuman beings and things.

Perhaps this collective disavowal helps explain the truncated trajectory of Derrida's interaction with his cat. Seized by his cat's gaze, he had enough awareness to recognize the address as calling for a response, but he remained too trapped within "his textual canon of Western philosophy and literature," as Haraway puts it, to actually respond.[73] To bring respect for nature into being we need to insist on it as a political imperative, and to actively cultivate it through our political institutions and public practices. This means constituting robust political protections for nature alongside our protections for people, and it means promoting richer forms of relationality between people and non-human nature as part of the public ethos of democratic citizenship.

Practicing Political Respect

Political respect for nature puts us into political community with nonhuman beings and things, but in extending the boundaries of political community in this way it also transforms the meaning of political community. In the centuries since the Age of Revolution when democratic political forms began to overturn the hierarchical orders of the old regime in Europe and the Americas, political equality conceived as the same set of rights and duties for all members of the polity has come to be seen as the only legitimate meaning of political community. The identification of political community with political equality was an important step in the historical break from the old regime with its many forms of domination, and equality among persons remains crucial today as a central element of legitimate politics. At the same time, it constitutes a roadblock to the inventiveness and political imagination that are now needed to effectively address our environmental problems, and it is an obstacle to creating political communities that are more emancipatory for both people and the Earth.

We do need to insist on political equality for people, albeit in the nuanced, difference-respecting forms that many feminists, disability theorists, and Indigenous peoples have called for. Yet we need to combine political equality for people with forms of political inclusion for nature that allow for differentiation in the rights and responsibilities of membership. It makes no sense to ask cows and rainforests to obey the law, or cast a ballot on election day, or pay taxes, or deliberate with others while respecting their rights, but this fact should not prevent us from extending political consideration and certain forms of inclusion to cows and rainforests. Respect for nature requires us to constrain our action with reference to the well-being of nonhuman others, and to formally incorporate responsiveness to their well-being into political decision making. It means that there are principled limits to what we may do to cows and rainforests, and that their well-being must be part of the discussion when we make public decisions about, for example, animal agriculture or resource extraction. In this way it reflects the basic democratic idea that the power of individuals and groups should never be unlimited but is legitimately constrained by the well-being of others.

Familiar mechanisms such as rights and political representation, which formally establish respect for persons, can help us institutionalize respect for nature too. Various approaches to nonhuman rights and representation have been pursued in recent years, including offices of animal and environmental welfare, proxy representation for endangered species or habitats, and constitutional protections and legal standing for animals and the environment.[74] These mechanisms are crucial resources for securing the structural conditions of nondomination for Earth others, and we shall explore some of them in more detail in chapter 6. In addition to the structural role they play, rights and representation also can help foster a public ethos of respect for nature. For example, to be a holder of rights is to be publicly recognized as having worth and dignity that are independent of one's use value or benefit to others.[75] This recognition has both a "legal-operational" side and a "cultural-psychological" one, as Christopher Stone puts it.[76] It simultaneously structures the objective context of our relationships with others and shapes our subjective experience of how we see and value them. As Stone points out, it is difficult for people living in modern democratic societies to conceive of something that lacks rights "as anything but than a *thing*" available for their use.[77] Granting rights can therefore be a powerful engine of cultural reform insofar as it reconstructs the perceptions and public practices that instrumentalize particular kinds of others. Historically, as Stone shows, "each successive extension of rights to some new entity has been, theretofore, a bit unthinkable," but in each case the extension of rights eventually helped transform how the new rights holders were regarded by others.[78] Over time, what became unthinkable was that those groups had once been denied rights, that it had ever seemed reasonable that they should be treated as the mere instruments of other people's wills.

Stone argues forcefully on these grounds for the extension of certain rights to nonhuman beings and things. Nature should not have all the rights—or the same rights—that people have, as he acknowledges. Yet his argument suggests that appropriate sets of rights for some nonhuman beings and things are a necessary step, both for establishing the structural conditions of respect for nature and in cultivating respect as a public ethos.[79] Like rights, political representation also nourishes the more-than-instrumental status of those it covers. It signals the public expectation that their well-being is to count with decision makers, that it may reasonably constrain state action and the behavior of others. So rights and representation are integral parts of political respect for nature, not only by establishing basic protections for nature in the laws that constitute the political community but also by enshrining them at the core of citizenship and embedding them in the reigning public ethos.[80] Rights and representation are not by themselves enough to guarantee respect for nature, but then they have never been enough to guarantee respect for persons, either. In fact, both rights and representation can be misused, and both can generate unintended effects. Consequently, we will need to pursue these practices in a critical way that is sensitive to how they can fail to achieve or even undermine their desired ends, and we must be ready to respond accordingly.[81] We shall have more to say about this in chapter 6.

The practice of political respect for nature poses substantial challenges. For one thing, the category of nature is large and diverse, including nonhuman life forms together with the nonbiotic entities and ecosystems that sustain them. Given this diversity, conflicts are endemic. In practicing respect for nature, we may find that being responsive to the well-being of certain Earth others causes unavoidable harm to others. The practice of respect may therefore require us to mediate between the needs of different organisms, and sometimes it will require mediating between the well-being of nonhuman individuals and that of species and ecosystems. For example, human development has led to the near extinction of caribou in Canada and the northern United States. Anthropogenic factors have also contributed to a rise in the wolf population in that area, and the wolves are rapidly eradicating the last of the caribou. To mitigate this human disruption to the ecosystem, government-paid hunters have begun to cull individual wolves.[82] They are right to do so, but respect requires that they minimize the suffering of the individual animals they kill, and that they watch for and respond to unintended harms that may accrue to local packs and ecosystems.

Then, too, some species and ecosystems are more central to the flourishing of life on Earth than others, and we may have reason to prioritize their well-being over that of more marginal things when unavoidable conflicts arise in the context of mitigating human impacts. For instance, Aldo Leopold's description of land as "a fountain of energy flowing through a circuit of soils, plants, and animals" reminds us just how much life depends on "the microscopic flora and fauna of the soil."[83] These tiny beings determine the land's fertility, the "ability of soil to receive, store, and release energy" into the food chains that sustain other species and broader ecosystems.[84] In practicing respect for nature we may sometimes need to give priority, as we work to mitigate our own effects, to parts of the Earth on which many other beings and things depend. In navigating conflicts like these, we will need to use our best judgment, drawing on the most reliable information available and ameliorating our harm as far as possible. Such conflicts will rarely be resolved without remainder, given the complexity of ecosystems and the diverse forms of well-being within nature. Respect for nature does not demand the perfect reconciliation of needs any more than respect for persons does. Needs will conflict, and practicing respect is often messy. Respect asks for our best efforts and good faith in being attuned and responsive to others. This is a perpetually unfinished business, an iterative process marked by continuing effort, learning, progress, mistakes—and more effort.

Respect for nature will also put pressure on human interests. Does respect require us to protect the well-being of bacteria and viruses that are deadly to us? Does it demand that we forsake human security, comfort, prosperity? Respect is a principle for regulating human life in relation to others, meaning that human life is a condition of its possibility. Consequently, respect cannot require action that would systematically undermine the survival of our species or make it impossible to meet basic human needs. Just as the principle of respect for persons allows for acts of self-defense, then, respect for nature is compatible with efforts to protect ourselves from pests and predators, and compatible more generally with pursuing the conditions of human well-being. Indeed, respect for nature must be practiced in ways that are consistent with respect for persons, who are, of course, parts of nature, and this will include respecting human rights. Yet if the two forms of respect can put pressure on one another, they are also mutually reinforcing in certain ways. Among other things, persons with human rights are better positioned to be able to practice political respect for nature. Their rights empower them politically, economically, and socially to insist on environmental protections and to demand that their societies foster practices of nondomination in relation to Earth others. Likewise, where animal and Earth rights are strong, environmentally damaging practices that also harm people, such as toxic dumping and resource depletion, are more difficult for large corporations and governments to impose on them.

Still, conflicts between human interests and the well-being of nonhuman parts of nature will regularly arise. When this happens, respect for nature requires us to distinguish between important human needs and superfluous human desires. Feeding, clothing, and housing ourselves are basic needs and justifiable enterprises, compatible in principle with respect for nature, but unlimited consumerism, profit-driven extractivism, and cruelty are not. Moreover, while a secure and comfortable life is a perfectly legitimate aim for human beings to have, the unlimited growth of the human population is an illegitimate imposition on Earth others. A human population that exceeds the carrying capacity of the Earth puts the satisfaction of even basic human needs systematically at odds with the well-being of nonhuman beings and things. It necessarily causes avoidable harm to them, effectively instrumentalizing them for human purposes.[85]

The distinction between legitimate aims and superfluous desires is not something that can be specified once and for all in the abstract. It is subject to reasonable disagreement and ought to be open to contestation, and we will need to look beyond the principle of respect for nature to resolve disputes when they arise. An eco-politics that incorporates respect for nature cannot hope to rest on a single, settled agreement about this matter but instead will put contestation about it at the center of public debate and decision making. This means continuously seeking to incorporate new learning and input that results from communicative and other interactions with nonhuman others alongside the input from people. This kind of iterative and inclusive deliberation must be a constitutive feature of any political community that means to establish political respect for nature. And even when we have good reason to consider something a substantial threat or to regard a particular use of nature as legitimate, we should be careful in how we manage the threat and attentive in how we carry out the use. Things that are threats to us may be important food sources for other animals or otherwise contribute to the health of ecosystems. Likewise, the effort to eradicate a pest can pose risks to other living things, as when the indiscriminate use of pesticides contributes to the collapse of bee colonies. Our ecological knowledge is in its infancy; we should always assume that there is more to the picture than we can presently see, and act accordingly.[86] Still, respect for nature does allow for human beings to defend ourselves and to provide for our own well-being, even when this requires the sacrifice of nonhuman beings and things. What it rules out is the unreflective destruction of nature for the purpose of satisfying endless consumerist desires and the boundless pursuit of profit. Respect asks us instead to bring a more discriminating sensibility to the pursuit of our own well-being and to pair it with attunement and responsiveness to the well-being of nonhuman others.

It bears repeating that the use of nonhuman beings and things is a necessary condition of human existence, as of all existence. This use regularly, ineluctably involves destruction and violence. Even the most sustainable way of life embodying the greatest respect for nature would require the continuing destruction of many Earth others. Facing up to this inevitability is sobering. It could easily generate guilt and paralysis. Guilt and paralysis need to be resisted, however, both because we cannot avoid impacting the Earth and because such sentiments are deeply disabling in the environmental context. Yet we ought not disavow the sacrifices we impose on nature, either. Knowing that we cannot avoid harming nonhuman others may too easily allow us to disavow our harm or rationalize unlimited harm, including harm driven not by the basic terms of human well-being but by proliferating, superfluous human desires. We need to actively counter our tendency to disavow the sacrifices that human existence inevitably imposes on nature but without being paralyzed by guilt about the scope of our impact.

One way to resist disavowal without generating guilt-ridden paralysis is through public rituals of mourning and memorialization. Such rituals simultaneously mark a loss or sacrifice and embody a collective commitment, as Simon Stow puts it, to "go on together as a polity in the face of [that] loss."[87] Recent work in political theory has demonstrated the long-standing and very central place of public mourning in democratic societies from Pericles's funeral oration in ancient Athens to the AIDS quilt, the 9/11 memorial, and street theater in Black Lives Matter protests.[88] The right kinds of speeches, memorials, and rituals can simultaneously be a salve for grief and an acknowledgment of accountability that spurs critical reflection and sometimes collective transformation. The AIDS quilt, which began traveling the United States for display in public spaces in 1987, is a good example. Conceived as a public expression of mourning for the many people who had died of the disease, it was also intended to make American citizens more aware of the stigma and bias against gay people that was hindering effective treatment and care, and to generate political and cultural change. As one activist put it, the quilt was "a weapon to deploy against the government; to shame them with stark visual evidence of their utter failure to respond to the suffering and death that spread and increased with every passing day." The quilt was therefore "both a memorial—and a call to action."[89] It was meant to express grief but also to transform the country's public ethos.

The public mourning most often discussed in democratic theory today is limited to the mourning of human losses, meaning sacrifices imposed on human beings and on the polity conceived as an exclusively human community. Because so many of us fail to recognize the sacrifices we impose on nature as ethically and politically significant losses, part of the work of public mourning in this context must be to establish for nature the condition that Judith Butler calls "grievability."[90] As Butler points out, mourning speeches, monuments, and rituals often do more than simply call attention to losses for which the polity already feels grief; they may also call forth grief by marking certain losses as publicly significant and worthy of regret. The AIDS quilt identified people with AIDS for the first time as publicly grievable and entitled to collective response. Moreover, even as the quilt was a reminder of the losses suffered by those with AIDS and their loved ones, and an effort to hold the country accountable for its bias against gay people, the quilt also called for a public commitment to go forward together on more inclusive terms.

A more recent public memorial—this one for a tree—suggests how we might begin to make use of public mourning to both express and catalyze a public ethos of respect for nature. On April 27, 2018, roughly thirty members of the Brown University community including faculty, students, university chaplains, and groundskeepers gathered under the massive canopy of the 110-year-old Angell Street beech tree to hold its funeral. The tree was slated to be cut down over the summer to make room for a new performing arts center. A faculty member from the History Department, whose office looked into the branches of the tree, decided that its life and impending death needed to be commemorated. The service she organized included readings from the Bible and the Koran as well as some poems, a Chinese proverb, and excerpts from the writings of Thoreau, John Muir, and the German forester Peter Wohlleben. Along with sadness about its imminent demise, people expressed gratitude for the tree's long life, for its cooling shade in summer, for the habitat it provided to birds and other things, for its sheer beauty. The service also included reflections on the university's decision to destroy the tree, noting other exceptional trees taken down over the years to make way for new buildings, and criticizing the university's repeated failure to plan its development in ways that would accommodate such trees, or at least protect spaces where replacement trees planted today could grow to maturity over time. One could sense a bit of self-consciousness in the crowd: A funeral for a tree! Was there not something a little ridiculous in this ceremony, in us? But the unease was trumped by a palpable, shared desire to forge a new kind of relationship between people and the Earth, one premised on respect rather than domination. Like the AIDS quilt, the memorial service for the Angell Street beech captured the powerful way that public mourning can mark a particular loss or sacrifice as grievable, generate reflection on collective accountability for the loss, and catalyze a public commitment to create more respectful practices going forward.

So along with rights and representation, ritualized practices of public mourning and memorialization can help us practice political respect for nature. When we cannot avoid damaging nature to meet our legitimate needs, respect requires us to recognize rather than disavow the damage, and to publicly acknowledge both the loss itself and our role in it, however unavoidable this role may have been. It also elicits collective reflection on the conditions that made the loss unavoidable (or made it seem unavoidable) and invites us to reimagine and, where possible, to reconstruct these conditions. Public mourning is another way of "facing" others in Levinas's sense because it means resisting disavowal, insisting on the considerability of Earth others even when we find ourselves having to harm them. It also offers an alternative to guilt-ridden paralysis, a means for going forward in good faith, even as we acknowledge the costs to nonhuman others that our life on Earth inevitably exacts.

Public mourning can be misused, of course. If it is invoked merely to appease a guilty conscience without generating critical reflection, it will not serve political respect for nature. Moreover, it should be balanced with public rituals that attune us to nature's many vitalities and not only to its vulnerability and destruction. Earth Day is too generic to do much work in this regard at present, but it could be enhanced by the addition of more concrete holidays and festivals that turn our minds and hearts to particular parts of nature and their ways of life. Perhaps along with the local Octoberfest we might have festivals marking the annual migrations of birds or (in coastal communities) the hatching of sea turtles. After all, we have public holidays and rituals to remind us about the founding of the country, about our veterans, past presidents, and most important political activists, even about our mothers, fathers, and sweethearts. These formal markers of appreciation stimulate awareness of our debts to others and the sacrifices they have made for our well-being. Public holidays and rituals that attune us to nonhuman beings and things, acknowledge our dependence on them, and commemorate both their sacrifices and their vitality could be a valuable way to practice and to nourish respect for nature.

In practicing respect, we must be mindful of the different subject positions we inhabit and the attenuations of agency they may imply. True, the large literature documenting the environmentalism of the poor demonstrates that people who are impoverished and politically marginalized can be effective practitioners of respect for nature and powerful agents of environmental change.[91] Indeed, wealthy societies have much to learn from the environmentalism of the poor and from the varieties of human/more-than-human relations found outside the so-called developed world. Still, where people find themselves trapped in poverty with the only available jobs requiring them to engage in harmful resource extraction, or when the only food and clothing they can afford to buy are produced through practices that torture animals and poison the Earth, they will need help in addressing the broader political, economic, and social conditions that constrain their agency and that hinder the practice of respect for nature. This consideration has implications for the accountability of individual agents within particular societies, given their distinctive dynamics of inequality, but it also applies at the global level. Wealthy societies bear a special responsibility for supporting political respect for nature. This means not only practicing respect themselves but also promoting changes that can empower those in other countries to practice it as well—for example, by helping to pay for green technologies and food systems that would enable poor countries to meet their people's needs in genuinely sustainable ways.

Conclusions

So political respect for nature means orienting ourselves to nonhuman beings and things in more than merely instrumental ways. It means constraining our use of power in relation to them and being responsive to their well-being along with our own. It means acknowledging the normative force of their being-for-themselves, the irreducibility of their existence as exceeding their use value to people. It means restraining our inclination to subject them to the unbounded force of human desires and perspectives. And it means orienting ourselves toward nonhuman others *as others*, meaning as more than simply objects. It means listening harder and watching more closely for what they have to teach us about themselves and about us, and cultivating more cooperative forms of relationality and interaction. Finally, it means humility, acknowledging our own nonsovereignty, the limits of our control, our vulnerability to the ultimately unmasterable wildness of Earth's more-than-human parts, and our frequent fragility in the face of what they can do. This alternative relationality is another aspect of what is political about political respect for nature: in shift-ing our sensibilities away from domination and toward more respectful forms of interaction with nonhuman beings and things, we begin to reconstitute the power relations among us.

In practicing respect for nature, we will face plenty of conflicts and compet-ing needs, some of them irreducible. Respect for nature is not a solution to these conflicts but an approach to navigating them. It asks us to treat human needs and interests as parts of a larger whole that has value, rather than as trump cards, as the only things with value. To interrupt the destructive dynam-ics of our environmental domination, we need to affirm respect for nature as a public ethos that is authoritative, even imperative, for us as democratic citi-zens and to establish it in the political institutions that govern our collective life. Respect for nature needs real politics, meaning the backing of legal rights and institutional representation as well as the collective action embodied in public rituals of mourning and appreciation.

These changes are tremendously demanding, and the challenges can be overwhelming. Still, we should remember that large-scale transformations of selves and societies have happened before. Christianity once was new, after all. Capitalism, too, at one time did not exist. Human rights, representative democracy, and the idea of the intrinsic dignity of the person all had to be invented. This is not a triumphalist narrative; none of these developments has been unambiguously positive—not by a long shot. The point is the scale of the changes to self and society that they have generated. The transformation that political respect for nature requires is every bit as deep and wide as those transformations were, but it is also just as possible. Political respect for nature will not solve all our environmental problems, but it is an important part—and it is an attainable part—of moving beyond environmental domination to a politics of emancipation for people and the Earth. Still, it cannot succeed alone. To be successful, efforts to foster respect for nature must proceed hand in hand with the development of a new culture of responsibility. Like environ-mental domination, eco-emancipation is a multifaceted phenomenon, and our best chance of achieving it lies in a holistic approach that engages our efforts across the domains of politics, economy, and culture, an approach that not only transforms how we relate to nonhuman nature and one another but also makes us new to ourselves. Eco-responsibility can help.

5

Eco-Responsibility

TODAY THE CONCEPT OF responsibility is saddled with associations that instead of supporting ecological emancipation actually help to sustain environmental domination. For one thing, in societies marked by neoliberal policies and culture, responsibility is overwhelmingly understood in highly individualized ways. The "responsibilization" of the individual subject, as Wendy Brown calls it, treats people as if they are responsible as individuals for outcomes that are in fact produced by complex, interacting structural forces and authorities.[1] It undercuts collective problem solving, undermines solidarity, and disempowers us in the face of large-scale consolidations of economic and political power. More generally, prevailing views of responsibility treat individual intentionality and control as preconditions of responsibility. This way of thinking about responsibility is at odds with the structure of most environmental problems, in which people contribute to environmental damage largely without intending to do so or controlling their effects. Climate change is perhaps the most obvious example, but the environmental domain is replete with cases in which many people participate in harmful outcomes for which they cannot reasonably be held responsible, given existing notions of responsibility with their emphasis on intentionality and control. This disjunction undermines effective environmental action because when no one is responsible, little gets done. Finally, conventional conceptions of responsibility fail to factor in the nonsovereignty of agency and the intersecting effects of domination, which position people differently within prevailing relations of power and shape the kinds of impact they can have.

At the same time, the practice of responsibility when rightly conceived is the seed of all political transformation and an integral part of liberation. It is crucial to overcoming environmental domination and to creating more ecologically emancipatory communities. For responsibility to serve this empowering and transformative purpose, however, it needs to be radically reconfigured. That is the purpose of this chapter. I draw from recent work on responsibility for structural injustice, arguing that responsibility consists most fundamentally in an *ability to respond*, and that it is deeply entwined with power.[2] This means that those who are already privileged and powerful will have special responsibilities for redressing environmental domination, but also that cultivating responsibility in the right ways can be empowering for everyone. Taken together, these considerations suggest the value of a plural approach to responsibility, one that enables us to distinguish among types and degrees of responsibility in ways that attend to the structural complexity of environmental problems, the nonsovereignty of human agency, and the differential effects of power.

In addition to changing how we think about responsibility, we need to generate new practices of responsibility, including networks of what one commentator calls "connected activism," in which people cultivate their ability to respond to environmental domination together with others.[3] Moreover, because existing social epistemologies shape what we think we are responsible for, including what we even regard as a problem requiring a response, new practices of responsibility will need to shake up some of our core assumptions about the world and our place(s) in it. Here contestatory political activism can be an important resource for change if it causes us to confront forms of environmental damage and creaturely suffering that have been masked by existing epistemologies of ignorance.[4] Disruptive politics can force social and cognitive crises that open the door to more reflective thinking and to behavioral change.

To foster eco-responsibility at the highest level will require new institutional arrangements. Existing political and economic systems stand in the way of the fullest realization of eco-responsibility, and these systems are maintained through institutions that channel power and shape behavioral incentives in particular ways. Chapter 6 explores some institutional changes that could make a difference. Yet we cannot wait for institutional changes to happen. In pursuing eco-responsibility, we must begin from where we are today. The experience of activists across a wide range of issue areas demonstrates that, despite the obstacles, it is almost always possible to make a start on political transformation, and it is often possible to have an impact. As Brooke Ackerly's work on human rights activism shows, people regularly take up responsibility for making a better world even when the world they are currently in is shot through with domination in ways that interfere with their efforts.[5] There are no guarantees of success, but there are countless possibilities for creating changes that, if pursued over time, have the potential to generate meaningful transformation.

Engaging in this effort through practices of eco-responsibility is an intrinsically liberatory activity. It releases us from the bondage of passively accepting our entrapment by forces that exploit the Earth and our own bodies for profit and power, and that make us complicit in the domination of human and nonhuman others. In this regard, practicing eco-responsibility, even imperfectly and in the context of existing domination, is an emancipatory experience. However partial and incomplete, it offers us a measure of freedom here and now, even as it opens the door to a wider and deeper emancipation over time. The first part of the chapter lays out the dominant view of responsibility as resting on intention and control and shows why it proves inadequate to contemporary environmental problems and the realities of human agency as a nonsovereign phenomenon. The second part draws on recent work in political theory that seeks more capacious ways to understand responsibility, particularly in the context of structural injustice, and it elaborates an alternative repertoire of responsibility that distinguishes responsibility as *culpability* from responsibility as *accountability* and *responsiveness*, arguing for a pluralist approach that gives all three a role in the environmental domain. The third part explores initiatives that could support the cultivation of eco-responsibility in its plural forms.[6]

The Limits of Liability in a "Sea of Agency"

The most familiar views of responsibility in moral philosophy and political theory theorize responsibility through the lens of legal liability, which requires both intentionality and control on the part of the agent.[7] We do not normally hold people responsible for something if they did not mean to do it or could not control what happened. Indeed, the "control condition," as the second criterion is known, is regularly treated as "the very essence of moral responsibility."[8] Yet many environmental problems today result from dynamics that are far too complex for any single agent to control, whether individual or collective, and they often involve effects that are generated without anyone having intended them. Nobody consciously sets out to warm the Earth, for example, and no single participant or group of participants can stop it, yet the effect transpires only because of the contributions that all participants make. Moreover, while their aggregated, interacting effects are harmful, the effects of each agent taken individually are negligible, disrupting the causal connection between agent and outcome. To compound the problem, agents often have few if any alternatives, given existing structural conditions that may include not only poverty, systemic inequality, and political marginalization but the basic terms of modern existence for all of us. Finally, all agents, both individual and collective, operate in the context of pressures exerted by intersubjective but nonagentic forces, such as global markets, and these pressures often contribute to environmental harms. Together, these factors create what Dale Jamieson and Marcello Di Paola call a "shifting and only partially coherent landscape of agency" that is fundamentally at odds with our existing conceptual resources for ascribing responsibility.[9] The result, as Jamieson and Di Paolo say, is that "in this sea of agency it is difficult to assign responsibilities, both because responsibilities are enmeshed across units and levels of analysis" and because "it is often just not clear who is responsible for doing what." Consequently, "everyone, even the worst actors, can claim 'plausible deniability.'"[10]

One might think that this deniability would be freeing. Like the ring of Gyges depicted in Plato's *Republic*, which enables those who wear it to act under a cloak of invisibility that liberates them from the consequences of their actions, the "sea of agency" regularly lets us off the hook for our environmental effects.[11] Yet far from feeling like a liberation, for most of us the experience is more commonly one of diminished agency, a sense of inefficacy and entrapment by forces beyond our control. We find ourselves participating whether we like it or not in the "unintended effects of systemic, interlocking forces and structures" that generate environmental damage we may regret or even abhor.[12] The light-switch example considered in chapter 3, in which simply turning on a living-room lamp forces us into "a global network of eco-altering" forces that we do not fully understand and cannot evade, illustrates this disempowering dynamic.[13] Then too, we know that even if we were to go off the grid our individual refusal would have little effect.

The awareness of our negligibility together with the sense of forced complicity alienates us from our own agency, leaving us "disoriented and skeptical about our capacity to manage our ecological entanglements."[14] The flip side of our inability to attribute responsibility is therefore not liberation but disempowerment. This disempowerment helps explain why so many of us remain so passive in the face of escalating environmental crises. Exacerbating the problem is the interaction between the structural conditions that make up the contemporary sea of agency and our culture of responsibility, meaning the particular repertoire of beliefs and values, focusing on liability, that shape our experience and practices of responsibility. We need to reconstruct this repertoire.

The complex causality that characterizes many environmental problems and conceals the contributions of relevant actors is not the only reason to rethink the liability view of responsibility, either. With its emphasis on individual intentionality and control, the liability view assumes an overly sovereigntist conception of the individual agent. As we saw in chapter 2, agency is a socially and materially distributed phenomenon that combines initiative with uptake in ways that are not reducible to the intentions or control of the individual. This means that we are regularly agents of outcomes we did not mean to bring about. And because our effects on the world are always the result of how our initiatives interact with the initiatives and responses of others, they also regularly exceed our control. If responsibility tracks agency, as it must, then these considerations suggest that our responsibilities extend beyond what the liability view would allow by including outcomes we may not have intended and did not control. To complicate the picture, power affects both the initiative and the uptake sides of agency, with the result that how our actions unfold in the world—and hence what we are responsible for—depends in part on existing configurations of power.

Taken together, these considerations call for a different way of understanding responsibility and new ways of practicing it. This alternative approach must be alive to the fact that our responsibilities often exceed our intentions and control, and thus have a wider scope than on the liability model, and it must be sensitive to the differential effects that power has on differently placed persons. In addition, it must enable us to identify reasonable bounds for responsibility. The nonsovereignty of agency should not be understood to make everyone responsible for everything. A nonsovereign model of responsibility needs to distinguish varying degrees and types of responsibility in light an agent's relationship to the outcome and the agent's position within prevailing relations of power, and it must help us see that the practice of responsibility, like the exercise of agency, is always an intersubjective and intercorporeal affair.

Reconstructing Responsibility

Recent work on responsibility for structural injustice has begun to reimagine responsibility, challenging the dominance of the liability view. As Chad Lavin notes, the liability view rose to predominance in the mid-twentieth century as European and Anglo-American theorists were grappling with events such as the Holocaust and the massacre at Mai Lai.[15] Their focus was on establishing grounds for assigning blame in the context of particular events caused by

clearly identifiable agents. What Lavin calls "impersonal conditions of deprivation" were not the primary concern.[16] In the intervening period, issues of structural injustice have come to the fore in political theory as ostensibly democratic
societies have been forced to confront their own persistent inequalities and the
impersonal dynamics of injustice that help drive them. The upshot, Lavin says,
is that contemporary discourse is marked by a significant "shortcoming,"
namely, "the incommensurability" between current "political urgencies" and
our "dominant conceptions of responsibility."[17] In the decade and a half since
Lavin's book was published, a surge of new work has emerged that is intended
to address this shortcoming, rethinking responsibility in the context of injustices that are sustained through large-scale, impersonal social systems, rather
than by a clearly identifiable, "competent agent's willed causality."[18]

The most influential of the new approaches to responsibility is Iris Marion
Young's "social connection model."[19] The model addresses problems of structural injustice in which unfairness is perpetuated systemically through large-
scale economic, political, and social forces instead of through intentional acts
of domination by discrete agents. Young uses the global apparel industry as an
example, where products are often made by impoverished people in developing countries working under exploitative conditions, while the products are
consumed by relatively privileged people in wealthy societies. The consumers
do not mean to be unjust, often know little about the labor conditions that
produce the goods they purchase, and do not control the system. Yet their
purchases help to sustain the system, and in Young's view "all those who contribute by their actions to structural processes with some unjust outcomes
share responsibility for the injustice."[20] Our responsibility tracks the force of
our effects, as Young sees it, and those whose contributing effects carry more
weight in bringing about the harm will have more responsibility for it. For
example, wealthy people who spend large sums of money on clothing made
by sweatshop workers in the developing world play a more significant part in
sustaining the exploitation of those workers than do people who buy little.
Those wealthy consumers may also be better positioned to purchase from fair
trade enterprises, and to use their privilege and resources to press for changes
in the industry more broadly.[21]

This view of responsibility focuses less on blaming people for what they
have done in the past than on changing their actions for the future.[22] Moreover, although responsibility here applies to individual persons, it calls for
coordinated, intersubjective action. Responsibility for justice "is a responsibility I *personally* bear," as Young puts it, "but I do not bear it alone" because this

responsibility arises through my participation in social, systemic processes that incorporate but also exceed my own agency.[23] As a result, I can exercise my responsibility for justice only through action in concert, meaning working with others to reconstruct the relevant systems and structures so as to make more just outcomes possible.[24] In view of the interactive sources of injustice and the need for cooperation to remediate them, Young describes the social connection model as a form of political responsibility.[25] Yet although she characterizes it as political, responsibility so conceived is not grounded in one's membership in a particular political community or state. Indeed, one of the animating concerns of Young's project was to theorize responsibility for justice outside state boundaries because the dynamics of structural injustice frequently cut across these boundaries. The political character of responsibility here is tied to its intersubjective engagement with power. Responsibility intervenes in unjust configurations of power that are sustained through intersubjective relations, and it asks us to interact with others in new ways to reconfigure how power operates.

Eco-responsibility is political in a similar way: it connects individual efforts to concerted collective action and public engagement aimed at reconstructing prevailing relations of power. Although eco-responsibility calls for collective action, however, it would be wrong to equate it with collective responsibility. Indeed, eco-responsibility troubles the familiar binary between individual and collective forms of responsibility. Most environmental problems are produced through intersubjective interactions but not always or exclusively as a result of collective action per se, in which participants share a common goal and consciously coordinate their behavior with one another to achieve it. Environmental problems from climate change to toxic waste to species extinctions typically do involve some collective agents such as states, corporations, and international organizations, but often these agents interact with one another more like individuals pursuing separate ends than like participants in an organized collective that pursues a common end. In this context, collective responsibility is an insufficient framework, if not a wholly inapt one. In fact, insofar as collective responsibility applies in a blanket fashion to all participants in a group, it may occlude important differences of power and capacity among them.[26] On the other hand, conventional models of individual responsibility also fail to capture the dynamics in play because the outcomes result not from what individuals do but from how what they do interacts with the actions of other individuals and collectives, along with impersonal structural forces. In other words, eco-responsibility operates on terrain that includes not only individual and collective actors but interactive processes that incorporate while exceeding them both. The interactive but not always collective character of this terrain sets the context for eco-responsibility.

Although Young was right to suggest that responsibility for justice extends beyond the things for which we can reasonably blame people, an account of eco-responsibility does need to make a place for blame in some cases. At the same time, because the structure of many environmental problems and the non-sovereignty of agency problematize the conditions of liability (intention and control), we might do better to understand blame in terms of *culpability* rather than traditional liability.[27] Culpability as it is conceived here acknowledges not only the structural complexity of many environmental problems but also the fact that agency is always a function of assemblages. Culpability recognizes that one's effects regularly outrun one's intentions and exceed one's control, and that the interactive dynamics that sustain individual agency are shot through with inequalities of power. By the same token, culpability registers the fact that in any given case some agents are positioned to exercise more conscious influence over outcomes than are others, and that a consciously influential agent may reasonably be held responsible in a way that makes blame, and potentially punishment, appropriate. Still, responsibility as culpability will capture only a part of what we are responsible for in the environmental domain.

We can productively broaden our thinking about responsibility by supplementing culpability with a notion of responsibility as *accountability*. Accountability has a parallel in the legal concept of "strict liability," found especially in litigation around commercial products that have inadvertently caused harm to consumers. Strict liability holds producers responsible for compensating harms caused by their defective products, even if the producer was not intentional about the harm or negligent in its actions.[28] Responsibility as accountability has a similar form but a broader scope. It gives us a measure of responsibility for any harm to which we contribute, however unintentional the contribution may have been, and even when we lacked control over the outcome. With respect to environmental harms, we are accountable for the often indirect and unconscious parts we play in outcomes such as climate change, species extinctions, and pollution.

In contrast to culpability, holding someone accountable for a harm in this sense does not imply blame or justify punishment. In view of the fact that the harm was neither intended nor controlled (nor consciously influenced), blame and punishment would be out of place. The woman who must commute by car every day to keep the job that puts bread on the table for her young children deserves no blame for her carbon emissions and the role they play in climate change. Instead of blame, accountability in this context involves acknowledging the harm, making a clear-eyed assessment of the causal dynamics in play, taking honest stock of our contributions, and doing what we can to remediate our effects going forward.

Accountability also entails an obligation to work for changes in the conditions that form the broader context of our harmful effects. For example, in thinking about my accountability in the context of climate change, my responsibilities include not simply switching to LED light bulbs to illuminate my home, but also joining with my neighbors to advocate for a cleaner power plant in our area, and electing public officials who support renewable energy development. Seen from this angle, even paying one's taxes can be a (partial) way of exercising accountability, provided that the state directs some of its revenue to remediate environmental harms to which all citizens contribute, and to fund the development of more sustainable technologies for meeting collective needs in the future. The responsibility to change my effects going forward, in other words, requires me to work cooperatively with others to reconstruct the sea of agency, creating new conditions of action for all of us, conditions that will make it possible for us to avoid reproducing environmental harms and perpetuating environmental domination in the future.[29]

A third form of eco-responsibility involves *responsiveness* to harm and to the legitimate needs and claims of those affected by it, whether or not one had a role in producing the harm or benefited from it. Responsibility so conceived presupposes no causal connection at all between the agent and the harm, but it does assume that the agent has some capacity to render assistance. Peter Singer's famous example of a child who has fallen into a pond and is in danger of drowning points to responsibility as responsiveness.[30] Despite the fact that you did not cause the calamity or gain from it in any way, the responsible thing to do if you find yourself passing by the pond is to help the child, however you can. Certainly there are limits—no one would say that responsibility in this instance requires sacrificing your life—but helping as you are reasonably able is what responsibility requires.

Responsibility in this form involves judgment, not only to determine what response is reasonably required but also because not all needs and claims deserve a response. The point of responsibility as responsiveness is not to cater to the whims of others, or to desires that are harmful or otherwise misplaced. In exercising this form of responsibility, then, we regularly find ourselves having to make judgment calls that draw on our sense of right, our faculties of discernment, and our best understanding of the situation. Challenging as these judgments can be in the context of human-human relations, they may be even more difficult in the environmental context, where our knowledge of ecological harms and the relevant needs of Earth others is inevitably incomplete. Yet complete knowledge is not required. As Ackerly has argued in the context of human rights crises, "understanding the details of any particular case of injustice . . . is not a precondition for taking responsibility" for helping.[31] Where conditions of complex causality apply and relevant information is imperfect, to make responding conditional on complete understanding of a crisis and its effects would be paralyzing. It would guarantee inaction. Instead, responsibility as responsiveness requires our best effort at understanding the situation, together with a measure of humility in the face of our own limitations, a commitment to learning as we go, and a willingness to change course as new information arises.

It is important to see that responsibility in this form is available to and appropriate for people from all walks of life in the environmental context, both privileged and oppressed. In many cases of environmental domination, as we have seen, people are among the parts of nature that suffer harm. In such instances, it will be incumbent on those with more privilege to be responsive to those with less. At the same time, people who have suffered harm also can exercise responsibility as responsiveness by articulating their own claims and needs, and by bringing their distinctive perspectives to bear on the issue. Thus eco-responsibility as responsiveness includes attending not only to nonhuman parts of nature but also to the people who are subjected to environmental domination, and this responsiveness is not limited to activism by privileged people on behalf of others but may also take the form of self-affirming resistance and activist engagement by people who themselves are affected.

This three-dimensional way of understanding eco-responsibility as including culpability, accountability, and responsiveness lets us make sense of the different roles and positions that various agents have in contexts of environmental domination. It expands the scope of responsibility for most people, but without attaching all responsibility to blame, and without treating all agents as equally responsible, or responsible in the same ways. It enables us to differentiate among types and degrees of responsibility so that we can legitimately punish wrongdoers when appropriate, can encourage forward-looking behavioral changes in the people who contribute to environmental damage without intending or controlling it, and can nourish the potentially transformative agency of us all, including people who are privileged as well as those subject to more debilitating forms of domination. Eco-responsibility has a plural character in this sense.[32] As we shall see presently, this plurality has implications for how we go about cultivating responsibility, suggesting the need for diverse tools and techniques.

Eco-responsibility understood in this multidimensional way knits together conceptual threads we have explored in connection with environmental domination, respect for nature, and agency. We have seen that environmental domination involves treating Earth others in merely instrumental ways, as if they are simply for us, and assuming that human interests are the only things that need count in our personal actions and public decision making. Insofar as eco-responsibility makes us responsive to and accountable for, sometimes even culpable for, harm to nonhuman beings and things, it makes Earth others count with us in noninstrumental ways and thereby tempers domination. It also offers another approach to the noninstrumentalizing and responsive orientations that constitute political respect for nature. Like respect for nature, too, eco-responsibility is a uniquely human practice, even as it enhances the quality of our relations with Earth others. It embodies the new exceptionalism sketched in chapter 2 because it is a way of recognizing and managing our uniquely human impact on the Earth, an impact that is distinctive both in its scale and in its ability to be guided in some measure by reflective decision making, principles of right, and coordinated social action, hence able to remediate its own harms and to work toward a better future. The demands of eco-responsibility bind only human beings because they address these uniquely human impacts and abilities. Moreover, while eco-responsibility eschews sovereignty, it does presuppose agency. Only beings who are capable of norm-responsive, socially coordinated reflection and choice can be responsible in the ways described here.

As with respect for nature, then, an asymmetry exists in the practice of eco-responsibility, meaning that it will not always be reciprocated. In calling myself to account for the impact that my automobile emissions have on the climate, I cannot expect the climate to make itself accountable to me in return. In a very broad sense, it is reasonable to think that regulating our emissions will affect how the climate affects us, and there is a kind of metaphorical reciprocity in this dynamic. This metaphorical reciprocity is meaningful and significant. Indeed, part of the larger project of eco-emancipation is to enhance our awareness of the complex interactions and mutual impacts that constitute the Earth systems of which we are a part. Yet metaphorical reciprocity lacks the normative valence that is central to eco-responsibility. Eco-responsibility is not an inevitable result of mutual impacts. It is an orientation that we ought to take up with other people and in our relations with more-than-human nature, an obligation we have, an ethical and political ideal to strive for. Because this orientation is not available to nonhuman others—at least so far as we now know—it is not something that we can reasonably expect them to cultivate. Consequently, eco-responsibility is not likely to be reflected back to us by nonhuman beings and things in a genuinely reciprocal way.

Still, as we saw in the context of respect for nature, this asymmetry does not imply a moral or political hierarchy that would justify human domination of nonhuman others. Think again of the child in the pond: the child is in no position to reciprocate the responsibility I exercise in rendering assistance. Yet the one-sidedness of my responsibility-as-responsiveness in this context by no means implies moral superiority on my part; it does not make me better or more significant than the child, much less entitle me to dominate the child. Different people are differently positioned relative to any particular harm and are endowed with different capabilities. These differences affect how they should respond to the harm but say nothing about how much they should count. The same is true for the differences between people and nonhuman parts of nature.

Responsibility so conceived is demanding. To embody it perfectly would mean perpetual engagement on a virtually endless set of environmental effects and the complex conditions that give rise to them. No one could be expected to do that. Still, the impossibility of perfectly embodying responsibility does not undermine its value. Just as asking people to be generous does not entail that they must give everything they have to others, so holding ourselves responsible for our environmental harms need not require us to spend every waking hour trying to prevent or repair environmental damage. Different people will engage in different ways and to different degrees. There are many ways to be generous, after all—some people tithe 10 percent of their income to their mosques; some deliver meals to old people; some go out of their way to help a colleague at work or a stranger in trouble. Yet no one practices generosity in every possible way all the time. While the virtue of generosity suggests that some kind of contribution to others should be a regular part of one's life, it does not demand that generosity take up all one's life, although trying to perfect the ideal certainly *could* take up all one's life because the world is full of people in need. Likewise, there are many ways to act on the value of eco-responsibility, but none of them need consume us.[33]

It may be useful here to think of responsibility in the way that Aristotle described generosity and all the moral virtues: as a mean between extremes. Generosity on his account is a mean between the extremes of being stingy and being a spendthrift.[34] It means giving the right amount, in the right way, at the right time, for the right reason, to the right recipient.[35] In a similar way (and without endorsing the whole architecture of Aristotle's ethical theory), we might say that eco-responsibility is a mean between answering only for harms that you as a discrete individual caused by yourself and can fix for yourself, on the one hand, and indiscriminately trying to fix every form of anthropogenic damage to nature, on the other. Responsibility well executed involves being attentive to the big picture of our actions and effects as this bears on environmental harms, remediating them as best we can, and making sensible, focused efforts to create the kinds of change that would enable us to generate better effects in the future. So conceived, eco-responsibility is a real advance beyond conventional conceptions of responsibility, and one that could have a transformative impact, but it is not an impossible standard to meet.

In contrast to both Aristotle's virtues and Young's social connection model, however, eco-responsibility situates us firmly in relation to nonhuman beings and things. This means that the sea of agency in which we are asked to exercise responsibility includes natural systems and forces along with human ones. To exercise responsibility in the context of deforestation or carbon emissions or the question of how to dispose of my old batteries, I need to grasp how my individual actions and the human systems that aggregate their effects interact with Earth systems to generate the environmental harms in which my agency is implicated. Scientific knowledge contributes crucial information here. It should help shape the background of social understanding and the broader field of sensibilities that guide the exercise of responsibility, including collective decision making about how to reconstruct the human institutions and structures that shape our agency and its effects going forward.[36]

Yet eco-responsibility does not require us all to be experts about Earth systems. As we have seen, perfect knowledge is not a precondition for taking up responsibility. Consider the way that medical knowledge about the effects of smoking has become a part of the cultural background that informs the ways in which many people today exercise responsibility for their health.[37] Much as we do not need to be medical researchers to appreciate that smoking can cause cancer, so we need not understand the complex chemistry behind anthropogenic climate change to grasp the fact that our use of fossil fuels is interacting in powerful ways with Earth systems, and to acknowledge that our role in these interactions gives us a share of responsibility for the harms being generated and the domination they entail. Eco-responsibility therefore involves attending to how our agency interacts not only with human structural forces but also with natural forces.[38]

So eco-responsibility means that we can sometimes be responsible for helping to repair damage that we cannot be blamed for having caused, but it does not make all of us equally responsible for everything. As individuals we are subject to multiple forms of responsibility based on the different roles we play in generating or sustaining particular environmental harms, and on our capacities to help remediate these harms. The kinds of responsibility we bear in any given instance may shift over time as well, and the line between them is somewhat porous. For example, the more I learn about factory-farmed meat or climate change, the less unconscious my participation in these systems will become, and the more my responsibility will approach culpability as opposed to accountability. Likewise, the culpability that one bears as an individual for environmental damage that results from ostensibly intentional actions may be mitigated by political and economic conditions that systematically constrain one's options. I may be fully aware that my job at the petrochemical plant contributes directly to environmental domination because the job involves secretly dumping toxic waste from the production process into the waterway running alongside the plant.[39] Yet if this job (or one like it) is the only viable source of income for my family and me, and if whistle-blower protections for employees who report illegal dumping have been dismantled by a government influenced by corporate money and resentment of public authority, and if political pressure for privatization has eroded unemployment benefits and other social services that would otherwise help me to make ends meet if I were to lose my job for reporting the dumping, then my responsibility in this instance may be better understood in terms of accountability than culpability.

This last consideration reminds us that in assessing responsibility for environmental harms we must be attentive to power differentials and varying scales of impact. Relative to individuals, large multinational corporations have far more power in determining environmental policies and practices, and their direct effects on the environment can be orders of magnitude greater than that of individuals.[40] For both these reasons, some commentators are critical of efforts to cultivate a stronger sense of eco-responsibility among average persons. They worry that this focus will turn attention away from the kinds of political activism needed to contest the power and effects of large-scale agents such corporations. Think of Naomi Klein's insistence that "you, me and Exxon

(Mobil) are not all in this together," and her conviction that treating us all as equally guilty is "demobilising because it prevents us directing our anger at the institutions most responsible."[41] Klein is partly right. It is crucial for us to hold corporations culpable for their environmental harms when the conditions of culpability are in play, and to hold them accountable for harms to which they contribute even when their actions do not meet culpability standards. At the same time, however, the power of corporations is subject to the choices of consumers and to pressure from citizens, at least in democratic societies. Indeed, the power of corporations is itself partly sustained through the participation and acquiescence of large numbers of individuals, as Horkheimer and Adorno made clear. To simply blame corporations for all our environmental problems obscures the power that individuals, acting in concert, can have.

We would do better to cultivate a more capacious repertoire of responsibility, one that enables us to differentiate among the kinds and degrees of responsibility that can be reasonably attributed to various sorts of agents under distinctive sets of conditions. A pluralist view of responsibility acknowledges the multiplicity of sites, sources, and forms of responsibility that operate in the environmental domain, given the complex sea of agency in which all participants act. In some cases, attributions of responsibility will have legal or regulatory implications; in others, their force may be cultural, ethical, or political, orienting us to different patterns of consumption, to new forms of production and exchange, to the reform of political institutions, or to vigorous forms of activism. The pluralist approach allows us to attribute blame in the places and measures warranted, but it does not stop there; it also calls us in a forward-looking and potentially empowering way to work with others, using whatever resources and influence our particular positions in life allow, to create the conditions for more emancipatory ways of living with other people and with nonhuman beings and things. In this sense, eco-responsibility is a crucial component of liberation, even itself a practice of freedom.[42]

Cultivating Responsibility

Reconceiving responsibility is an important step toward overcoming environmental domination, but it is nowhere near enough. We will also need to construct new practices of responsibility. Jade Schiff's work on responsibility for structural injustice is valuable in this regard. Her approach to cultivating responsibility rests on a rethinking of power. Instead of understanding power as a commodity to be utilized for the willed purposes of a sovereign subject,

Schiff draws on Arendt's "constitutive conception of [power] as the ability to act in concert." She combines this Arendtian lens with Foucault's idea of power as circulatory and productive to suggest that the right "constellation of regulated practices" can create subjects who are responsible in an emancipatory way, meaning people who are empowered by "the capacity to respond."[43] This approach challenges the common assumption that the large-scale, impersonal forces that sustain structural injustice (and environmental domination) embody power that is simply wielded over us in a unidirectional way by others, power that is inaccessible to us and therefore inexorable. Power is not a commodity owned and controlled by particular people, on Schiff's account, but an emergent property of assemblages to which we all contribute and which we can help to reconstruct. And while it is true that power circulates through "micropractices" that discipline us (with our participation) into certain kinds of behavior rather than others, Schiff points out that there is no reason why disciplinary power must produce docile subjects who acquiesce to injustice, rather than dynamic subjects who contest it.[44] A different set of micropractices—and macro ones—could produce flows of circulatory power that instead generate "subjects ready to respond to conditions of structural injustice."[45] In this sense, she says, "the makings of response-able subjects are already immanent in contemporary life," including existing flows of power.[46]

Resources for redirecting the flow of circulatory power toward the more emancipatory practices and selves of eco-responsibility are available to us across multiple domains. In the United States, efforts to change public attitudes and behavior on several issues have had remarkable success in recent years, including substantial reductions in smoking rates and a sea change in the country's orientation to gay people. Differences of opinion still exist on both issues, but the transformations are undeniable. They have resulted from a combination of information dissemination, legal action, new legislation, and the deliberate promotion of alternative repertoires of beliefs, values, and social practices. Some of these efforts were carried out by the state, including through regulatory changes, public education, and public service announcements. Others emerged through cultural forms independent of the state (movies, television, music, visual art), through civic activism, and through informal, personal interactions. In cultivating eco-responsibility, we can make use of a similar range of cultural resources and techniques.

Another model we might look to is the Civilian Conservation Corps (CCC) established in the postwar United States as part of FDR's New Deal. The CCC trained more than three million men in resource conservation between 1933 and 1942. In addition to providing professional training leading to good jobs and a pool of technical expertise in pollution and resource management, it inculcated values of environmental responsibility and "active care" for the Earth.[47] The focus of a reconstituted CCC would need to be adjusted for contemporary conditions and challenges, and eco-emancipation requires far more than conservation, but the basic model could prove valuable. More generally, the public promulgation of what Isabelle Stengers has called "sustainability stories," which exemplify the exercise of environmental responsibility, "sharing learning and success," could help nourish a public sensibility of eco-accountability and responsiveness. As Stengers puts it, we need to publicize such stories so that "where one group achieves something, what they learn, what they make exist, becomes so many resources and experimental possibilities for others."[48]

Although one important site for the cultivation of eco-responsibility is political communities, Young's social connection model reminds us that political responsibility transcends citizenship. The sources of environmental domination are not contained within state borders, and taking up the responsibility for transforming it will involve us in assemblages that cut through political identities and cut across state lines. It is helpful in this regard that eco-responsibility, like respect for nature, can be affirmed from within a variety of worldviews. And much as global interdependence and advancing communications technologies have combined to spread human rights as a repertoire of shared values, albeit imperfectly, so they have the potential to help nurture cultures of environmental responsibility across borders as well.

Ackerly's work is important in this connection. Her account of "just responsibility" brings into view a vast array of both local and international assemblages in which differently positioned people work together to take up responsibility for creating the conditions of more just communities. Her study of the Bangladesh Center for Worker Solidarity (BCWS) lets us see how people from distant parts of the world are "participating in a global web of garment worker activism" that "transforms political community and its power dynamics."[49] She documents both wins and losses, acknowledging that the practices of responsibility for justice pursued by BCWS are best conceived not as a solution to injustice that promises a permanent fix but rather as a process for creating "a political community of, and for engagement in, the ongoing political process of transforming political communities in the face of injustice."[50] The process is a fraught and sometimes dangerous one, and its outcomes are always uncertain.[51] At the same time, her research offers countless examples of concrete

institutional changes that have made workers' lives better, and of personal nar-
ratives of empowerment among people as differently placed as impoverished
Malaysian garment workers and privileged Vanderbilt undergraduates.

Ackerly emphasizes that responsibility for justice must start from where
we are, and where we are is almost always shaped by injustice to one degree
or another. The fact that "all efforts to confront injustice begin in a context of
injustice" means that attempts to take up responsibility for justice will regularly be impeded.[52] It makes our efforts in any given instance inevitably imperfect and incomplete, as residual injustice not only throws up external obstacles
but also inflects the inner beliefs and values that guide our action. Still, the
stories that Ackerly tells prove that while "taking responsibility for justice
is hard," it is "not beyond our abilities."[53] In the environmental context, Kenya's
Green Belt movement and the Sioux people's resistance to the Dakota Access
Pipeline offer examples of this reality, as do contemporary food movements and
transition towns supported by more privileged people living in prosperous
democracies. These mobilizations embody multiple forms of responsibility,
including ascriptions of culpability, a responsiveness to the well-being of
human and nonhuman others, and a willingness to be accountable for helping
to create more ecologically emancipatory communities going forward. We also
see people, in varying degrees of struggle and always in the face of uncertainty,
making a difference.

Ackerly emphasizes that it matters not only *that* we take up responsibility
for justice but *how* we do so, and here again her analysis has important implications for eco-responsibility. Ackerly mines her case studies of connected activism for what she calls normative "principles-in-practice" that are to guide the
exercise of responsibility. These principles are drawn from the practices of
organizations such as BCWS engaged in struggles for justice. They include

(1) utilizing intersectional analysis; (2) thinking about narrow issues with
awareness of their cross-issue dimensions; (3) promoting the capacity for
self-advocacy and other political skills of ourselves and of those throughout
our web of partners and allies; (4) working against the complex forces that
create obstacles to rights enjoyment by building community through connected activism; and (5) working in ways that enhance our learning.[54]

Together these principles-in-practice attune us to the intersecting effects of
existing power relations, reminding us not only that differently positioned
people are differently resourced for making change but also that domination
takes multiple forms that often interact across issue areas. The principles alert

us to the fact that every action we might undertake in the exercise of responsibility has the potential, as Ackerly puts it, "to exploit or reify power inequalities."[55] They encourage us therefore to support agency and self-advocacy on the part of all participants, and to be responsive to what others tell us about their experience and desires.[56] Finally, they build learning into the normative framework that orients action, making humility, openness, and reflexivity central to the practice of responsibility.

These principles-in-practice apply in a direct way to the human assemblages that figure in the exercise of eco-responsibility, in the sense that they should guide how we interact with other people in this context. They are also valuable for orienting us to the more-than-human parts of our political communities. They can help us avoid an anthropocentric paternalism by challenging us to practice eco-responsibility not simply on behalf of nonhuman beings and things but always also *with* them, in ways that are attentive and responsive to the capacities of Earth others, as well as to the conditions of their well-being. This means active listening, including listening for nonlinguistic forms of communication, and it means watching for cues from nonhuman animals and ecosystems about the effects of our efforts.

Above all, the principles direct us to take a holistic approach to the environmental problems we find ourselves facing, to think about these problems through the lens of intersecting dominations, cross-issue connections, existing power configurations, and possible alternative flows, and to make active learning a part of the process of responding. They bring us back to the idea that although eco-responsibility applies to us as human individuals, its exercise requires more than just individual action, and always involves us in more-than-human assemblages. Recycling our plastic bottles and changing our lamps to LED lightbulbs are good things to do, but only if we are also working to eliminate the ubiquitous use of plastics and to transition at scale to renewable energy, thus fostering new forms of relationality with Earth systems and with nonhuman beings and things. Yet when we do exercise responsibility in this more capacious, intersubjective, and more-than-human way, we will be changing the broader dynamics of environmental domination that not only ravage the Earth but also entrap and exploit people, including us, whoever we are. Once again, the practice of eco-responsibility is an assertion—an enactment— of freedom.

Disruptive politics can be another resource for the cultivation of eco-responsibility, insofar as epistemologies of ignorance make it difficult for people to see and care about the environmental domination that their conventional practices help sustain. The idea of epistemologies of ignorance is familiar from the literature on racial inequality, where Charles Mills introduced it to describe how privileged people cultivate a willful blindness to the violations and suffering that their privilege imposes on others, a blindness that helps perpetuate racial injustice.[57] Drawing on his work, Clarissa Hayward has argued quite powerfully that disruptive politics can be an effective tool for "interrupt[ing] motivated ignorance" and hence for "dismantling structural injustice."[58] What Hayward calls "disruptive civil action" includes "boycotts, mass protests, sit-ins, die-ins, and other forms of unruly political action associated with the mid-century Civil Rights Movement," as well as the more recent Occupy and Black Lives Matter movements, among others.[59] The goal of such action, she argues, is not primarily "moral suasion" aimed at convincing "those who are systematically advantaged by structural injustice that they ought to 'do the right thing.'"[60] Instead, the main objective is "to make it all but impossible for the privileged to *not hear* the voices of, to not know the political claims of, the oppressed."[61] Once the privileged can no longer claim to be unknowing about the experiences of the oppressed it is far more difficult for them to see themselves as good people while continuing to support the status quo.[62] Hayward traces the effects on public opinion of the early Black Lives Matter movement and shows substantial shifts from 2014 to 2015 signaling growing support for the idea, as one survey put it, that "our country needs to continue making changes to give blacks equal rights with whites."[63]

Environmental domination also draws on epistemologies of ignorance, epistemologies that make the suffering of nonhuman beings and things (and people) invisible or meaningless to many of us.[64] These epistemologies are supported by the old exceptionalism and by material features of many societies, including increasing urbanization, which severs people from Earth others, and by concerted efforts by industries and governments to hide from view the environmental ravages and animal suffering that our current ways of life entail. Disruptive civil action that makes these violations visible and helps us to see nonhuman harm and suffering has an important role to play in cultivating eco-responsibility.

Important as they are, the achievements of disruptive politics are often "partial" and "impermanent," as Hayward puts it.[65] They can open a door to the dismantling of environmental domination, but by themselves they do not exhaust the demands of responsibility in this context. Disruptive politics must therefore be paired with institutional changes that can make shifted epistemologies and behaviors durable over time. Hayward's example is the consent decree entered into by the US Department of Justice and the City of Ferguson, Missouri, in April 2016 "implementing major revisions to the city's municipal code, police policies and practices, and municipal court policies and procedures."[66] Her insistence on institutionalizing change is important. We saw in chapter 3 that environmental domination is in significant measure a function of institutional arrangements that subject people and nature to insufficiently constrained human power and exploitation. Undoing domination will require changing these institutional arrangements. Beyond that, because institutions structure incentives, they shape our habits and sensibilities. In the case of the Ferguson police department, the relevant incentives included things like "jobs, promotions, and salaries," which under the consent decree were connected to job performance in ways that were intended to support a culture of racial equity and to habituate officers to practices of policing that would "enhance rather than undermine public safety" for all citizens.[67]

Like racial equity, eco-responsibility rests in part on habits of heart and mind, habits that depend on support not only from arts, culture, education, and activism but also from political institutions. This is another way that eco-responsibility resembles Aristotle's virtue of generosity. As with all the moral virtues, generosity is learned through habituation, and habits are formed through practice.[68] Thus Aristotle points out that one becomes generous by doing generous things, much as builders hone their skills by building things and lyre players perfect their art by playing the lyre.[69] For this reason, he continues, creating the right political institutions is crucial to the cultivation of virtue because institutions structure our practices and incentivize our behavior in particular ways, thereby shaping our habits. So while disruptive politics has an important role to play in cultivating eco-responsibility, the openings in public sentiment that it can create need to be followed up with institutional changes that give these openings durability, broaden their impact, and help create new habits of heart and mind. We shall explore some institutional changes that could contribute to this effort in chapter 6.

Conclusions

Our current culture of responsibility is ill suited to the problem of environmental domination and tends to disable environmental action because it presupposes intentionality and control, emphasizes blame and punishment, and saddles the individual with responsibility for changes that no one can accomplish alone. If the conventional view is how most of us think about responsibility most of the time, there will be many environmental harms for which no one can reasonably be held responsible, and remediating environmental domination will remain difficult if not impossible. Supporting a new culture of eco-responsibility—conceived pluralistically to include accountability and responsiveness as well as culpability—will require the same diversity of approaches that has led to other cultural changes in recent years, from reduced smoking rates to increased support for gay rights. They include modifications to existing institutions as well as legal initiatives, educational outreach, political activism, and inspiration from the art world, the entertainment industry, and social media.

The complexity of the political and economic systems that structure our action and our environmental impact cannot be wished away. Yet we can learn to navigate this complexity in ways that answer more effectively to ecological demands and to our own need for empowered agency and freedom from domination. In fact, a new culture and new practices of eco-responsibility can help us gain influence over the complex forces that govern our lives even beyond the environmental domain. Just as it gives us tools to motivate environmental action, responsibility properly conceived equips us to more effectively contest the whole range of structural conditions in politics and the economy that so often entrap us in the contemporary sea of agency. The widespread sense that people have lost control of these forces is reverberating through many parts of the world today. It is being exploited by politicians promoting populist cultural agendas that promise to restore the lost agency of people who feel left behind by globalization and by democratic deficits in their governments.[70] A culture of eco-responsibility cannot solve all these problems, but it has the potential to be broadly transformative by enhancing human agency and by reconstructing the configurations of power that have generated so much alienation. It is also an important step in constructing new relationships of nondomination among people and the Earth, and creating the conditions for ecological emancipation. What this emancipation consists in, and the broader constellation of practices and institutions that could bring it into being, is the subject of chapter 6.

6

Ecological Emancipation

THE ARGUMENT OF THIS BOOK is that cultivating more respectful and responsible relationships with nature would make us freer—all of us, rich and poor, privileged and marginalized, human and nonhuman. Environmental action is not simply a matter of doing justice to nature and to the people who suffer disproportionately from the effects of pollution, extractivism, and climate change. Nor is it only about the interest that human beings share in sustaining a planet that is livable for our species over time. Environmental action *is* about justice and human survival, but it also holds the promise of release from the multiple, intersecting forms of domination that currently entrap and exploit us all, albeit in different kinds of ways depending on who and what and where we are. I do not mean to suggest that freedom is a more important objective than justice or human survival, or that it can be fully detached from them. Environmental justice and the survival of our species are also goods worth pursuing, and pursuing them may sometimes generate more freedom for people and for nature. Still, the justice we owe to others and the future survival of our species are not the only things at stake for us here. The stakes of environmental action include our own liberation from domination, and not at some point in an unimaginably distant future, but here and now.

I use the language of ecological emancipation to characterize this liberation. The choice of terms is driven by the conceptual and historical associations between emancipation and domination. Emancipation is a form of freedom that operates against the background of domination, and it draws its meaning and significance from the violations wrought by this background. To emancipate means, literally, to "unhand" something, to turn it loose, to release it from bondage or from the power of another.[1] Other forms of freedom exist that do not share this conceptual linkage. One might think of Isaiah Berlin's concepts of positive and negative liberty, for instance, or Hannah Arendt's notion of freedom as collective worldmaking. All are real forms of freedom, but none responds to the distinctive condition of domination in the direct way that emancipation does. To experience emancipation is to gain release from the dynamics of insufficiently checked power and exploitation that constitute domination.

The language is familiar to us from the historical struggles of American slaves before abolition, the working class under industrial capitalism, and women subjected under patriarchy to the tutelage of husbands and fathers, among other things. In each case, emancipation was conceived as a release from domination that involved a change in the structural conditions of one's life—the systems of property law, capitalist production, and the patriarchal family. People who struggled for emancipation in all these contexts knew, or came to understand, that the institutional change in status that constituted abolition or the collectivization of property or women's enfranchisement was not by itself sufficient to reverse domination. Emancipation includes not only a change in formal status but also a transformation of selves, and a shift in the wider interpersonal relations that constitute culture and society. We shall explore these various dimensions of emancipation in what follows. The point for now is that an important feature of emancipation as a form of freedom is its distinctive— even constitutive—connection to domination. Emancipation is a release from domination, and for this very reason it is always entwined with domination.

To speak of *ecological* emancipation is to flag the fact that the liberation of people from environmental domination is inextricably entwined with the liberation of nonhuman beings and things and the networks of interdependence that make up ecosystems. Ecological emancipation has some affinity with republican notions of nondomination. Like them, it emphasizes institutional constraints on power. At the same time, the view of emancipation developed here also looks outside the expressly political domain to the economic, cultural, and personal changes that are needed to overcome environmental domination. In addition, it pairs institutional constraints on power with an emphasis on participatory, often contestatory mobilizations for collective transformation. Above all, it situates ecological emancipation in more-than-human processes and relations, thinking not only of protections for people and for nature *by* people but of engagements across types of being that could be more liberatory for all.

It is true that the ideal of freedom, at least in certain guises, has often been invoked by people to justify or excuse environmental domination. Bathsheba Demuth's magisterial history of whaling in the Bering Strait demonstrates in excruciating detail how an American capitalist conception of freedom as the individual pursuit of profit and the Soviet socialist notion of freedom as the people's liberation from want wreaked equal havoc on the fragile Indigenous communities, human and nonhuman, of Beringia throughout the nineteenth and twentieth centuries.[2] Likewise, ideals of freedom as autonomy and self-determination can lead us to disavow the ways in which human selves and human agency are dependent on countless nonhuman beings and things, a disavowal that enables us too easily to countenance their abuse. In similar ways, the belief so prevalent in the United States today that freedom consists in choosing from the wide array of cheap consumer products available to us perpetuates a continuing cycle of toxic and energy-intensive extractivism, production, and dumping that is depleting and polluting the Earth as well as warming it. Elizabeth Anker has referred to freedom in this sense as "consumptive sovereignty," meaning the unlimited "choice to consume natural resources that one pays for."[3] Then too, conceptions of freedom that valorize property rights and noninterference prevent communities from constraining corporate activities and individual behaviors that harm nonhuman beings and things even as they also compromise the health and well-being of many people. In all these ways, certain conceptions of freedom have helped fuel environmental domination. Still, not every form of freedom need end in domination, and freedom in some forms is a necessary condition of human flourishing and the flourishing of many nonhuman others. In fact, caring about freedom is crucial to making progress on our environmental problems. Yet as with agency, domination, respect, and responsibility, we need to understand the concept of freedom differently than we have done until now.

There are many ways to understand freedom differently, but eco-emancipation is an important one. It consists partly in continuing practices of worldmaking in tandem with human and nonhuman others, practices that reflect both institutional constraints and extra-institutional mobilizations geared toward limiting how human power may be exercised over nature and people. Eco-emancipation also incorporates a public ethos of respect for nature and persons, along with a culture of responsibility that makes us accountable and responsive to Earth others. And even as it orients us to the more-than-human world, it avoids resting the emancipation of nature on the domination of people who are poor and marginalized. Eco-emancipation does not promise perfect harmony, either among persons or between people and nature. What it promises is release from the entrapment and exploitation that constitute environmental domination; it prevents us as human beings both from exercising domination in this form and from suffering it.

Eco-emancipation affects differently positioned people in different ways, as we shall see, and it affects human beings differently from other parts of nature. It is a plural, diversified phenomenon in this sense. Moreover, the freedom it entails is a nonsovereign kind of freedom. Instead of individual or collective mastery, eco-emancipation unfolds through relations of interdependence across individuals, communities, and types of being. And while it does involve greater influence over the human forces that shape our lives and affect the Earth, this influence is far from an experience of perfect control because emancipation always coexists with uncertainty and precarity. It is marked by continuing contestation among people, and by regular recalcitrance and unpredictability on the part of nonhuman nature. Then too, emancipation is never complete because domination is a permanent possibility of power. We live on a continuum in which domination and emancipation are perpetually in play, which means that there is always work to be done and we regularly face irresolvable remainders, but also that there is ever a reasonable hope of progress toward greater liberation. Envisioning what this liberation could be—its meaning, its mobilization, its institutions—can help us make good on that hope. The first part of this chapter lays out the meaning of ecological emancipation as combining a status condition of nondomination with political respect for nature and a culture of eco-responsibility, and identifying its plural, nonsovereign character. The second part takes up techniques for mobilizing eco-emancipation. The third part explores mechanisms for institutionalizing it.

Understanding Eco-Emancipation

Emancipating people. We have seen that environmental domination affects human beings in diverse ways. For the people who make the Niger delta their home, it has involved a vivid despoiling of their land and water by the petro-chemical industry, which has undercut their ability to make a living through agriculture and fishing, and brought poverty, sickness, and conflict. Their efforts to mobilize opposition to the oil companies have been met with violence and repression, paid for by the corporations and sanctioned (and often carried out) by the state. In Black and brown neighborhoods of the United States, environmental domination is evidenced by more brownfields and dumps than one finds in predominantly white areas, as well as less green space and higher levels of air pollution. Those who experience environmental domination in these forms are being instrumentalized and exploited by other people, people who profit from the extraction of local resources and labor, and who enjoy greater health, higher property values, and a better quality of life because of being insulated from the dumps and pollution they (indirectly) impose on others. The experience of domination in such contexts is typically a painful one, both in terms of material suffering and in the awareness of one's own lack of standing and respect, the knowledge that one counts with others as little more than a tool of profit and pleasure. Another wrenching aspect of environmental domination among people is to find oneself engaged, by the pressing necessity of putting food on the table, in activities that destroy the land and more-than-human members of one's own community, as when Indigenous peoples of the Amazon end up with no choice but to work for the mining companies.

The experience of environmental domination is different for middle-class and privileged people living in prosperous societies that have ostensibly democratic institutions. They too are trapped and exploited by structural forces that exceed their understanding and elude their grasp. Yet their exploitation is veiled by the consumer satisfactions the system makes available to them and a cultural ideal that equates freedom with consumer choice, and by the presence of electoral political systems that make them feel they have a say in public decisions. Even as they are themselves exploited by corporate practices of data mining, planned obsolescence, toxic products and production practices, and the capture of government, their consumerism and their labor contribute to the domination of nature and less privileged people. In contrast to the environmental domination of the poor and the marginalized, which so often is painful and violent, the environmental domination of the privileged is frequently blind, both in the sense that they do not feel their own exploitation and in the sense that they are often unaware of how their behavior exploits human and nonhuman others.

Just as the experience of environmental domination differs across persons and contexts, so eco-emancipation will be experienced differently depending on one's status and location. Where environmental domination involves illness, impoverishment, and violence at the hands of soldiers and mercenaries hired by oil companies, as in the Niger delta, emancipation will mean greater physical security, reconnection with one's land and livelihood, a cleaner and healthier environment, and more influence in public decision making. Where domination takes the form of entrapment and exploitation that feed our own destructive desires and make our support of rapacious environmental practices a necessary condition of modern existence, emancipation will mean access to ways of living that meet our needs and nourish our souls fairly and sustainably, with respect and responsibility. It will mean being able to live well in our more-than-human communities without having to enrich and empower a few (and be complicit in their exploitative practices) simply to get to work, eat dinner, and heat our homes.

The changes that constitute emancipation in this context involve a wide range of practices and institutions across the domains of politics, culture, and the economy. We shall explore such changes in more detail presently. What is crucial to see now is that the new relationships they make possible will be quite diverse and cannot be fully specified in advance. There are common threads that run through eco-emancipation in every form, such as protections against insufficiently constrained human power and exploitation. Yet the process of gaining these protections and what happens in their presence will be a function of how human and nonhuman beings and things in each place make community. Every eco-emancipatory community will be distinctive because no two ecosystems, including the peoples within them, are the same.

Along with institutional constraints on human power, respect for nature and eco-responsibility are portals to this freer life. The instrumentalization of nature leads to the great consolidations of economic and political power that make the domination of people possible, including privileged people as well as the poor and the marginalized. These consolidations of power then fuel ever-greater exploitation of the Earth, generating more profit and more unconstrained power over people. Respect for nature can interrupt this cycle, opening the door to forms of life not driven by domination. It also releases us from the confines of a totally self-referential subjectivity through which the vastness of the wide world can be experienced only in the narrow terms of human use value. The emancipatory force of eco-responsibility, for its part, lies in how it effectuates human agency and counters disempowerment. Acknowledging our shared (albeit diverse) accountability for environmental degradation, and cultivating responsiveness to the well-being of nonhuman others, can help us navigate the sea of structural forces shaping modern life in ways that affirm our agency instead of leaving us impotent and ineffectual. And even as respect for nature and eco-responsibility help protect us from being trapped and exploited, they also prevent us from feeling entitled—entitled to make use of nonhuman others without attending to their well-being or our impact on Earth systems, entitled to count only ourselves in what matters, entitled to rule nature instead of being in partnership with it. Our sense of entitlement in this regard goes hand in hand with our own subjection; to give it up is to gain a new freedom.

Some aspects of this new freedom are familiar, or at least resonant with experiences of freedom that many of us would recognize easily. Release from the exploitative labor conditions of gold mining in Amazonia and the ability to make a living through labor that sustains instead of destroys one's native ecosystems surely would feel liberating. The same is true for being able to stay warm in a New England winter without in the process having to enrich and empower the fossil fuel industry and the political officials who abet its ravages on human and more-than-human beings in places like the Niger delta or Louisiana's petrochemical "Cancer Alley." At the same time, the liberation that comes from forsaking our sense of human entitlement clashes with some things that we have seen are commonly identified with freedom today, including unfettered consumption and consumer choice, ideals of personal autonomy that deny any constitutive relations of interdependence, and property rights conceived as sovereign control over parts of the Earth. For people invested in these conceptions of freedom, eco-emancipation will entail real losses. Part of the work of eco-emancipation therefore must be to reconfigure what we expect from the experience of freedom. The practices that constitute emancipation need to include educational, literary, artistic, musical, and experiential efforts that make us aware of how our familiar concepts of freedom and our sense of entitlement promote environmental domination, including our own entrapment and exploitation, and that help us understand and feel freedom differently. We shall have more to say about this presently in connection with mobilizing emancipation.

Some aspects of the freedom that eco-emancipation promises may be difficult to envision under current circumstances and in light of present subject formations, meaning how people conceive themselves and how they understand what it means to be a human being. In this regard, eco-emancipation requires an existential orientation of openness to the unknown. For in advance of establishing the institutional and extra-institutional conditions of nondomination that eco-emancipation requires, and cultivating the respect and responsibility it needs, we cannot say for sure how it would feel to live this way. Then too, living this way could mean many different things because the more-than-human communities it gives rise to will take a plurality of forms based on who and what participates, and where. There is no getting around the fact that for many human beings the experience of eco-emancipation will involve being undone in some respects, because it means abandoning the sense of human entitlement and the identities that go with this sensibility. Yet the same is true for every kind of emancipation. The reason is that emancipation, in contrast to forms of freedom that focus exclusively on external conditions such as legal status or civil and political rights, always entails an inner transformation of self and of the desires and aspirations that orient the self. The transformation happens in part through participating in new social practices, political institutions, and material configurations, but it also requires periodic leaps of faith and a willingness to share in becoming something that one cannot quite see yet.

The willingness to be undone in this way is a tall order. Being undone is discomfiting at best, terrifying at worst, and it does not always take us to a freer place or otherwise improve things. In this sense, it is not only demanding but inherently risky. Still, the demands and risks associated with eco-emancipation, however real, are not unique to it. They are unavoidable in any well-lived human life, and they are fundamental to democratic life. Although decision making in healthy democracies is constrained by democratic principles, the practice of collective self-government even within such constraints is indeterminate in ways that parallel the uncertainties of eco-emancipation. For example, as the United States reckons with its past and present racial injustice, American citizens are being asked to become something they have never been before, to forge a collective in which the structures of white supremacy and the selves of white privilege come undone. Periodically being undone in the sense of abandoning practices that are unjust or unfree but that have been constitutive of one's world and identity is a necessary feature of any democracy that aspires to freedom and justice for all, and it is a duty of democratic citizens. The same is true of eco-emancipation. The existential orientation of openness that eco-emancipation requires is no more difficult than and essentially no different from the orientation needed by democratic citizens to make good on the promises of democracy.

Emancipating nature. As challenging as it is to envision and articulate the experience of eco-emancipation for people, making sense of what emancipation might mean for nonhuman beings and things is far more difficult. Must nature also be undone or transformed to enjoy emancipation? Can it be free? Can waterways and animals enact emancipation—or when we talk about the emancipation of nature are we talking about a gift endowed on the nonhuman parts of nature by the human ones? The first thing to emphasize here is the uncertainty that we inevitably face in theorizing on this terrain. Our knowledge of the inner experience of most nonhuman beings is incomplete at best. Even with concerted efforts to know more, our understanding is bound to be limited by the constraints of our own physiology and subjectivity. This is not to say that we can never see beyond the bounds of our present perspectives—we can do so, and eco-emancipation is only possible if we make the effort—but there are undeniable limits to how fully we can comprehend the experience of a whale or a tree. The second thing to emphasize is the plurality that emancipation takes in this context, which is perhaps even greater than the plurality of emancipation among people. Some nonhuman parts of nature have consciousness, can suffer and love, can choose and communicate. Others lack these capacities, based on our best understanding so far. How emancipation affects these different parts will vary enormously.

Still, as with eco-emancipation among people, there are some common threads. The emancipation of nonhuman nature is partly a status condition, or rather the alleviation of the status of domination. This reversal requires more robust and reliable institutional constraints on how human power may be exercised in relation to nonhuman beings and things, and legal protections against their exploitation. As we saw in chapter 3, the environmental domination that concerns us here is a product of human action and institutions. Although it is conceivable that some nonhuman beings may dominate others, such violations, if they exist, are not for us to manage. We are neither obligated nor entitled to police the Earth. Insofar as environmental domination is a human product, the institutions and practices of eco-emancipation that reverse it will be a distinctly human responsibility.

At the same time, it would be wrong to conceive eco-emancipation as a gift bestowed by people on a passive nature. Everything we do as human beings is made possible by the nonhuman beings and things that act with, around, and through us. Moreover, human practices of eco-emancipation involve attunement and responsiveness to signals from nonhuman nature, and they are facilitated by engagements that rest on continuing communication and interaction with it. So although eco-emancipation is a distinctly human project in the sense that only human beings are responsible for pursuing it, human beings can pursue this (like any) project only as parts of more-than-human assemblages. Finally, in the many different practices that constitute eco-emancipation, people themselves will be transformed in ways that reflect the influence of nonhuman beings and things. We should think of eco-emancipation as an iterative process with multiple directionalities. It does not flow exclusively from people to nonhuman nature but continuously circles back again in layers of influence, learning, and responsiveness.

It may help to recall the eighteenth-century republican distinction between domination as living "at the mere mercy of another" and liberty as living "on one's own terms." Emancipation for nature allows nonhuman beings and things to manifest the possibilities of their existence—as individuals, species, and interdependent parts of ecosystems—without having the terms of this existence distorted by insufficiently constrained, exploitative human power. We cannot know in advance what the countless varieties of nonhuman existence will be like in the absence of human domination, but there are a few things we can assume with some confidence. The lives of nonhuman domesticated animals will be marked by less physical and emotional suffering at human hands, and by opportunities for greater experiential engagement and richer relationships with one another and with people. Nondomesticated animals will find their habitats free not of all human influence but of the rapacious extractivism, enclosures, and thoughtless dumping that have made them unlivable for so many. Mountains, waterways, forests, and other ecosystems will reflect their emancipation in the multiple possibilities of existence that can unfold within them when the effects of human power are more reliably constrained and more responsive to nonhuman nature. People are parts of many of these ecosystems, so the possibilities of existence that unfold within them will include new ways of being human and new kinds of relationships between people and nature, relationships that are marked by respect and responsibility on the part of people, and that help us to appreciate the multitudes within and around us that enliven us.

Understanding eco-emancipation requires coming to terms with the always-unfinished quality of this project as active struggle against existing conditions of environmental domination. Neil Roberts's notion of "freedom as marronage" offers inspiration in this regard. As it emerged in the context of nineteenth-century Caribbean and Latin American slave communities, marronage was a shared refusal of the condition of slavery and the creation of alternative, self-governing collectives.[4] It involved flight from the physical site of one's bondage to occupy distant terrain beyond the borders of the plantation and the bounds of the state.[5] True, the sites of environmental domination today cover the whole of the Earth, leaving us nowhere to flee. Yet Roberts makes it clear that the experience of marronage can involve metaphorical flights as well as literal ones, flights of imagination and collective effort that refuse and reconstruct the current terms of a community's existence.[6] Whether literal or metaphorical, the flight that constitutes marronage is a "dynamic, active struggle" against domination.[7] It includes a "continuing process of release from bondage," and the ongoing effort to enact "a new political order."[8] Roberts distinguishes marronage in this regard from freedom understood as an "inert" condition or final achievement.[9]

In a similar way, the meaning of eco-emancipation cannot be fully captured by articulating the relevant institutions of nondomination, important as they are. Even including the political ethos of respect for nature and a culture of eco-responsibility is not enough. Eco-emancipation is activity, the continuing process of remaking existing environmental relations across types of being. This activity must be collective in the sense that individual human efforts need to be coordinated with one another for the shared purpose of reversing domination. Yet the relevant collective is more than merely human, and the activity of reversing domination will regularly generate new ways of being what we are, human and otherwise. In this sense, the collective in eco-emancipation perpetually exceeds itself in ways that cannot be predicted or controlled. This marks another aspect of the nonsovereignty of freedom in this form. Its activity is a process of what Haraway calls "becoming-with" others.[10] This becoming-with is not so much an intermingling of fixed essences as an iterative, layered process of mutual influence among beings and things that are always in the midst of becoming something else.[11] The activity of eco-emancipation therefore involves not just doing things that refuse environmental domination and reconstruct political communities but being in new kinds of relationships, relationships in which we ourselves become new.

Conceiving eco-emancipation as a more-than-human marronage also helps us appreciate its transitional character and the highly contingent ways it inevitably unfolds. Marronage is a flight from one way of life to another, a journey through terrain that is unknown and often treacherous. Roberts emphasizes that the "process by which people emerge from slavery to freedom" rarely has a linear trajectory, and it is never an all-or-nothing affair.[12] Even legal manumission was only one step on a much longer path, as African Americans learned in the post-Reconstruction years, and the path was marked by many obstacles and reversals. Because the dynamics of environmental domination are so complex, they cannot be reconfigured all at once, and no single effort could ever take us to the finish line, if such a line even exists. Then too, domination exists on a continuum, and in most societies life is lived somewhere between the two endpoints. Progress is possible—and in some places evident—but it is inevitably partial and uncertain.

Roberts is right to draw our attention to the in-between character of freedom in this form, as the transitional, precarious activity of emerging from domination rather than as the once-and-for-all achievement of a condition marked by the perfect absence of domination. The uncertainty and incompleteness of this emergence contribute to the nonsovereignty of eco-emancipation. Just as human agency is an emergent property of intersubjective and intercorporeal exchanges, rather than an internal experience of individual sovereignty, so eco-emancipation emerges through interactions between informal practices and formal institutions, and through doings and inter-becomings that no one person, group, or species could possibly control or even fully understand. Our freedom in this sense is never wholly our own, and it is never finished.

Mobilizing Emancipation

Trajectories of mobilization will vary just as domination and emancipation do. The large literature on the environmentalism of the poor demonstrates the rich plurality of mobilizations among people for whom environmental domination has been a vividly felt experience of suffering and loss. This experience makes people aware of the contradictions between their most pressing needs and the terms of existence that result from their domination. From Kenya's Green Belt movement to the Dudley Street Neighborhood Initiative in Boston, these mobilizations typically combine civic empowerment and challenges to entrenched power structures with new or restored relations of sociality between people and the nonhuman beings and things that compose their eco-systems.[13] Sometimes the movements are marked by the leadership of singular individuals such as Wangari Maathai in Kenya, or Ken Saro-Wiwa in the Niger delta, or Chico Mendes in the Brazilian Amazon, but other times they are more diffuse. They are often networked to other groups, both locally and internationally, including (but not only) other environmental groups. They typically focus their efforts on issues that have an immediate impact on the lives of local residents, such as deforestation that makes traditional livelihoods impossible, or toxic dumps that poison local children. Visual art, music, film, literature, and other cultural productions frequently are engaged to help shape minds and hearts; to instill hope, commitment, and courage among participants; and to get people moving.[14]

For privileged people in prosperous societies, the contradictions that result from environmental domination, which are so palpable among the poor and the marginalized, are often invisible. People may feel these contradictions implicitly, but the immediate gratifications of consumerism and the trappings of ostensibly democratic institutions tend to blunt their force. In this context, there is important work to be done in bringing the contradictions into view because, as Marcuse insisted, liberation depends on the consciousness of servitude.[15] A key component here is publicity. This means finding ways to publicize the links between what we consume and the domination of nature and people, including ourselves, that our consumption produces. This publicity may take the form of undercover YouTube videos of industrial poultry farms in Petaluma; or documentation by Montana farmers and ranchers of pollution to local water supplies from fracking;[16] or studies of the impact on human health of industrialized agriculture, the superfluous use of pharmaceuticals, and the proliferation of toxic chemicals in everyday household products. It is also important to make visible the ways that growing corporate influence over government is eviscerating our political institutions of meaningful democratic rule. Our political institutions, like the systems that satisfy our consumerism, subjugate us to the insufficiently constrained, instrumentalizing power of for-profit industries and the political officials increasingly beholden to them. The mystifying forces of advertising and neoliberal political ideology further occlude this domination by reinforcing ideals of freedom as consumer choice, sovereign self-reliance, and unfettered property rights. To counter these forces, we need cultural productions that illuminate the contradictions in our lives associated with environmental domination, and that bring alternative images of freedom into view.

Publicity alone is not enough, of course, in part because of the pacifying effects of prosperity and privilege. The poor and the marginalized in some ways face greater obstacles to mobilizing for environmental action than the privileged do, given the violence and deprivation that mark their circumstances. Yet the pressing nature of these circumstances can also be a natural catalyst for action. Part of the challenge in mobilizing the privileged is the absence of such catalysts. This perhaps explains why Horkheimer and Adorno's *The Dialectic of Enlightenment* ended in what Michael Hardt and Antonio Negri call "bitter resignation rather than . . . any active project."[17] We need not acquiesce to bitter resignation, however. A powerful catalyst for resistance to domination is indignation, as Hardt and Negri remind us. They characterize indignation as "a first expression of strength" and "a first step toward finding adequate modes of resistance" among people who are subject to injustice.[18]

Art can be a powerful force in stimulating indignation. Hardt and Negri mention Picasso's famous painting *Guernica* in this regard, in which a woman "cranes her neck out the window and holds a lamp to illuminate the destruction and suffering" of a city brought to ruin during the Spanish Civil War.[19] The painting, they point out, inspired among many viewers outrage about fascism and the ravages of modern warfare. They go on to say that "documentary film has today become the central art form of indignation."[20] The insight is an apt one when applied to the environmental context, as influential documentaries such as *Gasland* and *An Inconvenient Truth* attest.[21] Art in many forms can help catalyze indignation—think of hip-hop's rhymed critiques of white supremacy and police violence, or the impact on gay (and other) audiences of Larry Kramer's 1985 play *The Normal Heart* and the 2005 film *Brokeback Mountain*. Art and other forms of cultural production not only help us see contradictions and injustices that have escaped our conscious understanding but also engage our affective sensibilities in ways that can prod us to act. They make the suffering of others sensate to us, but they can also set our own experience in a new light and change our feelings about it.

Along these lines, Macarena Gómez-Barris argues that "we need many aesthetic strategies" to unmask existing environmental domination and to inspire alternative trajectories.[22] Although they involve human artistry, many of the strategies she documents involve collaboration with more-than-human parts of nature, as in the film by Columbian multimedia artist Carolina Caycedo that Gómez-Barris describes, in which the protagonist is a river.[23] The river's "submerged viewpoint" offers us "ways to see what lies in ecologies all around us but is not visible to the naked [human] eye."[24] Or consider the visual and performance art included in the Twenty-Third Biennale of Sidney, Australia (2022), entitled *rīvus*. The exhibition "invites several aqueous beings into a dialogue with artists, architects, designers, scientists, and communities, entangling multiple voices and other modes of communication" to stimulate "a fundamental shift in understanding our relationship with the rest of the natural world as a porous chronicle of interwoven fates."[25] As Gómez-Barris puts it, such efforts can help to "decolonize our vision," changing our sensibilities in the process and opening up new directions for action.[26]

We need more art that makes our subjection palpable to us and inspires indignation about it. Countless works have been produced over the last generation aimed at educating people about the human destruction of nature, and soliciting empathy for nonhuman beings. They are valuable resources for cultivating the respect for nature and the broadened sense of responsibility that emancipation requires. Yet we also need cultural productions that sting us with the painful recognition of our own entrapment and exploitation. Particularly in a society like the United States with its various freedom cults, to awaken privileged people to our own domination—to show us that what we thought was freedom has instead made us the unwitting tools of industries and governments that profit at our expense, make us complicit in their violence, and leave us with no real way out—should make us very angry. Although many of our contemporary freedom cults contribute to the problem of environmental domination, they can also be enlisted for the purpose of emancipation in this regard. The pride we take in regarding ourselves as free has the potential to fuel a productive indignation when we are led to see beyond the veil, to grasp the reality of our own entrapment and exploitation, and our forced complicity in the entrapment and exploitation of others. Eco-emancipation requires liberating ourselves from many of our existing conceptions of freedom, then, but our attachment to some of these very conceptions can be profitably employed to overturn them. They can help foster what Luke refers to as the "emancipation of consciousness" and "the senses."[27]

The idea that certain features of the problem of environmental domination could be mobilized to catalyze emancipation resonates with another insight suggested by Hardt and Negri. Their focus in *Assembly* is on contemporary capitalism in its neoliberal form, and they mean to show how capitalism's enlistment of individuals as agents of their own exploitation can be mobilized to reverse it. As they put it, certain "weapons of struggle are born of contemporary developments of capitalist society."[28] Consider the data-mining operation in Google's PageRank algorithm, in which "with each click" one's "living labor, living intelligence, living relationships, and living cooperation" are being "captured and transformed into fixed capital."[29] This capital not only is owned by others but is used by them to consolidate economic and political power that is then wielded over the users in ways that exceed users' understanding and influence, and often compromise their well-being. The genius of the system is that users carry out the processes by which they are entrapped and exploited— and they like it.

Yet the "fact that users experience both enjoyment and interest while employing the search engine," as Hardt and Negri say, "does not diminish the fact that the algorithm effectively absorbs what they produce to be accumulated by Google" and mobilized in ways that undercut basic interests that users have in privacy, truth, and sustainability, among other things.[30] If the genius of the system is to enlist users in their own exploitation, however, the genius of the emancipatory alternative that Hardt and Negri suggest is to enlist individuals in using technologies such as Google to articulate and reproduce new social and material values. The new values they have in mind emphasize a solidarity in which people are "defined no longer by their possessions but by their connections," and are assembled into "a new world of cooperative networks" that entail freedom from domination along with "relations of care and use regarding the common in all its forms."[31] The key insight is that "power is always a relationship . . . of many forces." It is "never as secure and self-sufficient as it pretends to be. The image of an omnipotent Leviathan is just a fable that serves to terrify the poor and the subordinated into submission."[32] Power is partly constituted through the force that is wielded by those it subjects. This Foucauldian insight implies that the exercise of power inevitably entails opportunities for resistance and redirection.[33] Against the sense of powerlessness that pervades so many ostensibly democratic societies today, *Assembly* means to show "the power of coming together and acting politically in concert," and thus to point the way to "new democratic political possibilities."[34]

From this perspective, recognizing our role in environmental domination can be a catalyst for emancipation. For while our experience of forced complicity in the political and economic systems that drive environmental domination today mostly feels disabling, it contains the seeds of something more liberatory. Our complicity in these systems is also their vulnerability. Romand Coles presses this point forcefully, saying that the "colossal rivers of grain, animals, goods, oil, labor, military, finance, medicines, water, and so forth" that seem to flow inevitably to environmental domination, capturing us as well as nonhuman beings and things in their ostensibly irresistible currents, could not exist without our participation.[35] Like Coca-Cola or Marlboro, which "have no more power than the power people give to them by 'believing' in what they offer," the political economy of environmental domination is more contingent than it often seems.[36]

The sense of powerlessness so common today partly reflects what Coles calls a "Wizard of Oz effect," in which "the order projects an ideological mirage of its omnipotence"—or at least projects the idea that things could not possibly be other than they are.[37] We see this effect in operation all the time, as in the notion that the only way to feed the world is through toxic, industrialized monocultures and the torture of animals; that the sole path to job creation is to allow industries to pollute our air, water, soil, and bodies; that after eviscerating our retirement savings through reckless profiteering, the banks must be bailed out by us or the world will fall apart, but that they cannot possibly be regulated to protect us against the danger that they will eviscerate us again—or the world will fall apart; that politics is by nature a dirty business and hence the power of money in politics simply cannot be curtailed; and on and on. Yet the Wizard of Oz effect depends on "our uptake and dissemination" of its projections, on whether we "accept and proliferate the frozen image of a totally implacable order," and on the degree to which we contribute materially to its survival.[38] It is true that as individuals we are no match for the forces of environmental domination, but in combination with others—human and nonhuman—we can make a difference. Coles points us to "alternative patterns of material flows and powers" that are now emerging as a result of social movements oriented around organic agriculture, food politics, and renewable energy.[39] These counterflows include farmers' markets, community-supported agriculture (CSA) arrangements, grassroots community-gardening initiatives, food policy councils, farm-to-school collaborations, fair-trade practices, and transition towns, among other things.[40] They demonstrate the possibility of a politics that resists domination of both the human and the nonhuman; they are mobilizations for eco-emancipation.

Another resource for mobilizing emancipation is the wilderness within that Mark Cladis finds in the literary tradition he calls "radical Romanticism."[41] Cladis reads figures such as Wordsworth, Thoreau, and W.E.B. Du Bois as offering a vision of the more-than-human world in which nature is not idealized as a sublime other but rather is seen to make possible a "wilderness" within human beings that entails a "capacity to challenge and unsettle" existing norms, and "to incite hope and transformation."[42] In radical Romanticism, Cladis writes, "wilderness is understood not only as a place but also as a condition and a process of that which is beyond complete control, as that which surprises and disorients, and as that which gives rise to newness and creativity."[43] The radical-Romantic wild is the part of us not fully captured by the existing terms of our existence. It "threatens to lift 'the veil of familiarity'" from prevailing relations of power; it "fires the imagination and challenges long-standing (often oppressive) practices."[44] It sees the Wizard for what he is and responds accordingly, meaning in a way that "cannot be subject to radical control" by dominant forces, but instead manifests "a wild democratic spirit."[45]

Cladis emphasizes that the wilderness within not only exceeds the control of dominant forces but is "beyond complete control" more generally, including the control of the subject him- or herself.[46] In this sense, although wilderness is an irrepressible source of individual agency and collective democratic transformation, it is far from a mark of sovereignty.[47] Instead, it suggests a nonsovereign way of understanding the dynamics through which existing configurations of power can give way to alternative formations, and how people who currently participate in their own domination can come to take part in their liberation. The wild within may not always spark activity and change that is emancipatory. Part of its nonsovereignty is that its trajectories are

unpredictable and therefore risky. Still, the wilderness that Cladis describes
helps us make sense of why, no matter how entrenched environmental domination may be, progress toward emancipation is always possible. And it points
us to another resource for activating emancipation. For as Cladis emphasizes,
while the wild is a naturally occurring aspect of all things, if we are to benefit
from its liberating potential, we will need to nourish it. Wilderness, he says, "is
something we *find*, something we *make*, and something we ought to *cultivate*
in our lives and culture."[48] Radical Romantics such as Wordsworth, Thoreau,
and Du Bois can help here, but resources can be found in other sites too, and
not only in art, literature, and film but also in the "wild" relationships we forge
with Earth's more-than-human parts.

Cultivating a radical-Romantic wilderness should not lead us to seek some
idyllic return to a pretechnical age.[49] Such returns are never possible. Moreover, if technological innovation is pursued within a framework that includes
institutions and social practices of nondomination, political respect for nature,
and a culture of eco-responsibility, it has the potential to serve ends that do
not result in extractivism and exploitation. Indeed, technology is a crucial tool
for creating more sustainable societies and living with Earth others in more
emancipatory ways. Technology is no silver bullet, of course; it cannot by itself
solve our environmental problems because the roots of these problems are not
fundamentally technological. Green technologies are a tool that must be
paired with the right political institutions and economic practices, and with
ethical and cultural transformation. When combined in this way, their potential
value for supporting eco-emancipation is significant. In this sense, eco-
emancipation is a forward-looking enterprise, one that seeks to create alternative modernities rather than to reject modernity.[50] It is true that the unfettered
expansion of consumerism will need to be brought in check, but limitless
consumption need not define modernity. Better modernities are possible for
us, in which we use technology to help us pursue peaceful and prosperous lives
in respectful, responsible community with one another and with Earth's more-
than-human parts.

Just as the meaning of emancipation admits of multiplicity, then, so the
methods for mobilizing it will be plural. In practicing eco-emancipation, we
enact and make possible a wide variety of new relationships among human
beings, and between people and nonhuman nature. These relationships are
dynamic, participatory inter-becomings that reflect a generative wilderness
running through us as people and linking us to all things. This wild consists in
the forces within and between us that cannot be fully captured by prevailing

relations of power, or domesticated by domination. It keeps the prospect of liberation perennially in view and provides the sparks that set it in motion. Eco-emancipation is in part an experience of coming home to this wilderness, not in the sense of abandoning modern life and human society, or living in perfect harmony with the nonhuman world, but in the sense of feeling our own power of transformation as a function of our Earthly life with others.

Institutionalizing Emancipation

So the alternative flows of power that help compose ecological emancipation connect sensibilities such as respect for nature and cultural norms such as eco-responsibility to collective mobilizations that aim to resist environmental domination and reconstruct political communities. Important as these connections are, eco-emancipation also needs the support of institutions. Hardt and Negri emphasize the importance of pairing extra-institutional mobilizations for liberation with what they call "the institutionalization of free and democratic forms of life."[51] Because the forces of domination are large, powerful, and enduring, eco-emancipation, like democracy, has a chance at a lasting life only if it can be given durable institutional forms. Moreover, insofar as domination is partly a status condition—a function of how power is institutionally constrained (or not)—then transforming the institutions that regulate power will be crucial to enacting a politics of emancipation. The objective of institutional change in this context is to ensure that power is (1) constrained within principled limits; and (2) answers to the well-being of its subjects, both human and nonhuman, and is responsive (where applicable) to their influence.

At the same time, it is important to understand the institutions of eco-emancipation in nonsovereign terms, as reliable sources of constraint and protection but also as dynamic sites of contestation, learning, and change. Along these lines, Hardt and Negri call for "the invention of new, nonsovereign institutions" to meet the durability needs of contemporary democratic assemblages. What they have in mind is institutions that incorporate "counterpowers" that "function antagonistically," checking and balancing one another so as to "subvert capitalist sovereignty."[52] Nonsovereign institutions channel and constrain power, but they do not effect a unitary source of control; in fact, they disrupt unitary control even as they allow for participatory decision making and action. Hardt and Negri are onto something important with the idea of nonsovereign institutions, but we need to think beyond their focus on capitalist power. Eco-emancipation requires preventing the large-scale consolidation not only of capitalist power but of all human power, including political as well as economic power. Even the assembled power of what Hardt and Negri call "the multitude"[53] itself must be subject to principled constraints if we are to put ourselves and nature on a path toward liberation. Moreover, the nonsovereign institutions they envision are limited to human beings, whereas institutions for eco-emancipation will need to incorporate more-than-human others.

A nonsovereign, eco-emancipatory institutional framework will include counterpowers in multiple forms: (a) *as countervailing sites of authority among political institutions*, such as contestations between governments or between states and international political bodies, or checks and balances within a particular government between its different branches and federated parts; (b) *as contestations across the political, economic, and social domains*, as when governments check the power of corporations through regulatory frameworks, or international lending agencies impose conditions on states that affect their behavior, or social movements challenge the actions of governments and industries; and (c) *between formal institutions and extra-institutional collective mobilizations*. The first principle of nonsovereign, eco-emancipatory institutions, then, is the multidimensional limitation of human power.

The second principle is inclusion, meaning inclusion of both marginalized people and nonhuman parts of nature. In other words, the multiple counterpowers that make up the nonsovereign institutional framework of eco-emancipation must incorporate more-than-human assemblages. Although this framework will be an artifact of human laws and public policies, at its best it will have what Coles refers to as a "polyface" quality. Borrowing the term from Joel Salatin's regenerative Polyface Farm, and inspired by Levinas's notion of "the face" as a catalyst for ethical engagement, Coles speaks of "polyface flows" as "profoundly receptive engagements" on the part of human beings with "myriad forms of life and interconnections that 'are not of one's own making.'"[54] As in Levinas's notion of the face, which "demands that I extend myself ethically beyond my ecocentric perception" toward an other "that can never be subsumed within it," polyface flows are "relational practices with nonhuman beings that . . . draw us into *eccentric*—rather than egocentric—ethical-corporeal movements."[55] Coles emphasizes that the "receptive resonance" in polyface flows is not the same thing as perfect harmony among the members of the assemblage. Salatin, he points out, eats the chickens and cows whose flourishing he otherwise serves.[56] The "receptive circulations in Salatin's pastures cultivate a more symbiotic thriving among myriad species" than one finds in conventional agricultural operations, but it is "not without a sacrificial dimension."[57] Coles also acknowledges the uncertainties that must inevitably attend our efforts to extend ourselves beyond our "egocentric perceptions," insisting that "a polyface ethos" includes a "sensibility" about all that we cannot know about others, and an appropriate humility.[58]

Despite their sacrificial dimensions and the uncertainty that permeates them, polyface flows are relational practices that orient people to one another and to nonhuman beings and things in more than merely instrumental ways. They embody the receptivity that we have identified with respect for nature and the responsiveness associated with eco-responsibility. Polyface flows are forms of relationality that situate us respectfully and responsibly within broader "flows of other beings and things," in communities that are both "human and non-human."[59] The institutions of eco-emancipation are inclusive in the sense that they aspire to embody polyface flows, meaning relational practices of receptivity and responsiveness across types of being.

In thinking about how eco-emancipation limits human power, it is important to see that structural constraints on both economic and political power are essential. A company that is "too big to fail" is also too big to be reliably checked by states and citizens, which leaves both people and nature vulnerable to arbitrary power and exploitation. Consequently, reversing neoliberal policies that abet the large-scale consolidation of economic power and minimize oversight is crucial. We need to enforce and expand antitrust laws to curtail mergers and monopolies, and we need to restore the regulatory power and will of governments. In addition to the scale of corporate power, its capacity to influence public decision making must be constrained. We need to prevent corporations and industries from directly shaping political outcomes through campaign financing and paid lobbying. This means providing public financing for political campaigns, subjecting corporate contributions to strict limits and to public disclosure requirements, and dramatically reducing (or outright eliminating) the amount that corporations can spend on lobbying efforts. We should also be cautious about privatizing the provision of public goods, from prisons and schools to hospitals, roads, and bridges. This is not to say that public-private partnerships never have a place. The point is to remind us that when combined with deregulation, relatively unrestricted free trade, the nonenforcement of antitrust laws, and the corporate capture of government, the privatization of public goods has the potential to increase both the scale and the capacities of corporate power in ways that foster environmental domination.

Efforts to pluralize the economy through the development of noncapitalist types of production and exchange also could help to limit the power of corporations by multiplying the sites and forms of economic activity, and deconsolidating economic power. Such alternatives could exist alongside some conventional (albeit constrained) capitalist practices in what J. K. Gibson-Graham refer to as a more "diverse" economy.[60] Many alternative economic practices already exist in most advanced democracies, if only in nascent form. Examples include "the exchange of commodities between and within worker cooperatives, where prices are set to enhance the sustainability of the cooperative; the ethical or 'fair' trade of products, where producers and consumers agree on price levels that will sustain certain livelihood practices; [and] local trading systems and alternative currencies that foster local interdependency and sustainability."[61] Gibson-Graham emphasizes alternative transactions involving the goods and services produced in households, often by women.[62] Among other things, they highlight "the incredible range of transactions, forms of labor, and kinds of enterprises through which the work of child care is performed around the world," including "community cooperative" child care, state-funded child care, and "community trade networks and baby-sitting clubs."[63] In the environmental context, farmers' markets and community-supported agriculture arrangements provide alternative economic frameworks that reduce the role of large corporations in both the production and the exchange of food.[64] Or consider the decentralized energy networks arising in many places around the world today involving wind and solar power that Coles writes about. In transition towns and other sites of local energy production, communities take charge of both the production and the distribution of electricity "in ways that could release contemporary economies from the megapowers that proliferate circulations of fossil fuels."[65]

More generally, we should cultivate "more complex, diverse, and skilled societies of small producers," as Luke has argued, who are well integrated into local communities.[66] This multiplicity not only would counter the consolidation of economic power but would distribute knowledge about the environmental impact of local lifestyles, enhancing transparency and combating the invisibility of distant "sacrifice zones" and "agribusiness regions," thereby "making those who consume aware of the ecological, economic, and energy costs of modern production."[67] Small producers and alternative sites of exchange will need support to compete successfully with today's corporate behemoths.[68] Yet large corporations themselves regularly benefit from state support in both direct and indirect ways. Redirecting some of this support to foster a more diverse economy is one way to set principled constraints on the scale and capacities of economic power, and hence to support eco-emancipation.

The limitation of economic power requires a strong state, as Robyn Eckersley has argued, in part because the existing scale and scope of corporate power today call for equivalently forceful sites of counterpower.[69] The social power of mobilized activists is also a valuable counterforce, but by itself it is not sufficient. This need for an appropriately scaled state recommends against Luke's "localistic, ecological populism" and Murray Bookchin's "libertarian munici-palism."[70] Luke insists on the "downsizing" of "nation-states" and "lessening the scope of centralized bureaucratic state control," while Bookchin regards the state as the irredeemable "destiny" of domination and holds that it must be dissolved for freedom to be possible.[71] The power of states also must be checked, of course, both as it bears on persons and as it affects nonhuman nature. Yet a political landscape that combines robust states committed to nondomination with multiple sites and sources of counterpower, from associations of local producers to municipal government councils to cross-national economic and political alliances, has the potential to take advantage of the environmental benefits of a strong state while preventing it from being a source of domination.

A state that is committed to nondomination of both people and the Earth will combine checks on political power with inclusive representation of more-than-human assemblages.[72] Because rights can serve the goals of both political inclusion and the limitation of power, eco-emancipatory institutions will incorporate regimes of animal and Earth rights alongside human rights. Human rights themselves are increasingly coming to include environmental protections for people such as "a right to environmental information" as well as "a right to participate in environmental impact assessment processes, and the right to environmental remedies when harm is suffered."[73] Yet rights for nonhuman beings and things are also important, both for nonhuman animals and for other parts of nature.[74] Donaldson and Kymlicka have advanced a sophisticated theory of animal rights that identifies different sets of rights for domesticated, wild, and what they call "liminal" nonhuman animals.[75] And as we have seen, Christopher Stone's generative *Should Trees Have Standing?* makes a forceful case that rivers, forests, and mountains should also have rights.[76] In both instances, rights are understood to offer protections against the abuse of power by human beings (individuals as well as states) and to be mechanisms for formally incorporating their holders into the political community.

Animal and Earth rights will need well-funded legal and administrative systems to support them, including (for instance) offices of animal and environmental advocacy. Donaldson and Kymlicka mention as an example the office of "animal advocate" in Zurich, which is occupied by "a lawyer with the power to represent animals in court, and with the mandate to focus on animal well-being."[77] In a similar way, Eckersley proposes the idea of "an independent environmental defender's office, staffed by a multidisciplinary team and charged with the responsibility of environmental monitoring, political advocacy, and legal representation," as a means for "ensuring that more systematic attention is directed toward the nonhuman constituency."[78] Such offices differ fundamentally from administrative units such as the US Environmental Protection Agency, whose purpose is to defend human interests.

It is also important for some animal and Earth rights to be entrenched at the level of fundamental law. As Bruce Jennings puts it, we must incorporate "new ecologically oriented norms and values into the constitutional structure . . . of a democratic mode of governance."[79] Like civil liberties and basic political rights, these norms must be difficult to reverse and must be insulated from partisan politics. The German constitution, for instance, incorporates provisions for animal rights intended to "protect the life and well-being of animals as fellow creatures."[80] Ecuador's 2008 constitution includes even broader protections for "the rights of nature" as a whole. Specifically, article 71 establishes that "nature . . . has the right to exist, persist, maintain and regenerate its vital cycles," while article 72 provides nature with "the right to restoration" from environmental damage. Bolivia's 2010 "Law of the Rights of Mother Earth" establishes similar protections.[81] These efforts to entrench rights for nature in fundamental law constrain political power, but they also make it more inclusive of the nonhuman by forcing the well-being of Earth others to count in political decision making.

We also need mechanisms for formally representing nature in decision-making bodies, from city councils to state and national legislative assemblies. Along these lines, Eckersley has discussed a "political trusteeship" model for representing "non-human species,"[82] and Andrew Dobson suggests the idea of "proxy representation of both non-human animals and future generations . . . by deputies elected from the environmental sustainability lobby."[83] Others have pressed for animal representation not only in legislative institutions but across a wider range of decision-making groups, from "municipal land planning" councils to "the governance boards of various professions and public services (police, emergency services, medicine, law, urban planning, social services, etc.)," and we could extend this idea to cover representation for other parts of ecosystems as well.[84] The idea is to build into a wide range of organizational forms mechanisms that force people to attend to nonhuman beings and things in their decision making.

It is true that representing nonhuman parts of nature is fraught with the potential for misrepresentation. Steven Vogel has written forcefully about the dangers of "ventriloquism" in this connection, or cloaking what are actually human interests in the guise of representing nonhuman ones.[85] Yet while we should be attentive to these dangers, we should also recognize that knowledge about the nonhuman world is available to us if we make an effort. We could not have survived as a species as long as we have done without some knowledge of what other things need to flourish. Moreover, we should not have to achieve "the perfect system of representation," as David Schlosberg puts it, before we attempt to improve the "obvious[ly] imperfect and biased system we have, and to bring a form of presence to those regularly left out of decision-making process[es]" that affect their well-being.[86]

Still, because our knowledge of nonhuman others is never perfect but evolves over time, a key feature of representative and other political institutions that incorporate Earth others must be what John Dryzek calls "ecosystemic reflexivity." This reflexivity is a feature of institutional design that allows decisions and practices to be changed in light of new ecological learning as it arises, thereby facilitating responsiveness to the claims of "the non-human world" in ways that evolve.[87] This openness to new information and the flexibility to change in light of it is another aspect of the nonsovereignty of eco-emancipatory institutions. Rather than reifying ostensibly fixed interests and ordering them inflexibly in relation to one another, we should understand these institutions as embodying frameworks for polyface flows that generate new insight over time, insight that can then be used to adjust the frameworks, potentially producing different rights and mechanisms of representation, and giving way to new forms of relationality.

The institutional apparatus of nondomination from rights to representation has never been enough to fully eliminate domination among people, and it has sometimes occluded existing domination or even been used to abet it.[88] Early efforts to extend rights and representation to nature have shown similar vulnerabilities. Gómez-Barris points out that Earth rights in Ecuador have been frequently co-opted, inverted, and ignored since the passage of its 2008 constitution.[89] She concludes that it is "wrong to assume that law is an appropriate site for nature's liberation from human authority."[90] Marisol de la Cadena similarly notes the disagreement, uncertainty, and inconsistencies that have plagued the rights of Pachemama announced by the constitutions of both Ecuador and Bolivia.[91] Yet if such mechanisms are admittedly insufficient, they are also necessary. A world without institutionally entrenched constraints on power and protections against exploitation is, by definition, a world of domination.

Moreover, rights and political representation can help to generate transformations in public ethos and political culture by articulating new values and collective aspirations, and by catalyzing political activism, which can then enhance the efficacy of the rights and representation.[92] Gómez-Barris's own account of artist-activists in Latin America makes it clear that both human rights and Earth rights, although never perfectly instantiated, have provided aspirational ideals that have spawned vibrant movements of resistance to environmental domination.[93] The insufficiency of legal-institutional mechanisms should lead us not to reject them, then, but to pursue them in a reflexive way that is always alive to how they can fall short or go wrong, and that is ready to respond. Moreover, the objective is not to pin all our hopes on some specific set of rights and representative mechanisms but to pursue what Donaldson and Kymlicka call "a commitment to constructing certain kinds of ongoing relationships" with more-than-human others—relationships that formally protect people and nature from insufficiently constrained power and exploitation, and that are responsive in decision making to their well-being.[94]

A final feature of eco-emancipatory institutions is transparency. We need to institutionalize more transparency about what is actually happening in the sea of agency today, and more transparency about how what we do contributes to environmental domination. We cannot enact respect or responsibility, and we cannot practice emancipation, without access to accurate information about the assemblages to which we contribute, and about the impact they have on other people and on nature. Some aspects of this need for transparency are obvious. We need to know more about what happens to animals, people, land, water, and climate in the agricultural and industrial practices that feed us, power our homes, and transport us from place to place.[95] Transparency means more access to better information and the effective dissemination of this information, beginning in early childhood. Doing a rough calculation of the carbon footprints of the products we find in the grocery store or the home improvement center should be as automatic for us by the age of ten as looking both ways before crossing a street.

Transparency also goes beyond increased access to information about agricultural, energy, and industrial practices.[96] It requires us to publicize the full costs of what we buy and what we do. The lower grocery-store prices for industrially produced food as compared with the prices for organic produce and meat that is humanely and sustainably raised conceal from view costs that consumers pay in other ways for their ostensibly cheaper food.[97] Similarly, the fossil fuel industry benefits from many unseen subsidies, which people mostly pay without realizing it. Efforts by environmental economists to make the full costs of our lifestyles evident are therefore important and have great transformative potential, even if economic costs are not the only ones that should count with us. In an even more general way, the efficiency of modern sewage systems as well as water and energy delivery make the effects of our waste and consumption invisible to us.[98] We need to find ways to combine efficiency with mechanisms that help us to see and feel the volume of our impact on others and on ecosystems.

It bears repeating that the institutions of eco-emancipation depend on collective mobilizations and activism, and depend on them not merely in a supplemental way but constitutively. Part of the nonsovereignty of the eco-emancipatory institutions explored here is their incorporation of contestation that introduces new information, generates new sensibilities, and fosters new, more-than-human flows of power and influence. The extra-institutional mobilizations of a healthy eco-democracy in this sense have an institutional role to play even though they also have a life that extends beyond formal institutions. And eco-emancipation itself extends beyond institutions, even the most emancipatory ones. We have seen that emancipation is more than just a status condition, although it is also importantly that. Eco-emancipation also includes worldmaking in tandem with human and nonhuman others, through the practice of respect and the exercise of responsibility, a more-than-human marronage that refuses entrapment and exploitation and brings into being new kinds of political community. The environmentalism of the poor exemplifies this emancipatory activity, from the Padres Hacia una Vida Mejor in Buttonwillow, California, who organized against a local dump expansion, to the Mnominee Nation's Sustainable Development Institute.[99] Equally important are the forms of activism arising among more privileged people that are generating "alternative patterns of material flows and powers" in local agriculture, food politics, and renewable energy.[100] All these counterflows tie what William Connolly calls "tactics of the self"—in this case oriented toward respect for nature and eco-responsibility—to a "collective politics of freedom."[101] They can also help to cultivate a "more-than-human sociality"[102] that awakens us to a sense of "citizenship in a broader commonwealth."[103] Like Leopold's land ethic, which enlarges the bounds of community to include the land and the innumerable beings and things that compose it, such counterflows expand "the ontological composition" of our political solidarities in ways that both complement and enliven the institutions of eco-emancipation.[104]

Conclusions

The multifaceted politics envisioned here is a politics of emancipation in the sense that it involves releasing nature and people from insufficiently constrained, exploitative human power. To emancipate something, as we have seen, is to unhand it, to relinquish one's putative authority over it, to free it from bondage. Eco-emancipation is a way of honoring the liberty of all things to live on their own terms, instead of making them live at the mere mercy of people. Emancipation is far from noninterference, of course. True noninterference is not an option for any of us in the environmental domain. We are too interdependent for that as individuals, communities, and species; to live on the Earth is inevitably to have an impact on others. Political institutions are crucial to eco-emancipation because reliable protection from insufficiently constrained power and exploitation requires an institutional apparatus sustained through the coercive power of the state. Yet eco-emancipation also is an activity of worldmaking together with others, human and nonhuman, one that depends on diverse economic practices, on the energy of collectively mobilized citizens, on a wilderness within each of us that "fires the imagination" and challenges domination, on a culture of eco-responsibility, and on a public ethos of respect for nature.

Eco-emancipatory political communities will be widely inclusive across types of being, but they will also be highly differentiated in the rights and responsibilities they ascribe to their various members; and the experiences of freedom they make possible will be diverse. And even as eco-emancipation redraws the boundaries of the political, it remains a distinctively human ideal, intended to guide us as people in our interactions with the rest of nature, not to reconstruct the relations that nonhuman beings and things have with one another. Eco-emancipation is not a matter of trying to force all nature to adhere to the ideal of nondomination but a matter of practicing this ideal ourselves in our relations with the more-than-human world we inhabit, and with one another.

Eco-emancipation is ecological in the familiar sense that it aims to protect the environment, but also in the sense that it can come about only by means of a new kind of political ecosystem, understood as the constellation of inter-connected human and more-than-human networks in which our relationships with other organisms unfold. A politics of eco-emancipation involves practices of care for this ecosystem, new kinds of assemblages, and a willingness on the part of human beings to be undone, to abandon our sense of entitlement to all things and be open to becoming-with others in ways we cannot fully control or predict. This politics is best seen as a process rather than an achievement, meaning that it will require continuing struggle, aspiration, and learning, a more-than-human marronage. It will not resolve all our environmental problems (they are too advanced for that), and it cannot promise perfect harmony, either among people or between people and nonhuman parts of nature. Still, it carries the seed of true and radical transformation because it opens the door to more sustainable and more liberated ways of life for all of us, privileged and poor, human and nonhuman—an Earthly politics of freedom.

Epilogue

MOST BOOKS OF political theory end with a conclusion. This book ends differently, without a conclusion, as a way of marking the fact that there is no end or finish line to the project of eco-emancipation. Eco-emancipation is a continuing process of liberation—or better, continuing practices of liberation—with no fixed end point. In these practices, uncertainty and reversals as well as conflicts and mistakes go hand in hand with the advance of understanding and with the cultivation of respect for others and responsibility for our common world. The more-than-human political communities of eco-emancipation point in many directions, with unpredictable trajectories. Eco-emancipation is a way of life, or many ways of life, in which people engage with nonhuman animals and ecosystems to contest existing conditions of domination and create more emancipatory ones. This polyface politics puts us into new kinds of relationships with one another and with the Earth, relationships that are freer because protected in reliable ways from insufficiently constrained, exploitative human power.

What political communities will actually look like when human power is exercised with respect and responsibility in relation to nature cannot be specified in advance. We can imagine it, and we can hope for it, but we will not know it until we *do* it. In the meantime, we may find it fortifying to reflect on a few current efforts to create more eco-emancipatory practices, and so I end the book with a small collection of such efforts. They are brief, and none of them is a story of complete liberation—far from it. Each one is partial, imperfect in its own ways, and situated within existing relations of environmental (and other) domination. But each one is also significant, creative, hopeful. Each offers inspiration, helps us see possibilities for a path forward, and demonstrates that human beings in collaboration with other parts of nature can indeed bring new worlds into being. They are liberation stories from the Earthly politics of freedom.

———

Menominee Nation Sustainable Development Institute. Founded in 1993, the Sustainable Development Institute (SDI) at the College of the Menominee Nation in Keshena, Wisconsin supports a wide range of activities and initiatives intended to "encourage, promote, and build upon Menominee approach to sustainable development," with the goal of educating students and the public about Menominee ways of living.[1] The institute grew out of efforts, following the 1992 Earth Summit in Rio de Janeiro, to formulate new approaches to integrating environmental protection with improvements in the socioeconomic conditions of people. It drew from the Menominee people's long history of sustainable forestry to develop a distinctive model of development.

Today there is a garden, a greenhouse, and a seed bank that support research for sustainable agriculture, teach students and members of the community about permaculture, and help promote food sovereignty for students and staff at the college and in surrounding tribal communities. The institute runs summer programs that bring students and teachers together for collaborative learning about Indigenous planning practices focused on "environmental sustainability, holistic healthcare, equitable business practices, and the pursuit of justice." It sponsors public forums (recent themes have included climate adaptation for tribal communities and renewable energy for Indian country) and fosters collaboration on practices of sustainable living between the college, the surrounding tribal communities, and external partners in sustainability. Although rooted in traditional lifeways, SDI is an example of the kind of forward-looking, alternative modernity that eco-emancipation calls for. While the institute focuses on serving Indigenous peoples, its model of sustainable development is a generative resource for all of us in thinking differently about human/more-than-human relations.

Lake Erie Bill of Rights. In February 2019, voters in Toledo, Ohio, passed by a wide margin the Lake Erie Bill of Rights, which "allows citizens to sue on behalf of the Lake if the Lake faces environmental harm."[2] The document holds that "Lake Erie, and the Lake Erie Watershed, possess the right to exist, flourish, and naturally evolve," and it provides for penalties to be imposed on governments and corporations "engaged in activities that violate the rights of the Lake Erie Ecosystem."[3] The bill faces significant "legal infirmities," as Richard Lazarus puts it, because its provisions may conflict with state and federal law and because the lake borders not only multiple US states but also Canada. Nevertheless, the 60 percent support it received from voters makes it significant, if only as an indication of public sentiment. Lazarus takes it as evidence of "a citizen rebellion" that "relates to a broader and important political movement by environmentalists across the globe."[4] This rebellion reflects the fact that "the residents of Toledo were fed up with the trashing of Lake Erie," and fed up with the weakness of political will on the part of elected officials who were doing nothing about it.[5] In Toledo, as in other places around the world where rights for nature are increasingly being codified in law, the Bill of Rights for Lake Erie was an effort on the part of citizens to establish more reliable constraints on human power in relation to nature, and to limit exploitation. It was an effort to force both environmental protection and political change: a refusal of environmental domination in multiple registers.

Southside Community Land Trust. In Providence, Rhode Island, the Southside Community Land Trust provides "access to land, education and other resources so people in Rhode Island can grow food in environmentally sustainable ways and create community food systems where locally produced, affordable and healthy food is available to all."[6] The group provides "training through apprenticeships and hands-on workshops for beginning farmers and others seeking to learn about small-scale, sustainable farming." They also run three production farms that employ principles of sustainable agriculture and that, together with their gardens, provide food to roughly three thousand local people each year who do not have enough to eat. The trust also offers summer jobs and internships for youth from the city's low-income neighborhoods, and free summer programs for low-income preschool and middle-school children geared toward growing food, eating healthy, and caring for the environment. The programs are particularly notable for their efforts to cultivate in the next generation political respect for nature and eco-responsibility, along with social justice.

Kenya's Green Belt Movement. Starting with a small group of rural women engaged in subsistence farming whose livelihoods were threatened by deforestation in their once fertile land, the Green Belt movement has grown into a formidable force for sustainable security, integrating environmental and democratic activism. The movement began with the planting of seven trees on Earth Day in 1977 "to commemorate Kenyan women who had been environmental activists."[7] By 2004—when their leader, Wangari Maatha, was awarded the Nobel Peace Prize—the movement "had created 6,000 local tree nurseries and employed 100,000 women to plant 30 million trees, mostly in Kenya, but in a dozen other African countries as well." As Rob Nixon notes, "the movement's achievements have been both material—providing employment while helping anchor soil, generate shade and firewood, and replenish watersheds—and symbolic, by inspiring other reforestation movements across the globe."[8]

Their work not only addresses the problem of deforestation (Kenya "has lost 98 percent of its . . . forest cover since the arrival of British colonialism in the nineteenth century"[9]), but it makes the movement "a powerful player in a broad based civil rights coalition that [has given] thousands of Kenyans a re-vived sense of civic agency and national possibility."[10] As Nixon points out, for Kenyans in the 1950s seeking an end to colonial subjugation, the forest was "a place of cultural regeneration and political refusal," and a "geographical and symbolic nexus of . . . peasant insurrection."[11] The Green Belt movement draws from this history of "forest resistance"[12] to embody a new kind of col-laboration between people and nonhuman nature for emancipatory purposes. Today the movement is still planting trees whose more-than-human vitalities are reconstructing landscapes, reseeding depleted ecosystems, and providing habitats for many species. The organization describes itself as working "at the grassroots, national, and international levels to promote environmental con-servation; to build climate resilience and empower communities, especially women and girls; to foster democratic space and sustainable livelihoods."[13] It is an example of the emancipatory potential of more-than-human assemblages engaged in collective worldmaking.

Ashton Hayes Community Energy CIC. In 2006 the town of Ashton Hayes, population one thousand or so, made the decision to try to become England's first carbon-neutral village.[14] Villagers agreed to reduce their personal carbon emissions and to seek carbon neutrality in public buildings and activities. Their efforts have mostly targeted low-hanging fruit. For example, "they use clotheslines instead of dryers, take fewer flights, install solar panels and glaze windows to better insulate their homes."[15] Together as a town they have also "built a new playing field with a solar-powered pavilion, which is the home of a community cafe three days a week," and they have "put photovoltaic solar panels on the roof of the primary school."[16] Still, the impact has been signifi-cant, according to the *New York Times*, which notes that "households that par-ticipated in surveys in both the first and 10th years shrank their energy use by about 40 percent."[17]

In 2011 the town established the Ashton Hayes Community Energy CIC (AHCE) to manage renewable generation assets on behalf of the community, and in 2020 the group established a "Junior Board" at the local school so that village children can participate directly in the project.[18] One of the secrets to the continuing vitality of the initiative is that "the people of Ashton Hayes feel in charge."[19] They are precisely the kinds of people—privileged, prosperous members of contemporary capitalist democracies—whom environmental domination often renders complacent and ineffectual in the face of large-scale environmental problems such as climate change. Instead, they are working together and using the resources their privilege and prosperity allow them to make a difference. They are literally generating their own power—and demonstrating to others that it can be done. They manifest the empowerment that eco-responsibility can unleash, and offer a window into one way of pursuing, together with others, a more emancipatory way of life.

The Path of the Pronghorn. Each year the antelope-like mammals known as pronghorns that inhabit the Green River valley of Wyoming migrate north with the spring to their summer habitat in Jackson Hole and Grand Teton National Park, returning south again as winter approaches. The migration covers more than two hundred miles round-trip along a river corridor, and hundreds of animals typically participate. In recent years, "housing developments, roads, and fences" have begun "threatening to sever the corridor at several crucial bottlenecks."[20] A number of nonprofit organizations together with the state of Wyoming have coordinated efforts to study the problem and remediate it. They have adopted a variety of approaches, including retrofitting or removing problem fences, purchasing parcels of land to protect them from development, limiting oil and gas leasing, and building highway overpasses and underpasses "to facilitate safe crossing of pronghorn during migration."[21]

The story is unfinished, and the achievements are precarious. In February 2020, according to the *Guardian*, "conservation groups filed a legal petition challenging the Trump administration's plan to allow 3,500 new gas wells in south-western Wyoming that would block the route."[22] The outcome of the case is uncertain, and the future of the herds hangs in the balance because the migration is essential to their survival. Still, the story exemplifies an effort by people to support the liberty of Earth others to live on their own terms rather than at the mere mercy of human beings. And it manifests the kind of learning, responsiveness, and creativity that eco-emancipation calls for, an effort by people to understand nonhuman beings better and to live among them with greater respect and responsibility.

The Theater of Negotiations, Les Amandiers, May 2015. Seven months ahead of the 2015 Paris climate talks, a group of students at the school of the political arts at Sciences Po in Paris gathered at the Théâtre des Amandiers to conduct "a simulated negotiation" over the problem of climate change,[23] initiated by Bruno Latour and others. Students from thirty countries participated over the course of six days, charged with negotiating their way to agreement about limitations on greenhouse gas emissions. The simulation was documented by the filmmaker David Bronstein, and it has come to have an enduring cultural life as the film CLIMATE, *Make It Work!*.[24] Although the meeting was intended to model the UN's COP21 negotiations, the participants at Les Amandiers represented a far more diverse range of ontological types. Nation-states were included, as in the real COP21, but alongside them and "equal in sovereignty" were delegations named "Forest," "Atmosphere," "Oceans," and "Endangered Species," as well as "Cities," "NGOs," "Indigenous Peoples," "International Organizations," and even "Stranded Petroleum Assets."[25]

The negotiation was a "scene of conflict" among actors "each capable of encroaching on the action of others" in ways that impact climate change.[26] It forced its human participants to contend with nonhuman beings and things in more than merely instrumental ways, and to incorporate inputs from Earth others into the deliberative process. The composition of the assembly as representing both human and more-than-human entities was intended to upend "the distinction between a nation-state and its environment," to make the point that "humans are not alone at the command post," and to model a more-than-human practice of "power-sharing."[27] It was also meant to make the full range of human participants in the decision process visible and accountable to one another, including certain nonstate actors and economic agents that under neoliberal globalization have made nation-states "mere marionettes in their hands."[28]

Acknowledging its fictional status, Latour nevertheless describes the negotiation as a "constitutive" event that called into being a political sensibility with "a radically new spirit."[29] He likens it to the 1789 Constituent Assembly in France, which transformed the Estates General into "something entirely different"—a sovereign people—and gave rise to the revolutionary new regime of modern democracy.[30] He reminds us about "the work of invention that was required, once upon a time, to bring to light the improbable being called *the people*," and he presses the continuing importance of "political simulations," of "models" and "fictions" that "[anticipate] what we hope to observe soon."[31] Les Amandiers offers, he says, "an image" of a *"res publica"* that embodies "a new nomos of the Earth."[32] We have no assurance of its becoming real. In fact, Latour says that the six-day negotiation "never stopped almost failing."[33] Yet if "politics is the art of the possible," as he rightly insists, then the value of such images, like the other liberation stories recounted here, is that they help us to "multiply the possibles."[34]

Perhaps in the end this is the truest way to understand eco-emancipation: as a raucous, unpredictable, always-in-danger-of-failing, never-ending collection of collaborations across beings, species, and systems, with respect and responsibility, to "multiply the possibles" of a freer, more sustainable life on Earth.

NOTES

Chapter 1: Awakenings

1. Nixon, *Slow Violence*.

2. Abbott, "Scientists Bust Myth"; Sender, Fuchs, and Milo, "Revised Estimates for the Number of Human and Bacteria Cells in the Body."

3. On this point, see Cronon, "Trouble with Wilderness"; McKibben, *End of Nature*; and Purdy, *After Nature*.

4. Connolly, *Facing the Planetary*, 10. See also Bruno Latour's discussion of how nature as "Gaia" exceeds the human in *Facing Gaia*, esp. lecture 3.

5. See White, Rudy, and Gareau, *Environments, Natures and Social Theory*, xix; and Whatmore, *Hybrid Geographies*, 3.

6. See Plato, *Republic*, book 9; and Montesquieu, *Spirit of the Laws*, books 3 and 4.

7. The German constitution, for example, includes provisions for animal rights intended to "protect the life and well-being of animals as fellow creatures." Ecuador's 2008 constitution includes broader protections for "the rights of nature" as a whole, and Bolivia's 2010 "Law of the Rights of Mother Earth" establishes similar protections. These examples are discussed in the chapters that follow. Although at present they remain largely aspirational, I see animal and Earth rights as offering potentially valuable mechanisms for constraining human power in relation to nature.

8. *Holy Bible*, Genesis 1:26.

9. Aristotle, *Politics*, book 1, chap. 8, p. 45 (1256bl, 15–23).

10. Locke, "Second Treatise of Government," paras. 6, 271.

11. Marx, "Economic and Philosophic Manuscripts of 1844," 75.

12. Unless otherwise specified, I use the term "Earth others" to refer to nonhuman beings and things.

13. Pettit, *Republicanism*, 31.

14. Forrest, "Interview with Naomi Klein." See also McKibben, "What Exxon Knew about Climate Change."

15. For discussion of the dynamics of agency under conditions of structural domination and oppression, see Krause, *Freedom beyond Sovereignty*.

16. Some Indigenous groups are isolated enough to still be more or less independent of modern social, economic, and political systems. However, the number of such groups is rapidly shrinking, and many of them increasingly find their ways of life affected by the domination of nature as practiced by more "advanced" societies, with the effects of climate change being just one example. Modern societies have much to learn from them, although the goal of ecological

emancipation is not to become "unmodern" so much as to forge "alternative modernities" that are more respectful of nonhuman nature and more environmentally sustainable. I borrow the idea of alternative modernities from Martínez-Alier, *Environmentalism of the Poor*, 145 (Martinez-Alier credits Victor Toledo for the phrase). Moreover, while modern societies can learn from Indigenous lifeways, it is not the responsibility of Indigenous groups to save white people from their own worst impulses, as Kyle Whyte has pointed out. The idea of mining Indigenous lifeways to guide alternative modernities risks "treating Indigenous peoples as resources that can be used . . . for the advancement of humanity." Still, we should take inspiration where we can find it, albeit always being careful to resist instrumentalizing the sources of our inspiration. Whyte, "Indigenous Science (Fiction) for the Anthropocene," 238.

17. I borrow the language of ecological emancipation from Eckersley, *Green State*, 14. I share Eckersley's conviction that "the project of emancipation" must include "both the human and the nonhuman world," but my understanding of the human side of emancipation is different from hers (9). In particular, she emphasizes the ways in which "privileged social classes have been able to remain remote" from the effects of environmental domination (10). For her, the ecological emancipation of human beings is primarily a matter of redressing the unequal burdens that environmental degradation has on the poor and the marginalized (10). It is true that ecological costs are distributed in unfair ways, with the poor and the marginalized bearing disproportionate burdens, but my concern also includes how the insufficiently constrained use of human power in relation to nature entraps and exploits human beings across the whole range of social hierarchies, compromising freedom for all of us, albeit in differentiated ways. Additionally, I mean to elaborate in more depth than Eckersley does the mechanisms through which the different forms of environmental domination among human beings interact with the domination of nonhuman nature by (different groups of) people. Emancipation as it is conceived here will require more than the redistribution of ecological costs and benefits from the poor to the privileged; it calls for fundamentally reconstructing the basic structure of human power as it bears on the relationships between people and the Earth. Still, Eckersley's account of "ecological democracy" is a valuable one (esp. 111–38), and I draw on her work in what follows.

18. Stefan Dolgert makes a similar point in discussing the human treatment of nonhuman animals, where "knowing what we are doing produces a longing not to know" and generates a willful blindness about animal suffering. Dolgert, "Sacrificing Justice," 264. Other important work exploring the political nature of our relationships with nonhuman animals includes K. Smith, *Governing Animals*; Donaldson and Kymlicka, *Zoopolis*; and Goodin, Pateman, and Pateman, "Simian Sovereignty." This work moves productively beyond an earlier generation of animal rights and animal welfare literature that treated the human/nonhuman relationship in primarily ethical terms rather than political ones. See, for example, Singer, *Animal Liberation*; Regan, *Case for Animal Rights*; and Sunstein and Nussbaum, *Animal Rights*. The present study has a broader scope than the animal rights and welfare literatures in that it covers our relationship with the whole of nonhuman nature. In this regard, it is more in keeping with work in environmental political theory that situates human beings in relation to all species and ecosystems (and the nonliving things that support them). See, for example Eckersley, *Environmentalism and Political Theory*; Eckersley, *Green State*; Schlosberg, *Defining Environmental Justice*; Coles, *Visionary Pragmatism*; Dryzek, *Politics of the Earth*; Luke, *Ecocritique*; Biro, *Denaturalizing Ecological Politics*; Meyer, *Political Nature*; Cannavò, *Working Landscape*; and Bennett, *Vibrant Matter*.

19. Schlosberg, *Defining Environmental Justice*; Lane, *Eco-Republic*; Jamieson, *Reason in a Dark Time*, esp. chap. 6; and Broome, *Climate Matters*.

20. See especially Merchant, *Death of Nature*.

21. Cited in Solomon, *Objectivity in the Making*, 62.

22. For rich discussions of these works from a contemporary environmental standpoint, see Cladis, "Radical Romanticism: Democracy, Religion, and the Environmental Imagination," 21; and Cladis, "Radical Romanticism and Its Alternative Account of the Wild and Wilderness."

23. Bookchin, *Ecology of Freedom*.

24. Plumwood, *Feminism and the Mastery of Nature*.

25. Horkheimer and Adorno, *Dialectic of Enlightenment*.

26. Leiss, *Domination of Nature*, 123.

27. Abram, *Becoming Animal*, 254. Abram is referring to the self in this passage, or personal identity, not to agency per se. I mean to extend his concept of the distributed circuits of the self to agency.

28. See Vrousalis, "Exploitation, Vulnerability, and Social Domination." Other accounts, by contrast, have insisted on the connection between domination and exploitation, especially in the context of the labor-republican tradition. See, for example, Gourevitch, *From Slavery to the Cooperative Commonwealth*; W. Roberts, *Marx's Inferno*; and Cicerchia, "Structural Domination in the Labor Market." Frank Lovett, too, characterizes exploitation as "a common feature of domination" in Lovett, *General Theory of Domination and Justice*, 131.

29. "Exploitation," Oxford English Dictionary. July 5, 2022. en.oxforddictionaries.com /definition/exploitation.

30. Derrida, *Animal That Therefore I Am*, 30–31.

31. Ackerly, *Just Responsibility*, 2–3, 60–65.

32. On epistemologies of ignorance, see Mills, "White Ignorance." For discussion of the value of disruptive politics to dispel epistemologies of ignorance, see Hayward, "Responsibility and Ignorance," 396, 404–6.

33. In theorizing beyond our existing human-dominant frames, *Eco-Emancipation* resonates with some work in posthumanism. See, for example, Braidotti, *Posthuman*; Massumi, *What Animals Teach Us about Politics*; and Wolfe, *What Is Posthumanism?* In particular, it shares the goal of thinking beyond the perspective of the old human exceptionalism. At the same time, however, I regard some of the achievements of humanism as a philosophical project, such as the ideal of moral and political equality among persons, to be tremendously valuable, even if their full promise has yet to be realized, and I have no wish to leave them behind. Consequently, although there are resonances between this book and some posthumanist ones, I do not regard *Eco-Emancipation* as a project in posthumanism per se. Additionally, in contrast to some posthumanists, my approach insists that there are some capacities in human beings as a part of nature that are distinctive relative to other parts of nature, and that are morally and politically significant in the sense that they entail a special accountability on the part of people for the harms effected through environmental domination and are necessary for mobilizing on behalf of emancipation. This issue is discussed in chapter 2 in connection with agency and what I call "the new exceptionalism." For these reasons, I have largely avoided the language of posthumanism throughout the book, despite the affinities between this project and that one.

Chapter 2: A New Exceptionalism

1. Abram, *Becoming Animal*, 254.

2. Arendt, *Human Condition*, 190–92.

3. See, for example, Donaldson and Kymlicka, *Zoopolis*, 65–66, 117–22, 176–77; and see Bekoff and Pierce, *Wild Justice*; de Waal, *Age of Empathy*; Denison, "Between the Moment and Eternity"; Reid, "Moral Agency in *Mammalia*"; and Sapontzis, *Morals, Reason, and Animals*.

4. Kateb, *Human Dignity*, 3–4.

5. Kateb, *Human Dignity*, 6.

6. Kateb, *Human Dignity*, 7.

7. See Kateb, *Human Dignity*, 20, 160.

8. Kateb, *Human Dignity*, 170–71.

9. Kateb, *Human Dignity*, 171.

10. Kateb, *Human Dignity*, 171.

11. Kateb, *Human Dignity*, 160; and see 132–33.

12. Kateb, *Human Dignity*, 5, 17.

13. Kateb, *Human Dignity*, 17.

14. Kateb, *Human Dignity*, 21–22.

15. Kateb, *Human Dignity*, 5, 115–17, 171.

16. Kateb, *Human Dignity*, 116.

17. Kateb, *Human Dignity*, 210.

18. Kateb, *Human Dignity*, 210.

19. Kateb, *Human Dignity*, 210, 135.

20. Kateb, *Human Dignity*, 162.

21. Kateb, *Human Dignity*, 151. On animal agency, see McFarland and Hediger, *Animals and Agency*; Carter and Charles, "Animals, Agency and Resistance"; Arruda and Povinelli, "Chimps as Secret Agents"; Spinka and Wemelsfelder, "Environmental Challenge and Animal Agency"; and Delon et al., "Consider the Agent in the Arthropod." On animal cognition and choice making, see Premack, "Animal Cognition"; Arnott and Elwood, "Information Gathering"; Arganda, Perez-Escudero, and de Polavieja, "Common Rule for Decision Making"; and Wright, "Testing Complex Animal Cognition." On norm responsiveness, see Fitzpatrick, "Chimpanzee Normativity"; Schlingloff and Moore, "Do Chimpanzees Conform to Social Norms?"; and Bekoff and Pierce, *Wild Justice*.

22. Agency so conceived is the foundation of the two moral powers in Rawls. See Rawls, *Theory of Justice*. Philip Pettit likewise understands agency as the capacity for control over action (whether rational, volitional, or discursive). See Pettit, *Theory of Freedom*. Nancy Hirschmann defines agency in terms of intentional choice, although she emphasizes the importance for freedom of ensuring that informal social conditions protect women's choices against domination. See Hirschmann, *Subject of Liberty*. Sovereigntist assumptions about agency can also be found in the communitarianism of Charles Taylor and feminist work on relational autonomy. See C. Taylor, "What Is Human Agency?"; Mackenzie and Stoljar, *Relational Autonomy*; and Friedman, *Autonomy, Gender, Politics*. In addition, poststructuralist views that associate agency with transgression and resistance sometimes recapitulate the sovereigntist identification of

agency with intentional choice. See Saba Mahmood's critique of Judith Butler on this point in Mahmood, *Politics of Piety*.

23. I focus here on individual agency not collective agency, although individual agency is conceived as an assemblage, which is a kind of collectivity. The main difference between collective agency and the assemblage view of individual agency is that collective agency involves consciously coordinated action among different individual agents guided by a shared purpose or intention, which is not the case for individual agency as an assemblage. The differences between individual and collective agency, and the ways that individual agency is both distinct from and dependent on collective agency, are discussed below.

24. Kateb, *Human Dignity*, 160; and see 132–33.

25. The idea of agency as a socially distributed phenomenon is elaborated at much greater length in Krause, *Freedom beyond Sovereignty*, chaps. 1 and 2. See also Krause, "Agency." The present discussion builds on that earlier work for purposes of contesting the role that human agency has played in justifying environmental domination via the old exceptionalism, and understanding the role that agency must play in overcoming this domination. My account of nonsovereign agency finds inspiration in Arendt but also departs from her view in some important ways. For analysis and critique of Arendt's view, see Krause, *Freedom beyond Sovereignty*, 29–42. For additional discussion of Arendt and the nonsovereignty of agency, see Zerilli, *Feminism and the Abyss of Freedom*; Markell, *Bound by Recognition*, esp. chap. 2; and Markell, "Insufficiency of Non-domination."

26. Arendt, *Human Condition*, 189.

27. Arendt, *Human Condition*, 188.

28. Arendt, *Human Condition*, 190.

29. Arendt, *Human Condition*, 190.

30. Action is not always subject to social uptake, of course. I can pour myself a cup of coffee without needing social uptake to bring the action to fruition. Arendt is concerned especially with explicitly political action, but her account applies to human action in the social and political domains in a general way.

31. Arendt, *Human Condition*, 184.

32. Arendt, "What Is Freedom?," 163. Arendt equates "sovereign" with "indivisible," meaning the function of a singular, unitary will, "independent of others and eventually prevailing against them" (163).

33. Arendt, *Human Condition*, 234–35.

34. Arendt, *Human Condition*, 173, 190–91, 197, 234. And see Markell, *Bound by Recognition*, esp. chap. 3; B. Williams, *Moral Luck*, esp. chap. 2; and B. Williams, *Shame and Necessity*, esp. chap. 3.

35. B. Williams, *Shame and Necessity*, 69.

36. Markell uses the language of "acknowledgement" to express recognition of the ways that our nonsovereign agency makes us complicit in injustice. Markell, *Bound by Recognition*, 177–89. Acknowledgment is indeed crucial, but often something more than acknowledgment is needed to reverse the injustices in which we find ourselves complicit, including actively taking responsibility for creating a more just future through concrete action in the world. We shall pursue the theme of responsibility in a nonsovereign way in chapter 5.

37. The notion that we can be held accountable for things that we did not control or intend is admittedly unnerving. The ideal of agency as sovereignty holds that no one should be responsible for what is outside their control, and there are some advantages in this way of thinking. It is an achievement of the sovereign view, for example, that in liberal democratic societies we no longer hold people responsible for deeds committed by their family members or punish women for being raped. Intentionality and control, or at least influence, are not irrelevant to responsibility, but neither are they the whole of it. Particularly in the context of complex social dynamics such as implicit bias or climate change, when we limit responsibility to the things we intended and controlled, we make it too easy to ignore our complicity in harms that depend on our participation even as they elude our full control and sometimes our awareness. We need to be able to distinguish between different degrees and types of responsibility, some involving intentionality and influence, and some exceeding these conditions. These issues are elaborated in depth in chapter 5.

38. Political and economic inequalities also pose problems for agency in related ways. I focus here on social inequality, meaning inequalities of power that attach to social identities (such as race, gender, or sexual orientation). These inequalities interact with political and economic inequalities, of course, so the contexts of social inequality are often also contexts of economic and political inequality.

39. Baldwin, "Notes of a Native Son," 68.

40. Baldwin, "Notes of a Native Son," 68.

41. Baldwin, "Notes of a Native Son," 68–69.

42. Baldwin, "Notes of a Native Son," 69.

43. Baldwin, "Notes of a Native Son," 69.

44. The disabling effects that social inequality has on agency can be mitigated by the solidarity and mutual recognition found within marginalized communities, which constitute alternative communities of bearers within the larger society, with its context of bias and oppression. For further discussion of this dynamic, see Nancy Fraser's work on subaltern counterpublics in Fraser, "Rethinking the Public Sphere"; and see Warner, *Publics and Counterpublics*; Stout, *Blessed Are the Organized*; and Krause, *Freedom beyond Sovereignty*, chap. 3.

45. Laura Ephraim has productively pushed Arendt in this regard, arguing for "an Arendtian environmental politics" that attends to "the involvement of nonhuman life forms in animating political life" (Ephraim, "Save the Appearances!," 2). Ephraim means "to theorize," with the help of Arendt, a "mode of hybridity . . . that serves the flourishing of political life and promotes respect and protection for biological life" (11). In contrast to the present study, however, her argument focuses not on the composition of human agency but on its context, the "stage" on which human actions "appear" (4). Her broader objective is to show that politics "requires not only the stability and beauty of the world's durable artifacts but also the freshness and novelty of the earth's shape-shifting organisms" (11). Human freedom depends on a stage that is both worldly and earthly, she argues, and consequently "biological and political life must be revalued and renewed together" (11). Ephraim's account is a valuable one, in part because it moves beyond Arendt's own narrow association of corporeality with necessity, and in part because of how it "contributes to recent efforts to theorize a more active role for nonhuman beings and matter in environmental politics . . . while resisting their tendency to flatten important differences between human and nonhuman beings by attributing 'agency' . . . to them all" (2n7). Yet

for Ephraim, as for Arendt, nonhuman nature operates mainly as a backdrop, as the "stage" for human action and sometimes as an inspiration for it (nature's significance lies in its inspiring, "entertainment value" for people, 8, 9, 12), not as a constitutive component of human agency. Moreover, politics and "political values like freedom and plurality," as she presents them, are limited to people (8). Or at least Ephraim offers no discussion here of incorporating nonhuman beings and things into politics or enhancing their experience(s) of freedom. For Ephraim, it seems, nature is important because (or to the extent that) it supports the political flourishing of people. Rich as it is, by neglecting the more-than-human constituents of human agency and by limiting politics to people, Ephraim's Arendtian environmentalism remains within the confines of the old exceptionalism.

For additional efforts to mobilize Arendt for environmental ethics and political theory, see Ephraim, *Who Speaks for Nature?*; Chapman, "Ways That Nature Matters"; Myers, *Worldly Ethics*; Rossello, "Animal Condition in the Human Condition"; Szerszynski, "Technology, Performance, and Life Itself"; Voice, "Consuming the World"; and Whiteside, "Worldliness and Respect for Nature," all cited in Ephraim, "Save the Appearances!"

46. Bennett, "Agency of Assemblages," 446–47.

47. Bennett, "Agency of Assemblages," 463. See also Connolly, who insists that there are many types of agency in "forcefields." Connolly, *World of Becoming*, 7, 21.

48. For examples of the new materialism, see Coole and Frost, *New*; Coole, "Rethinking Agency"; Coole, "Experiencing Discourse"; Coole, "Agentic Capacities and Capacious Historical Materialism"; Latour, *Reassembling the Social*; Knappett and Malafouris, *Material Agency*; Law and Hassard, *Actor Network Theory and After*; and Panagia, *Political Life of Sensation*. There is also a rich and diverse literature in environmental political theory and philosophy that explores what Teena Gabrielson describes as "the value of conceptualizing agency as emerging from the intra-action of a variety of actants, both human and non-human." Gabrielson, "Bodies, Environments, and Agency," 408. In addition to Gabrielson's work, see, for example, Bennett, *Vibrant Matter*; Alaimo, *Bodily Natures*; Whatmore, *Hybrid Geographies*; Morton, *Hyperobjects*; Barad, *Meeting the Universe Halfway*; and Cadena, *Earth Beings*.

Like these literatures, the present study "conceives of agency as collectively produced by a variety of participants, including non-human animals, plants, and things" (Gabrielson "Bodies, Environments, and Agency," 405) but, in contrast to much of the new materialism, *Eco-Emancipation* also means to acknowledge the special place of human agency in the politics of both environmental domination and eco-emancipation. The special place it makes for human agency is discussed below in connection with "the new exceptionalism."

49. Leopold, *Sand County Almanac*, 241.

50. Leopold, *Sand County Almanac*, 241.

51. Leopold, *Sand County Almanac*, 243.

52. Leopold, *Sand County Almanac*, 242.

53. Leopold, *Sand County Almanac*, 243.

54. Vogel, *Thinking Like a Mall*, 113.

55. Vogel, *Thinking Like a Mall*, 120, emphasis in the original.

56. Anker, *Ugly Freedoms*, 161.

57. Anker, *Ugly Freedoms*, 160.

58. Anker, *Ugly Freedoms*, 162.

59. Anker, *Ugly Freedoms*, 163.

60. See, for example, Hirschmann, "Feminist Thoughts on Freedom and Rights"; Hirschmann "Disability as a New Frontier"; Hirschmann "Disability, Feminism, and Intersectionability"; Hirschmann and Linker, *Civil Disabilities*; Arneil, "Disability, Self-Image, and Modern Political Theory"; Siebers, *Disability Theory*; and Shakespeare, *Disability Reader*.

61. Whyte, "Indigenous Science (Fiction) for the Anthropocene."

62. Abram, *Becoming Animal*, 254.

63. In this respect, the nonsovereign approach to agency resonates with recent work in posthumanist studies, which also contests this divide. See Braidotti, *Posthuman*, 49, 60, 67; Abram, *Becoming Animal*, 47; Agamben, *Open*, 12, 16, 26; Derrida, *Animal That Therefore I Am*, 23, 32, 126; and Massumi, *What Animals Teach Us about Politics*, 3, 52, 92–93. Jedidiah Purdy also insists on the "permeability" of the boundary between human and nonhuman beings. See Purdy, *After Nature*, 282.

64. Watts, "Indigenous Place-Thought and Agency amongst Humans and Non-humans," 23.

65. Or, as Ephraim puts it, there is a "tendency to flatten important differences between human and nonhuman beings by attributing 'agency' . . . to them all" (Ephraim, "Save the Appearances!," 2n7). Bruno Latour's actor network theory exemplifies this tendency (see Latour, *Reassembling the Social*). See also Law and Mol, "Actor-Enacted," 58; Jones and Cloke, "Non-human Agencies," 80–82; and Gell, *Art and Agency*, 6–7.

66. Bennett, "Agency of Assemblages," 447.

67. Bennett, "Agency of Assemblages," 453. Connolly likewise insists that we should "appreciate multiple degrees and sites of agency, flowing from simple natural processes, through higher processes, to human beings and collective social assemblages." Connolly, *World of Becoming*, 22.

68. Bennett, "Agency of Assemblages," 446.

69. Bennett, "Agency of Assemblages," 453.

70. Bennett, "Agency of Assemblages," 446.

71. Bennett, *Vibrant Matter*, 104.

72. For further discussion of the norm-responsiveness dimensions of agency and the limitations of the new materialism in this regard, see Krause, *Freedom beyond Sovereignty*, 48–51.

73. Donaldson and Kymlicka, *Zoopolis*, 117–18.

74. Donaldson and Kymlicka, *Zoopolis*, 117.

75. Donaldson and Kymlicka, *Zoopolis*, 117.

76. Donaldson and Kymlicka, *Zoopolis*, 118.

77. Donaldson and Kymlicka, *Zoopolis*, 118.

78. Donaldson and Kymlicka, *Zoopolis*, 118.

79. Puppies are taught how to behave with other dogs by adult dogs, through stern but nonviolent vocalizations, mouthing, and cuffing. The norms are remarkably consistent, and most puppies learn them pretty quickly.

80. Donaldson and Kymlicka, *Zoopolis*, 119.

81. Donaldson and Kymlicka, *Zoopolis*, 121.

82. In emphasizing the need to make ourselves bearers of animal agency, my argument resonates with that of Donaldson and Kymlicka, who defend a model of "dependent agency" in relation to nonhuman animals, according to which the "human companions" of domesticated

animals must be "prepared to enable the development of [agentic] capacities" in them in a way that parallels the obligation we have to "recognize and assist the expression of agency" in people with certain disabilities that put them in need of such assistance (*Zoopolis*, 104, 120). My view differs from theirs, however, in seeing all agency as nonsovereign and hence as in some sense dependent, rather than treating dependent agency as an exceptional case.

83. In this respect, the new exceptionalism I have in view contrasts with the approach defended recently by Joshua Dienstag, which insists on something closer to the old (morally hierarchical, politically exclusionary) human exceptionalism, arguing that care for nonhuman nature is impossible without it. Dienstag's account is a nuanced and powerful one, a worthy successor to Kateb's, although ultimately it seems to me to fall short of being able to sustain the kind of care for the Earth that it aspires to because it fails to attend to the necessarily political dimensions of establishing (and enforcing) this care. See Dienstag, "Dignity, Difference, and the Representation of Nature."

Chapter 3: Environmental Domination

1. Merchant, "Scientific Revolution and *The Death of Nature*," 517.

2. Leiss, *Domination of Nature*, 55.

3. Merchant, "Scientific Revolution and *The Death of Nature*," 517. It is perhaps worth noting that although modern science introduced new methods and technologies for attempting to master nature, the idea has an older lineage, going back at least as far as Aristotle's assertion that plants and animals "exist for the sake of human beings" as "instruments" to be used for human purposes (Aristotle, *Politics*, book 1, chap. 8, p. 45 (1256b1, 15–23).

4. See for example, Leiss, *Domination of Nature*; Plumwood, *Feminism and the Mastery of Nature*; Bookchin, *Ecology of Freedom*; and Eckersley, *Environmentalism and Political Theory*.

5. This chapter draws from Krause, "Environmental Domination."

6. In linking the status condition of systematic vulnerability to the practice of exploitation as a constitutive feature of domination, I depart from some republicans. Indeed, some have seen exploitation as the concern of a very different tradition of political thought, namely Marxism. The perspective on domination pursued here is no more Marxist than it is republican, strictly speaking, but it does have debts to both. The key insight it takes from republicanism is the idea that domination involves a status condition of systematic vulnerability that is a function of the existing political order. For further discussion of possible tensions between conventional republican conceptions of domination and exploitation, see Vrousalis, "Exploitation, Vulnerability, and Social Domination." Other accounts, by contrast, have insisted on the connection between domination and exploitation, especially in the context of the tradition of labor republicanism. See, for example, Gourevitch, *From Slavery to the Cooperative Commonwealth*; W. Roberts, *Marx's Inferno*; and Cicerchia, "Structural Domination in the Labor Market." Frank Lovett, too, characterizes exploitation as "a common feature of domination" in Lovett, *General Theory of Domination and Justice*, 131. For examples of republican theory applied to the environmental domain, see, for example, Cannavò, "Vulnerability and Non-domination"; Cannavò, "EPT and Republicanism."

7. See, for example, Cole and Foster, *From the Ground Up*; Martínez-Alier, *Environmentalism of the Poor*; Guha, *Environmentalism*; Nixon, *Slow Violence*; Plumwood, *Feminism and the Mastery*

of Nature; Salleh, *Ecofeminism as Politics*; MacGregor, *Routledge Handbook of Gender and Environment*; Bookchin, *Ecology of Freedom*; Leiss, *Domination of Nature*; Biro, *Critical Ecologies*; and Luke, *Ecocritique*.

8. "Exploitation," *Oxford English Dictionary*, July 5, 2022, en.oxforddictionaries.com /definition/exploitation.

9. For accounts of the connection between domination, slavery, and despotism, see Pettit, *Republicanism*; Pettit, *On the People's Terms*; Skinner, *Liberty before Liberalism*; and Lovett, *General Theory of Domination and Justice*.

10. See, for example, Hayward, "What Can Political Freedom Mean in a Multicultural Democracy?"; and see Nancy Hirschmann's discussion of this matter in *The Subject of Liberty*, esp. 26–28.

11. Horkheimer and Adorno, *Dialectic of Enlightenment*, 42, 134.

12. For recent data, see Mikati et al., "Disparities in Distribution of Particulate Matter Emission Sources by Race and Poverty Status."

13. For discussion of these issues in the US context, see Cole and Foster, *From the Ground Up*; Schlosberg, *Defining Environmental Justice*. The study that helped catalyze the environmental justice movement in the United States was United Church of Christ Commission for Racial Justice, "Toxic Wastes and Race in the United States."

14. See, for example, Guha, *Environmentalism*; Martínez-Alier, *Environmentalism of the Poor*; Nixon, *Slow Violence*; and Vanderheiden, *Atmospheric Justice*.

15. This evocative term is Nixon's from *Slow Violence*.

16. For an interactive map identifying documented killings of environmental activists by country, see Global Witness, "On Dangerous Ground." For discussion of an earlier version of this report and the "acute rise" in "ecosides" in Latin America and the Asian Pacific, see Gómez-Barris, *Extractive Zone*, xix and 141n16.

17. See, for example, Gómez-Barris, *Extractive Zone*; Nixon, *Slow Violence*; Coles, *Visionary Pragmatism*; and Shutkin, *Land That Could Be*.

18. Horkheimer and Adorno, *Dialectic of Enlightenment*, xiv.

19. Marcuse, *One-Dimensional Man*, 166.

20. Horkheimer and Adorno, *Dialectic of Enlightenment*, xiv.

21. Horkheimer and Adorno, *Dialectic of Enlightenment*, xvi.

22. Horkheimer and Adorno, *Dialectic of Enlightenment*, 120, xv.

23. Horkheimer and Adorno, *Dialectic of Enlightenment*, xv, 133–34.

24. Marcuse, *One-Dimensional Man*, 167, 243.

25. While direct subjection to the will of another person constitutes the exemplary case of domination for Pettit, he acknowledges that domination can also involve a "structure or pattern" of social arrangements that systematically limits your choice "without imposing the will of another as to what you should do" in a direct way, although Pettit's acknowledgment is somewhat ambivalent (see Pettit, *On the People's Terms*, 165). There are good reasons to insist on its importance as an analytic category. See Hayward, "What Can Political Freedom Mean in a Multicultural Democracy?"; Hirschmann, *Subject of Liberty*, 28–29; and Gourevitch, *From Slavery to the Cooperative Commonwealth*, 106–9. The present analysis treats domination as a function of arbitrary power and exploitation, which may involve subjection to the personal wills of particular agents but can also be manifest in subjection to the power of impersonal human forces such a markets, multinational corporations, racially stratified social systems, and the like.

26. Marcuse, *One-Dimensional Man*, 144.

27. Marcuse, *One-Dimensional Man*, 32.

28. Marcuse, *One-Dimensional Man*, 33, 33, 169.

29. Stengers, *In Catastrophic Times*, 22–23.

30. Jamieson and Di Paola, "Political Theory for the Anthropocene," 256–59.

31. Brown, *Undoing the Demos*, 222.

32. Plumwood, *Feminism and the Mastery of Nature*, 12.

33. Plumwood, *Feminism and the Mastery of Nature*, 12; and see Di Chiro, "Welcome to the White (m)Anthropocene?"

34. Horkheimer and Adorno, *Dialectic of Enlightenment*, 134.

35. Horkheimer and Adorno, *Dialectic of Enlightenment*, 29, 30.

36. Bookchin, *Ecology of Freedom*, 324.

37. Bookchin, *Ecology of Freedom*, 324.

38. Bookchin, *Ecology of Freedom*, 33.

39. Luke, *Ecocritique*, 24.

40. Luke, *Ecocritique*, 128, 121.

41. Classic treatments of responsibility that emphasize control include Feinberg, *Doing and Deserving*; Hart, *Punishment and Responsibility*; and Nagel, "Moral Luck."

42. Jamieson and Di Paola, "Political Theory for the Anthropocene," 263.

43. As Naomi Klein puts it, "a lot of environmentalist discourse has been about erasing responsibility: 'We're all in this together. . . . We're all equally responsible.' Well, no—you, me and Exxon (Mobil) are not all in it together. The idea we're all guilty is demobilising because it prevents us directing our anger at the institutions most responsible" (Forrest "Interview with Naomi Klein"). See also McKibben, "What Exxon Knew about Climate Change."

44. See, for example, Young, *Responsibility for Justice*; Krause, *Freedom beyond Sovereignty*, 76–97; Krause, "Creating a Culture of Environmental Responsibility"; and Jamieson and Di Paola, "Political Theory for the Anthropocene," esp. 264–70. This differentiated conception of responsibility is also compatible with the mobilizations aimed at reconstructing flows of power in the environmental domain that are documented by Schlosberg and Coles, "New Environmentalism of Everyday Life."

45. Other influential contributions on the domination of nature include Merchant, *Death of Nature*; and Plumwood, *Feminism and the Mastery of Nature*, cited above. See also Forsyth, *Critical Political Ecology*; and Castree, "Commodifying What Nature?"

46. Leiss, *Domination of Nature*, xxv.

47. Leiss, *Domination of Nature*, xxv.

48. Leiss, *Domination of Nature*, 55.

49. Leiss, *Domination of Nature*, xvii.

50. Leiss, *Domination of Nature*, 138. For discussion of how the gendering of nature as feminine is tied to the domination of both nature and women, see (among others) Plumwood, *Feminism and the Mastery of Nature*; Salleh, *Ecofeminism as Politics*; and Thompson and MacGregor, "Death of Nature."

51. Leiss, *Domination of Nature*, 138, 85.

52. Görg, "Politics of Science," 49.

53. Görg, "Politics of Science," 49.

54. Marcuse, *One-Dimensional Man*, 33.

55. To note a resemblance in this regard is of course not to deny the very real differences among those positioned as subordinates or the diverse harms involved.

56. Leiss, *Domination of Nature*, 121–22.

57. Leiss, *Domination of Nature*, 122.

58. Leiss, *Domination of Nature*, 122.

59. Leiss, *Domination of Nature*, 123.

60. Horkheimer and Adorno, *Dialectic of Enlightenment*, xvi.

61. Marcuse, *One-Dimensional Man*, 33.

62. For another way that the republican tradition is being appropriated to think through concerns central to environmental political theory, see Cannavò, "Vulnerability and Non-domination." Cannavò's focus is on articulating "a civic republican politics of limits" that connects nondomination to an acknowledgment of both ecological and human limits (para. 1, paras. 28–37). See also Cannavò, "EPT and Republicanism."

63. Pettit, *Republicanism*, 52.

64. Pettit, *Republicanism*, 36–37, 55; Pettit, *On the People's Terms*, 58–59.

65. On this point I depart somewhat from Pettit, who allows for this possibility in principle but maintains that "domination is generally going to involve the awareness of control on the part of the powerful, the awareness of vulnerability on the part of the powerless, and the mutual awareness—indeed, the common awareness among all the parties to the relationship—of this consciousness on each side" (Pettit, *Republicanism*, 59–60).

66. Pettit, *On the People's Terms*, 62.

67. Pettit, *On the People's Terms*, 63.

68. Pettit, *On the People's Terms*, 7–8.

69. On this point, see Donna Haraway's discussion of "sympoiesis" in *Staying with the Trouble*, chap. 3; Karen Barad's idea of "intra-action" as "mutual constitution of entangled agencies" (*Meeting the Universe Halfway*, 33); and Cadena's concept of "co-emergence" (*Earth Beings*, 102–3). See also Jane Bennett's reflections on "the agency of assemblages" in *Vibrant Matter*, esp. chap. 2; and Latour, *We Have Never Been Modern*.

70. Species and ecosystems change over time, of course, and so the terms of existence for any organism are not static.

71. While one way the domination of nature affects nonhuman beings and things is by undermining in a broad sense the environmental systems that support them, another way it can affect some nonhuman beings is to directly prevent particular individuals from living in a way that allows for the fullness of their existence, as in the effects that factory farming has on individual animals. Many nonhuman beings have individual subjectivity in the sense that they are distinctive sites of suffering, pleasure, emotional attachment, consciousness, and so on. Consequently, while it is important to think about the domination of nature in the broad terms of damage to ecosystems, we must also be attentive to the direct damage that domination can do to individual, nonhuman subjects.

72. There is a shift in the meaning of arbitrary power from Pettit's *Republicanism* to his *On the People's Terms*. In the earlier work, power counts as arbitrary when it fails to track the interests of those subject to it (*Republicanism*, 36–37, 55); in the later work, power is arbitrary when it is not effectively controlled by its subjects (*On the People's Terms*, 58–59). Pettit allows for

different types of control, not all of them direct, but what matters for nondomination in *On the People's Terms* is that people control the power that is exercised over them, not merely that this power be responsive to their interests.

73. There is a parallel here to the distinction between moral subjects and moral agents drawn by the environmental ethicist Paul Taylor. See P. Taylor, *Respect for Nature*, 14–19.

74. Marcuse, *One-Dimensional Man*, 7.

Chapter 4: Political Respect for Nature

1. On this point, see Pettit, *On the People's Terms*, 63.

2. This chapter draws from Krause, "Political Respect for Nature."

3. Kant, *Grounding for the Metaphysics of Morals*, 428–30.

4. Kant, *Grounding for the Metaphysics of Morals*, 428–30.

5. Kant, "Toward Perpetual Peace."

6. For discussion of the nonsovereign quality of human agency, see Zerilli, *Feminism and the Abyss of Freedom*; Markell, *Bound by Recognition*, esp. chap. 3; Markell, "Insufficiency of Nondomination"; and Krause, *Freedom beyond Sovereignty*. The animal studies literature demonstrates agentic capacities in a variety of nonhuman animals. See, for example, McFarland and Hediger, *Animals and Agency*; Shapiro, "Moral Agency in Other Animals"; Carter and Charles, "Animals, Agency and Resistance"; and Donaldson and Kymlicka, *Zoopolis*.

7. In taking inspiration from this aspect of Kant's philosophy for environmentally sustainable politics, my account aligns with Eckersley's notion of ecological democracy, which also rests on what she calls a "post-Kantian . . . ideal of respect." Eckersley, *Green State*, 112.

8. Eckersley, *Environmentalism and Political Theory*, 61.

9. Vogel, *Thinking Like a Mall*, 102.

10. Vogel, *Thinking Like a Mall*, 102.

11. Eckersley, *Environmentalism and Political Theory*, 61. In this passage Eckersley draws from Fox, *Toward a Transpersonal Ecology*, 172.

12. Haraway, *Staying with the Trouble*, 33.

13. Abbott, "Scientists Bust Myth"; and Sender, Fuchs, and Milo, "Revised Estimates for the Number of Human and Bacteria Cells in the Body."

14. Bennett, *Vibrant Matter*, 12.

15. The same is true for people. A post-Kantian perspective on respect for persons will be more responsive than Kant himself was to the nonsovereign character of human agency and to our constitutive interdependence with others, including other individuals, species, and Earth systems.

16. P. Taylor, *Respect for Nature*, 44, 45.

17. P. Taylor, *Respect for Nature*, 45.

18. P. Taylor, *Respect for Nature*, 75.

19. P. Taylor, *Respect for Nature*, 18.

20. P. Taylor, *Respect for Nature*, 18.

21. P. Taylor, *Respect for Nature*, 18.

22. P. Taylor, *Respect for Nature*, 75.

23. I borrow this language from Vogel, *Thinking Like a Mall*, 25.

24. McKibben, *End of Nature*; Purdy, *After Nature*; and Vogel, *Thinking Like a Mall*.

25. Cronon, "Trouble with Wilderness," 85. See also Luke's critique of how land conservation strategies can, however unintentionally, create more of a "nature cemetery" than anything else (Luke, *Ecocritique*, xiv). See also Shutkin, *Land That Could Be*, whose "civic environmentalism" focuses on urban and suburban experiences (and uses) of nature, xiv, 128–41, 240.

26. Cronon, "Trouble with Wilderness," 81.

27. *Holy Bible*, Genesis 1:26. Biblical citations follow the King James Version.

28. See, for example, Berry, *Unsettling of America*; T. Williams, *Open Space of Democracy*; and Linzey, *Animal Theology*. See also "Pope Francis's Speech to the UN in Full."

29. Derrida, *Animal That Therefore I Am*, 30–31.

30. Derrida, *Animal That Therefore I Am*, 9.

31. Derrida, *Animal That Therefore I Am*, 12.

32. Derrida, *Animal That Therefore I Am*, 66.

33. Derrida, *Animal That Therefore I Am*, 13.

34. Derrida, *Animal That Therefore I Am*, 30–31.

35. Derrida, *Animal That Therefore I Am*, 25.

36. Derrida, *Animal That Therefore I Am*, 23; and see 32.

37. Derrida, *Animal That Therefore I Am*, 29.

38. Haraway, *When Species Meet*, 20. For a collection of essays that fruitfully seek to extend Derrida's insights to animal studies and environmentalism in ways that go beyond his own work, see Fritsch, Lynes, and Wood, *Eco-Deconstruction*.

39. Haraway, *When Species Meet*, 23.

40. Haraway, *When Species Meet*, 21.

41. Haraway, *When Species Meet*, 22, 23, 27.

42. Haraway, *When Species Meet*, 19, 23, 20, 22.

43. Haraway, *When Species Meet*, 21–22.

44. Haraway, *When Species Meet*, 42, 71.

45. Derrida, *Animal That Therefore I Am*, 106. For examples of Levinas-inspired thinking beyond the human, see the excellent essays in Edelglass, Hatley, and Diehm, *Facing Nature*.

46. Levinas, *Totality and Infinity*, 199–200.

47. Levinas, *Totality and Infinity*, 77, 251.

48. Levinas, *Totality and Infinity*, 39.

49. Levinas, *Totality and Infinity*, 40, 51, 87, 90.

50. Levinas, *Totality and Infinity*, 84.

51. Levinas, *Totality and Infinity*, 40.

52. Levinas, *Totality and Infinity*, 51, 199–200.

53. Levinas, *Totality and Infinity*, 51, 81, 84.

54. Levinas, *Totality and Infinity*, 84.

55. Levinas, *Totality and Infinity*, 86.

56. As William Edelglass puts it, "responsibility for the other . . . is not dependent on or derived from prior entanglements, shared commitments or characteristics, or a debt owed." Edelglass, "Rethinking Responsibility," 221.

57. Levinas, *Totality and Infinity*, 77.

58. Levinas, *Totality and Infinity*, 74; see also 194, 214, 215.

59. Levinas, *Totality and Infinity*, 75. As Mick Smith says, ethical responsibility in Levinas arises "without and before any definable point of origin; it has no *arche* (beginning) in the ontology of the world," and in this respect it "resembles Arendt's understanding of the 'miraculous'" and what she calls "natality." M. Smith, "Earthly Politics of Ethical An-arche," 144. See also Mooney and Mower, who characterize the call for response in Levinas as "primal" because "nothing lies beneath it—not objects, Gods, force fields, or language—not knowers, actors, beliefs, or doctrines" (Mooney and Mower, "Witness to the Face of a River," 281).

60. Levinas, *Totality and Infinity*, 199.

61. Levinas, *Totality and Infinity*, 200.

62. Levinas, *Totality and Infinity*, 202–3.

63. Levinas, *Totality and Infinity*, 303.

64. Indeed, this approach productively elides the instrumental/intrinsic binary altogether. On this point, see Toadvine, "Enjoyment and Its Discontents," 161; and Simmons, "Toward a Relational Model of Anthropocentrism," 231.

65. Arne Naess makes a similar point in noting the "multiple roots" of the principles of deep ecology, which "can follow from several . . . comprehensive world views." Naess, "Deep Ecology Movement."

66. Levinas, *Totality and Infinity*, 53.

67. Levinas, *Totality and Infinity*, 75.

68. Nussbaum, "Beyond 'Compassion and Humanity,'" 317. Along these lines, Michael Pollan remarks on "the anguished hand-wringing" in some animal rights literature over the fact of predation in nature. He suggests that the effort to hold animals to human standards of justice, including treating predation as a "moral degradation," reflects "an abiding discomfort not just with our animality but with animals' animality too." Pollan, *Omnivore's Dilemma*, 321.

69. Atterton, "Facing Animals," 27–28.

70. Levinas, *Totality and Infinity*, 202–3.

71. See the important discussion of how a human "recognition of vulnerability and limits may actually promote non-domination" in Cannavò, "Vulnerability and Non-domination," para. 38.

72. On this point, see Stefan Dolgert's discussion of how "knowing what we are doing" in relation to nonhuman animals "produces a longing not to know," while "the whole weight of civilization must be marshaled to deny our guilt" (Dolgert, "Sacrificing Justice," 264, 283).

73. Haraway, *When Species Meet*, 20.

74. See, for example, the nuanced account of differentiated forms of political inclusion for different kinds of animals in Donaldson and Kymlicka, *Zoopolis*; and K. Smith, *Governing Animals*. For discussion of differentiated forms of political incorporation for other parts of the environment including plants, waterways, and ecosystems, see Stone, *Should Trees Have Standing?*, esp. chap. 1; Eckersley, *Green State*, 136–37, 214; Dobson, "Representative Democracy and the Environment"; Schlosberg, *Defining Environmental Justice*, 193–99; and Disch, "Ecological Democracy." See also the discussion of recent court cases in New Zealand, Australia, and India granting rights to rivers in O'Donnell and Talbot-Jones, "Creating Legal Rights for Rivers"; and Bruce Jennings's notion of "eco-constitutionalism," in Jennings, *Ecological Governance*, 179, 185–87. These and other forms of political inclusion for nonhuman nature are discussed in chapter 6.

75. Stone, *Should Trees Have Standing?*, 4.

76. Stone, *Should Trees Have Standing?*, 4.

77. Stone, *Should Trees Have Standing?*, 3.

78. Stone, *Should Trees Have Standing?*, 2–3.

79. Stone, *Should Trees Have Standing?*, 3–4. Introducing the language of rights into relations between human beings and more-than-human parts of nature has the potential to generate some negative consequences. Glen Coulthard notes, for example, that as Indigenous peoples have begun to adopt the language of property rights to reclaim stolen land or protect against further encroachments, there has been a concomitant change in how some people think about their relationship to the land, transforming what had been seen as familial relations into more instrumentalized ones. See Coulthard, *Red Skin, White Masks*, 78, 60–61. Still, the invocation of a human right to possess parts of nature as property is quite different from the invocation of rights envisioned here. Far from treating nature as a human possession, the invocation of rights in this context treats nature as a kind of an end in itself and gives it standing that is independent of its use value to human beings. Another reasonable concern is that rights talk tends to individualize its subjects, which may be detrimental to the more holistic understanding of ecosystemic interdependence that eco-emancipation requires. Yet rights for nonhuman beings and things need not be understood to individualize them in such ways; rights can be understood as tools for exercising (and enforcing) respect for nonhuman beings and things as the embedded, interdependent parts of Earth systems that they are. We shall return to the issue of rights for nature in chapter 6.

80. Stone, *Should Trees Have Standing?*, 2, 3.

81. John Dryzek has argued along these lines for political institutions that manifest "ecosystemic reflexivity" in the sense that they enhance ecological learning and responsiveness to the claims of (and new information about) "the non-human world." Dryzek, "Institutions for the Anthropocene," 938, 940. See also Schlosberg's discussion of "institutionalizing reflexive engagement and ecological reflexivity" in *Defining Environmental Justice*, 188–90.

82. Robbins, "America's Gray Ghosts."

83. Leopold, *Sand County Almanac*, 253, 191.

84. Leopold, *Sand County Almanac*, 254.

85. Research has demonstrated that human population growth can be staunched through noncoercive means such as enhanced freedom, economic opportunity, education, and health care for women. See, for example, A. Sen, *Development as Freedom*; G. Sen, Germain, and Chen, *Population Policies Reconsidered*; Lindahl-Kiessling and Landberg, *Population, Economic Development, and the Environment*; and Cassen, *Population and Development*. It is crucial that any efforts to constrain human population growth proceed in ways that respect the freedom and equality of all persons and are mindful of the potential for abuse, but active efforts will be required. They are an important part of cultivating political respect for nature.

86. This is not to deny that respect for nature will regularly require bold vision, creativity, and courageous action. The point is that a measure of humility is always in order too, along with sensitivity to our unintended effects and a readiness to rectify them.

87. Stow, *American Mourning*, 3. Stow borrows the language of "going on together" from Josiah Ober, *Athenian Legacies: Essays in the Politics of Going On Together*.

88. See, for example, Stow, *American Mourning*; Honig, *Antigone, Interrupted*, 26–29, 33–34, 43–44, 56–66, 96–97, 191–95; Butler, *Precarious Life*; and Butler, *Frames of War*.

It is true that rituals of public mourning are not always constructed in ways that make them salutary for democracy. Because expressions of grief are so emotionally powerful, they can sometimes shut down productive political discourse. As Stow points out, in the aftermath of the September 11 attacks in the United States, the country's collective grief made it difficult to have a critically engaged public discussion about the meaning and causes of the attacks against the background of American aggression abroad. In this sense, public mourning can inhibit both the critical reflection and the contestation that are central to a healthy democracy. Moreover, public mourning often is captured by nationalistic sensibilities that romanticize the polity and its losses in ways that are intended simply to reinforce cohesiveness. See Stow, *American Mourning*, 9–12.

89. Howard, "AIDS Memorial Quilt Still Traveling."

90. See Butler, *Frames of War*.

91. See, for example, Nixon, *Slow Violence*; Gómez-Barris, *Extractive Zone*; Martínez-Alier, *Environmentalism of the Poor*; Guha, *Environmentalism*.

Chapter 5: Eco-Responsibility

1. Brown, *Undoing the Demos*, 84, 131–34.

2. I borrow here from Loralea Michaelis and Genevieve Fuji Johnson, who define "to be responsible" as, "quite literally, *to be able to respond* in morally and politically appropriate ways." Michaelis and Johnson, "Political Responsibility Refocused," 5.

3. Ackerly, *Just Responsibility*, 2–3, 60–65.

4. On epistemologies of ignorance, see Mills, "White Ignorance." For discussion of the value of disruptive politics to dispel epistemologies of ignorance, see Hayward, "Responsibility and Ignorance," 396, 404–6, discussed below.

5. Ackerly, *Just Responsibility*, 13.

6. Parts of this chapter draw from Krause, "Creating a Culture of Environmental Responsibility."

7. Feinberg, *Doing and Deserving*; Nagel, "Moral Luck"; Hart, *Punishment and Responsibility*; Raz, *From Normativity to Responsibility*; and Schlosberg, *Defining Environmental Justice*. For further elaboration of the limits of the liability model in connection with responsibility for racial and gender-based inequities, see Krause, *Freedom beyond Sovereignty*, chap. 3.

8. Sommers, "Two Faces of Revenge," 48. Even sophisticated accounts of responsibility tend to share this emphasis. For example, Steve Vanderheiden's account of responsibility for environmental injustice is highly nuanced and attentive to the complexity of environmental problems but still retains a fundamental commitment to the control condition and the idea that we can be responsible only for things we choose to bring about (Vanderheiden, *Atmospheric Justice*, 208, 219–20, 227, 230).

9. Jamieson and Di Paola, "Political Theory for the Anthropocene," 262.

10. Jamieson and Di Paola, "Political Theory for the Anthropocene," 268–69.

11. Plato, *Republic*, 359d.

12. Jamieson and Di Paola, "Political Theory for the Anthropocene," 263.

13. Jamieson and Di Paola, "Political Theory for the Anthropocene," 263.

14. Jamieson and Di Paola, "Political Theory for the Anthropocene," 262–63.

15. Lavin, *Politics of Responsibility*, vii.

16. Lavin, *Politics of Responsibility*, vii.

17. Lavin, *Politics of Responsibility*, ix.

18. Lavin, *Politics of Responsibility*, vii. Examples of the more recent work include Young, *Responsibility for Justice*; Vázquez-Arroyo, *Political Responsibility*; Matravers, *Responsibility and Justice*; Zheng, "What Is My Role in Changing the System?"; Schiff, *Burdens of Political Responsibility*; Johnson and Michaelis, *Political Responsibility Refocused*; Hayward, "Responsibility and Ignorance"; and Ackerly, *Just Responsibility*.

19. Young, *Responsibility for Justice*, 96.

20. Young, *Responsibility for Justice*, 105.

21. Young, *Responsibility for Justice*, 144–45.

22. Young, *Responsibility for Justice*, 96–97, 109. As Martha Nussbaum points out (and as Young acknowledged), we do sometimes have reason to blame people for their contributions to global injustice. Nussbaum, "Foreword," xxi; and see Hayward's discussion of this critique in "Responsibility and Ignorance," 400.

23. Young, *Responsibility for Justice*, 109–10, emphasis in the original.

24. Young, *Responsibility for Justice*, 111.

25. See Young, "Responsibility and Global Labor Justice," 377.

26. Along these lines, see Connolly's warning against attributions of a "generic human responsibility" for environmental harms (Connolly, *Facing the Planetary*, 33).

27. The distinction between liability and culpability, along with the threefold schema for a plural theory of responsibility elaborated below (culpability/accountability/responsiveness), draws from my earlier work on responsibility for racial and gender-based injustice (Krause, *Freedom beyond Sovereignty*, chap. 3). Here I develop this framework for the specific challenges of theorizing responsibility in the environmental domain and working for eco-emancipation.

28. Legal Information Institute, "Strict Liability."

29. Accountability thus directs the individual to participate in "movements as a form of resistance to what Foucault called circulatory power" and also to participate in what Schlosberg and Coles refer to as "alternative circulations of power and material nature in new collectivities," hence to "reconstruction in addition to resistance." See Schlosberg and Coles, "New Environmentalism of Everyday Life," 13. This could include (among other things) food movements geared to constructing "food systems which are good for farmers, the health of consumers, and the environment," and energy movements that aim to change "the way that energy is produced and distributed" (14–15, 15).

30. See Singer, *Life You Can Save*, 3, 4, 12, 14, 16, 46, 60, 144–46.

31. Ackerly, *Just Responsibility*, 102, 105.

32. For discussion of responsibility as a pluralistic phenomenon in a different context, see M. Williams, "Political Responsibility for Decolonization in Canada," 78–79.

33. Along these lines, Zheng has argued for a role-centered model of responsibility for structural injustice in which one's responsibilities are tied to—and bounded by—specific roles that one inhabits, such as parent, worker, consumer, citizen, and so on. Each role is defined in terms of "some intuitive, salient, and relatively circumscribed range of associated actions" (Zheng, "What Is My Role in Changing the System?," 879). Being responsible for structural injustice is demanding but "manageable, because that responsibility is discharged through work that one is already always performing" in one's established roles (881). For example, parents choosing a

school for their children can exercise responsibility for structural injustice by considering not only the quality of instruction but the degree of diversity offered by different schools (881). There is value in this approach, but as Ackerly notes, we need to be cognizant of how existing social roles may reproduce norms that are unjust. Consequently, part of taking responsibility for justice is "to create new modes of political community," including new social roles, "rather than relying on existing structures of political economy—consumerism, charity, work, and citizenship—to condition our responses." Ackerly, *Just Responsibility*, 220.

34. Aristotle, *Nicomachean Ethics*, book 3, sections 9–13.

35. Aristotle, *Nicomachean Ethics*, book 2, section 5.

36. For discussion of institutional mechanisms for incorporating scientific knowledge into public deliberation about environmental matters, see Dryzek, "Institutions for the Anthropocene." See also Callon et al. on "hybrid forums" for decision making in contexts of uncertainty (Callon, Lascoumes, and Barthe, *Acting in an Uncertain World*, 21, 26, 181–89).

37. For documentation of the vastly reduced rates of smoking among American adults since 1965, see "Health, United States, 2019: Table 17."

38. The "ecovillages" that Litfin has studied in various parts of the world offer an example of this aspect of accountability. Litfin, "Ontologies of Sustainability in Ecovillage Culture." Ecovillagers, Litfin shows, "are unusually sensitive to the consequences of their actions, both near and far" (251). These communities "vary according to cultural and ecological context," ranging from wealthy suburban towns in the Global North to traditional rural villages in the Global South. Despite the diversity, however, they share a commitment to living "a low-impact way of life," which they pursue through various combinations of "ecological design, permaculture, renewable energy, community-building practices, and alternative economics" (249–50). Ecovillages offer concrete examples of how environmental responsibility could be reframed from a discourse that emphasizes liability and blame to one that focuses on accountability and responsiveness, including a shared approach to creating the conditions for a more sustainable way of life.

39. For an account of one Louisiana man's experience along these lines, see Hochschild, *Strangers in Their Own Land*, 28–30.

40. White et al. point out (citing William Freudenburg and collaborators) that in the United States in 1993 just "two companies—DuPont and Freeport McMoran—put out 400 million tons of toxic waste. Together these two companies generated 30% of total chemical toxic waste for the U.S." (White, Rudy, and Gareau, *Environments, Natures and Social Theory*, 107–8).

41. Forrest, "Interview with Naomi Klein." Timothy Luke similarly warns against focusing environmental responsibility on the individualized "sphere of consumption rather than on the vital sites of production." With this focus, he says, "a core supply-side changelessness is preserved by enveloping it in a demand-side mobilization for marginal change" (Luke, *Ecocritique*, 120, 132).

42. In his influential work on German guilt in the aftermath of World War II, Karl Jaspers makes the point that accepting responsibility "is the beginning of an inner upheaval which seeks to realize political liberty," and that "political liberty begins with the majority of individuals in a people feeling jointly liable for the politics of their community" (Jaspers, *Question of German Guilt*, 71, 115). We have seen that there is reason to move beyond the limited notion of liability, but the basic insight that taking responsibility is connected to the practice of freedom is important and highly relevant for the case of environmental domination and the aspiration to eco-emancipation.

43. Schiff, "Power and Responsibility," 44, 52, 58.

44. Schiff, "Power and Responsibility," 52, 54.

45. Schiff, "Power and Responsibility," 54.

46. Schiff, "Power and Responsibility," 54.

47. Mapes-Martins, "Household Maintenance and the Environmental Politics of Tending," 100–101.

48. Stengers, *In Catastrophic Times*, 31, 153. See also Schiff on the use of narrative—or storytelling—as a resource for social transformation in *Burdens of Political Responsibility*, 20–21.

49. Ackerly, *Just Responsibility*, 3, 49.

50. Ackerly, *Just Responsibility*, 223.

51. See Ackerly's sobering discussion of the violence suffered by some of the activists she studied. Ackerly, *Just Responsibility*, 62–64.

52. Ackerly, *Just Responsibility*, 18.

53. Ackerly, *Just Responsibility*, 247.

54. Ackerly, *Just Responsibility*, 193.

55. Ackerly, *Just Responsibility*, 217.

56. For example, Ackerly points out that workers sometimes suffer from boycotts that are intended to support them because boycotts can "harm workers by ending production" rather than making effective changes in the conditions of production. Ackerly, *Just Responsibility*, 227–30, 24–25, 59–60. Instead of jumping into boycotts, she recommends that privileged people wishing to take responsibility for injustice in the global supply chains that produce their consumer goods should be "maximally informed by what those in struggle are actually doing" and guided by "the connected activism of self-advocates and their allies," because "only if the workers who are impacted are calling for such action can they be considered instances of taking political responsibility" (25).

57. Mills, "White Ignorance"; and see Hayward, "Responsibility and Ignorance," 396, 404.

58. Hayward, "Responsibility and Ignorance," 396.

59. Hayward, "Responsibility and Ignorance," 405.

60. Hayward, "Responsibility and Ignorance," 406.

61. Hayward, "Responsibility and Ignorance," 406, emphasis added.

62. Hayward, "Responsibility and Ignorance," 406.

63. Hayward, "Responsibility and Ignorance," 406.

64. This analogy is not meant to equate the suffering of Black persons under white supremacy to environmental degradation but rather to notice a structural similarity in some of the conditions that sustain domination in the two cases.

65. Hayward, "Responsibility and Ignorance," 406.

66. Hayward, "Responsibility and Ignorance," 406.

67. Hayward, "Responsibility and Ignorance," 407.

68. Aristotle, *Nicomachean Ethics*, book 2, section 1.

69. Aristotle, *Nicomachean Ethics*, book 2, section 1.

70. Some of this populism, of course, is driven by darker sensibilities, such as resentment on the part of people long privileged by their race and gender who feel threatened by the increasing influence of women and members of minority groups.

Chapter 6: Ecological Emancipation

1. The word *emancipation* derives from the Latin roots *ex* (out of, from), *manus* (hand), and *capere* (to take). See "Emancipate," *Dictionary by Merriam-Webster*; and "Emancipate," *Online Etymology Dictionary*.

2. Demuth, *Floating Coast*.

3. Anker, *Ugly Freedoms*, 154. Anker points out that this form of freedom is consumptive not only in a consumerist sense but also in the sense that "the consumer will eventually be consumed by their practice of consumption. Like the disease of consumption, consumptive sovereignty eats away at its host" (158).

4. N. Roberts, *Freedom as Marronage*, 3–11.

5. N. Roberts, *Freedom as Marronage*, 4, 5.

6. N. Roberts, *Freedom as Marronage*, 116–17, 127–28.

7. N. Roberts, *Freedom as Marronage*, 56.

8. N. Roberts, *Freedom as Marronage*, 56, 23–24.

9. N. Roberts, *Freedom as Marronage*, 9.

10. "To be one," Haraway says, "is to become with many" (Haraway, *When Species Meet*, 4). See also Sarah Whatmore on the theme of cocreation among subjects in Whatmore, *Hybrid Geographies*, 161.

11. On this point see the valuable discussion of the "co-emergence" of subjects in Cadena, *Earth Beings*, 102–4; and see the related discussion in Barad of the "intra-activity of becoming" (Barad, *Meeting the Universe Halfway*, 178, 214, 235, 353).

12. N. Roberts, *Freedom as Marronage*, 4.

13. On the Green Belt movement see Nixon, *Slow Violence*, esp. chap. 4. On the Dudley Street Initiative, see Shutkin, *Land That Could Be*, chap. 4.

14. For a rich account of artist-activists working to mobilize people on environmental issues in Latin America, see the many examples throughout Gómez-Barris, *Extractive Zone*.

15. Marcuse, *One-Dimensional Man*, 7.

16. "Fracking in Montana."

17. Hardt and Negri, *Assembly*, 108. William Leiss makes a similar point in "Modern Science, Enlightenment, and the Domination of Nature," 24–25.

18. Hardt and Negri, *Assembly*, 259, 258.

19. Hardt and Negri, *Assembly*, 259.

20. Hardt and Negri, *Assembly*, 259.

21. Strikingly, however, Hardt and Negri's examples of indignation-based mobilizations focus almost exclusively on marginalized groups, including mobilizations by the Black Lives Matter movement, by poor women and girls protesting sexual violence, by Indigenous people protesting ecological violence, and by working-class movements protesting the exploitation of labor (Hardt and Negri, *Assembly*, 260–61). Crucial as these mobilizations are, Hardt and Negri miss an opportunity to illustrate how indignation might fuel mobilizations by the more privileged masses in prosperous societies, too.

22. Gómez-Barris, *Extractive Zone*, 91.

23. See the extended discussion of the film in Gómez-Barris, *Extractive Zone*, chap. 4.

24. Gómez-Barris, *Extractive Zone*, xiv, xv, 1, 80, 83, 102.

25. Quoted in Twenty-Third Biennale of Sydney. See also Elizabeth Fortescue, "If a Polluted River Could Speak." I am grateful to Macarena Gómez-Barris for calling my attention to the Biennale of Sydney.

26. Gómez-Barris, *Extractive Zone*, 91.

27. Luke, *Ecocritique*, 148. Luke is drawing on Marcuse in this passage.

28. Hardt and Negri, *Assembly*, 76. Along similar lines, note Bookchin's evocative assertion at the close of *The Ecology of Freedom* that "the ruins" generated by environmental domination "are mines for recycling the wastes of an immensely perishable world into the structural materials of one that is free as well as new" (Bookchin, *Ecology of Freedom*, 447).

29. Hardt and Negri, *Assembly*, 286.

30. Hardt and Negri, *Assembly*, 286–87.

31. Hardt and Negri, *Assembly*, 295, 294.

32. Hardt and Negri, *Assembly*, xvii.

33. Hardt and Negri, *Assembly*, 222.

34. Hardt and Negri, *Assembly*, xxi.

35. Coles, *Visionary Pragmatism*, 85.

36. Coles, *Visionary Pragmatism*, 85. Coles is quoting Gustavo Esteva and Madhu Prakash, *Grassroots Postmodernism*, 31. On a related note, Gunster points out that it is because we "forget that we are the collective producers of the world that surrounds us" that "the relation of most individuals to this world remains one of dependence and helplessness" (Gunster, "Fear and the Unknown," 213, 212).

37. Coles, *Visionary Pragmatism*, 119.

38. Coles, *Visionary Pragmatism*, 119, 147.

39. Coles, *Visionary Pragmatism*, 22, 23.

40. Coles, *Visionary Pragmatism*, 86–88.

41. Cladis, "Radical Romanticism and Its Alternative Account of the Wild and Wilderness."

42. Cladis, "Radical Romanticism and Its Alternative Account of the Wild and Wilderness," 848. In this sense, the wilderness within might profitably be seen as a feature of those whom Bruno Latour refers to as "esperados," meaning people who "resist anguish" in the face of environmental devastation and disempowerment. Latour, *Facing Gaia*, 13.

43. Cladis, "Radical Romanticism and Its Alternative Account of the Wild and Wilderness," 849.

44. Cladis, "Radical Romanticism and Its Alternative Account of the Wild and Wilderness," 838.

45. Cladis, "Radical Romanticism and Its Alternative Account of the Wild and Wilderness," 838, 844.

46. Cladis, "Radical Romanticism and Its Alternative Account of the Wild and Wilderness," 849.

47. Cladis, "Radical Romanticism and Its Alternative Account of the Wild and Wilderness," 838.

48. Cladis, "Radical Romanticism and Its Alternative Account of the Wild and Wilderness," 838, emphasis in the original.

49. Biro, "Ecological Crisis," 235. Cladis, of course, does not argue for such a return.

50. For further discussion of alternative modernities, see Martínez-Alier, *Environmentalism of the Poor*, 145.

51. Hardt and Negri, *Assembly*, xx, 224.

52. Hardt and Negri, *Assembly*, 257; and see 256.

53. Hardt and Negri, *Assembly*, 39.

54. Coles, *Visionary Pragmatism*, 24, 97.

55. Coles, *Visionary Pragmatism*, 98, 99.

56. Coles, *Visionary Pragmatism*, 99.

57. Coles, *Visionary Pragmatism*, 98–99.

58. Coles, *Visionary Pragmatism*, 100.

59. Coles, *Visionary Pragmatism*, 24.

60. Gibson-Graham, *Postcapitalist Politics*, xxii, 53. The discussion of Gibson-Graham here draws from Krause, "Creating a Culture of Environmental Responsibility."

61. Gibson-Graham, *Postcapitalist Politics*, 62.

62. Gibson-Graham, *Postcapitalist Politics*, 60.

63. Gibson-Graham, *Postcapitalist Politics*, 72, 74.

64. The food movements, transition towns, and decentralized energy grids described by Schlosberg and Coles offer additional examples of alternative economic relationships. Schlosberg and Coles, "New Environmentalism of Everyday Life," 16.

65. Coles, *Visionary Pragmatism*, 110.

66. Luke, *Ecocritique*, 204.

67. Luke, *Ecocritique*, 204.

68. Some of these changes might involve subsidies, but revising regulatory schemes that disadvantage small producers relative to large ones also could be valuable. On the difficulties of small-scale production in the agricultural sector, see Salatin, *Everything I Want to Do Is Illegal*, 3, 24.

69. For discussion of the importance, from an environmental perspective, of a properly scaled state, see Eckersley, *Green State*, 7; and Eckersley, "Ecological Democracy and the Rise and Decline of Liberal Democracy."

70. Luke, *Ecocritique*, 207; Bookchin, *Ecology of Freedom*, 57, 434–35, 442–47.

71. Luke, *Ecocritique*, 206; Bookchin, *Ecology of Freedom*, 213, 373.

72. This discussion draws from Krause, "Environmental Domination."

73. Eckersley, *Green State*, 137.

74. For recent treatments of rights for nonhuman animals, see Donaldson and Kymlicka, *Zoopolis*; and K. Smith, *Governing Animals*. On rights for nonanimal parts of the environment, see Eckersley, *Green State*, 136–37, 214. See also the discussion of recent court cases in New Zealand, Australia, and India granting rights to rivers in O'Donnell and Talbot-Jones, "Creating Legal Rights for Rivers."

75. Donaldson and Kymlicka, *Zoopolis*.

76. Stone, *Should Trees Have Standing?*, esp. chap. 1.

77. Donaldson and Kymlicka, *Zoopolis*, 154.

78. Eckersley, *Green State*, 134.

79. Jennings, *Ecological Governance*, 185.

80. Animal Legal and Historical Center, "German Animal Welfare Act."

81. "Constitution of the Republic of Ecuador"; and World Future Fund, "Law of the Rights of Mother Earth."

82. Eckersley, *Green State*, 114, 134.

83. Dobson, "Representative Democracy and the Environment." See also Schlosberg's illuminating discussion of political "inclusion and proxies" in *Defining Environmental Justice*,

193–99. On the participation of the nonhuman in democratic practice, see also Disch, "Ecological Democracy."

84. Donaldson and Kymlicka, *Zoopolis*, 154.

85. Vogel, *Thinking Like a Mall*, 190–94.

86. Schlosberg, *Defining Environmental Justice*, 195–96.

87. See Dryzek, "Institutions for the Anthropocene," 938, 940. See also Schlosberg's discussion of "institutionalizing reflexive engagement and ecological reflexivity" in *Defining Environmental Justice*, 188–90.

88. See, for example, Wendy Brown's classic critique of rights in *States of Injury*, esp. chap. 5, "Rights and Losses."

89. Gómez-Barris, *Extractive Zone*, 27–34.

90. Gómez-Barris, *Extractive Zone*, 28, 29.

91. Cadena, *Earth Beings*, 284.

92. See Stone, *Should Trees Have Standing?*, 2–4.

93. Gómez-Barris, *Extractive Zone*, 30, 31, 33–34.

94. Donaldson and Kymlicka, *Zoopolis*, 155. Donaldson and Kymlicka's work covers only relations between people and nonhuman animals, not broader environments, but the sensibility can be extended to cover a more inclusive collection of nonhuman others.

95. On the environmental importance of transparency and right-to-know laws, see Purdy, *After Nature*, 241–42, 244.

96. Transparency in regulatory agencies is as important as transparency in industries. A 2004 study found that "for ten of the most common hydrocarbons, the EPA's reports underestimated actual emissions by 25 percent to 440 percent." See Press and Mazmanian, "Toward Sustainable Production," 248.

97. Pollan, *Omnivore's Dilemma*, 200–201, 243. See also Stone, *Should Trees Have Standing?*, 25–26; and Shiva, *Earth Democracy*, 146.

98. Allon, "Household as Infrastructure," 52–54.

99. For examples, see Martínez-Alier, *Environmentalism of the Poor*; Guha, *Environmentalism*; Nixon, *Slow Violence*; Gómez-Barris, *Extractive Zone*; Cole and Foster, *From the Ground Up*; Coles, *Visionary Pragmatism*; Shutkin, *Land That Could Be*; and Whyte, Caldwell, and Schaefer, "Indigenous Lessons about Sustainability."

100. Schlosberg and Coles, "New Environmentalism of Everyday Life," 22, 23.

101. Connolly, *Facing the Planetary*, 56, 64, 74, 173.

102. Tsing, *Mushroom at the End of the World*, 152.

103. Abram, *Becoming Animal*, 9.

104. The language of ontological composition is Cadena's (Cadena, *Earth Beings*, 278, 281).

Epilogue

1. "Sustainable Development Institute."

2. Lazarus, "Rights for Lake Erie?"

3. Lazarus, "Rights for Lake Erie?"

4. Lazarus, "Rights for Lake Erie?"

5. Lazarus, "Rights for Lake Erie?"

6. Southside Community Land Trust, "Mission and Impact."

7. Nixon, *Slow Violence*, 129.

8. Nixon, *Slow Violence*, 129.

9. Nixon, *Slow Violence*, 132.

10. Nixon, *Slow Violence*, 133.

11. Nixon, *Slow Violence*, 137.

12. Nixon, *Slow Violence*, 138.

13. Green Belt Movement, "Who We Are."

14. "Ashton Hayes Going Carbon Neutral."

15. Schlossberg, "English Village Becomes Climate Leader."

16. Schlossberg, "English Village Becomes Climate Leader."

17. Schlossberg, "English Village Becomes Climate Leader."

18. "Ashton Hayes Going Carbon Neutral."

19. Schlossberg, "English Village Becomes Climate Leader."

20. Wildlife Conservation Society, "Pronghorn Migration on the Path of the Pronghorn."

21. National Fish and Wildlife Foundation, "Path of the Pronghorn," accessed March 14, 2021, https://www.nfwf.org/programs/path-pronghorn.

22. Randall, "'They Won't Survive.'"

23. Latour, *Facing Gaia*, 256.

24. Bronstein and Les films de l'air, CLIMATE, *Make It Work!*

25. Latour, *Facing Gaia*, 255, 262, 267.

26. Latour, *Facing Gaia*, 266.

27. Latour, *Facing Gaia*, 271, 283.

28. Latour, *Facing Gaia*, 267.

29. Latour, *Facing Gaia*, 255, 286.

30. Latour, *Facing Gaia*, 258.

31. Latour, *Facing Gaia*, 257.

32. Latour, *Facing Gaia*, 257.

33. Latour, *Facing Gaia*, 261.

34. Latour, *Facing Gaia*, 257.

BIBLIOGRAPHY

Abbott, Alison. "Scientists Bust Myth That Our Bodies Have More Bacteria Than Human Cells." *Nature*, January 8, 2016. http://www.nature.com/articles/nature.2016.19136.

Abram, David. *Becoming Animal: An Earthly Cosmology*. New York: Vintage Books, 2011.

Ackerly, Brooke A. *Just Responsibility: A Human Rights Theory of Global Justice*. Oxford: Oxford University Press, 2018.

Agamben, Giorgio. *The Open: Man and Animal*. Stanford, CA: Stanford University Press, 2004.

Alaimo, Stacy. *Bodily Natures: Science, Environment, and the Material Self*. Bloomington: Indiana University Press, 2010.

Allon, Fiona. "The Household as Infrastructure: The Politics and Porosity of Dwelling in a Time of Environmental Emergency." In *The Greening of Everyday Life*, edited by John M. Meyer and Jens Kersten, 47–64. Oxford: Oxford University Press, 2016.

Animal Legal and Historical Center. "German Animal Welfare Act." Accessed March 11, 2021. https://www.animallaw.info/statute/germany-cruelty-german-animal-welfare-act.

Anker, Elizabeth R. *Ugly Freedoms*. Durham, NC: Duke University Press, 2022.

Arendt, Hannah. *The Human Condition*. Chicago: University of Chicago Press, 1998.

———. "What Is Freedom?" In *Between Past and Future: Eight Exercises in Political Thought*, 143–71. New York: Penguin, 1993.

Arganda, Sara, Alfonso Perez-Escudero, and Gonzalo G. de Polavieja. "A Common Rule for Decision Making in Animal Collectives across Species." *Proceedings of the National Academy of Sciences* 109, no. 50 (December 11, 2012): 20508–13.

Aristotle. *Nicomachean Ethics*. Translated by Hippocrates G. Apostle. Grinnell, IA: Peripatetic, 1984.

———. *The Politics*. Translated by Carnes Lord. Chicago: University of Chicago Press, 1984.

Arneil, Barbara. "Disability, Self-Image, and Modern Political Theory." *Political Theory* 37, no. 2 (April 2009): 218–42.

Arnott, Gareth, and Robert W. Elwood. "Information Gathering and Decision Making about Resource Value in Animal Contests." *Animal Behaviour* 76, no. 3 (September 1, 2008): 529–42.

Arruda, Caroline T., and Daniel J. Povinelli. "Chimps as Secret Agents." *Synthese* 193, no. 7 (July 2016): 2129–58.

"Ashton Hayes Going Carbon Neutral." The Ashton Hayes Going Carbon Neutral Project. Accessed March 11, 2021. https://www.goingcarbonneutral.co.uk/.

Atterton, Peter. "Facing Animals." In *Facing Nature: Levinas and Environmental Thought*, edited by William Edelglass, James Hatley, and Christian Diehm, 25–40. Pittsburgh, PA: Duquesne University Press, 2012.

Baldwin, James. "Notes of a Native Son." In *Collected Essays*, 5–129. Edited by Toni Morrison. New York: Library of America, 1998.

Barad, Karen Michelle. *Meeting the Universe Halfway: Quantum Physics and the Entanglement of Matter and Meaning*. Durham, NC: Duke University Press, 2007.

Bekoff, Marc, and Jessica Pierce. *Wild Justice: The Moral Lives of Animals*. Chicago: University of Chicago Press, 2010.

Bennett, Jane. "The Agency of Assemblages and the North American Blackout." *Public Culture* 17, no. 3 (Fall 2005): 445–66.

———. *Vibrant Matter: A Political Ecology of Things*. Durham, NC: Duke University Press, 2010.

Berry, Wendell. *The Unsettling of America: Culture and Agriculture*. San Francisco: Sierra Club Books, 1977.

Biro, Andrew, ed. *Critical Ecologies: The Frankfurt School and Contemporary Environmental Crises*. Toronto: University of Toronto Press, 2011.

———. *Denaturalizing Ecological Politics: Alienation from Nature from Rousseau to the Frankfurt School and Beyond*. Toronto: University of Toronto Press, 2005.

———. "Ecological Crisis and the Culture Industry Thesis." In *Critical Ecologies: The Frankfurt School and Contemporary Environmental Crises*, edited by Andrew Biro, 229–54. Toronto: University of Toronto Press, 2011.

Bookchin, Murray. *The Ecology of Freedom: The Emergence and Dissolution of Hierarchy*. Oakland, CA: AK, 2005.

Braidotti, Rosi. *The Posthuman*. Cambridge, UK: Polity, 2013.

Bronstein, David, and Les films de l'air. CLIMATE, *Make It Work!* Theater of Negotiations. 2015. Accessed March 14, 2021. http://www.lesfilmsdelair.com/en/film/climat.

Broome, John. *Climate Matters: Ethics in a Warming World*. New York: W. W. Norton, 2012.

Brown, Wendy. *States of Injury: Power and Freedom in Late Modernity*. Princeton, NJ: Princeton University Press, 1995.

———. *Undoing the Demos: Neoliberalism's Stealth Revolution*. Brooklyn: Zone Books, 2015.

Butler, Judith. *Frames of War: When Is Life Grievable?* London: Verso, 2016.

———. *Precarious Life: The Powers of Mourning and Violence*. London: Verso, 2006.

Cadena, Marisol de la. *Earth Beings: Ecologies of Practice across Andean Worlds*. 2011. Durham, NC: Duke University Press, 2015.

Callon, Michel, Pierre Lascoumes, and Yannick Barthe. *Acting in an Uncertain World: An Essay on Technical Democracy*. Translated by Graham Burchell. Cambridge, MA: MIT Press, 2011.

Cannavò, Peter F. "EPT and Republicanism." In *The Oxford Handbook of Environmental Political Theory*, edited by Teena Gabrielson, Cheryl Hall, John M. Meyer, and David Schlosberg, 72–88. Oxford: Oxford University Press.

———. "Vulnerability and Non-domination: A Republican Perspective on Natural Limits." *Critical Review of International Social and Political Philosophy*, December 2019. https://doi.org/10.1080/13698230.2019.1698155.

———. *The Working Landscape: Founding, Preservation, and the Politics of Place*. Cambridge, MA: MIT Press, 2007.

Carter, Bob, and Nickie Charles. "Animals, Agency and Resistance." *Journal for the Theory of Social Behaviour* 43, no. 3 (2013): 322–40.

Cassen, Robert, ed. *Population and Development: Old Debates, New Conclusions.* New York: Routledge, 1994.

Castree, Noel. "Commodifying What Nature?" *Progress in Human Geography* 27, no. 3 (June 2003): 273–97.

Chapman, Anne. "The Ways That Nature Matters: The World and the Earth in the Thought of Hannah Arendt." *Environmental Values* 16 (2007): 233–45.

Cicerchia, Lillian. "Structural Domination in the Labor Market." *European Journal of Political Theory,* May 24, 2019. https://doi.org/10.1177/1474885119851094.

Cladis, Mark S. "Radical Romanticism and Its Alternative Account of the Wild and Wilderness." *ISLE: Interdisciplinary Studies in Literature and Environment* 25, no. 4 (Autumn 2018): 835–57.

———. "Radical Romanticism: Democracy, Religion, and the Environmental Imagination." *Soundings: An Interdisciplinary Journal* 97, no. 1 (2014): 21–49.

Cole, Luke W., and Sheila R. Foster. *From the Ground Up: Environmental Racism and the Rise of the Environmental Justice Movement.* New York: New York University Press, 2001.

Coles, Romand. *Visionary Pragmatism: Radical and Ecological Democracy in Neoliberal Times.* Durham, NC: Duke University Press, 2016.

Connolly, William E. *Facing the Planetary: Entangled Humanism and the Politics of Swarming.* Durham, NC: Duke University Press, 2017.

———. *Micropolitics: Thinking, Culture, Speed.* Minneapolis: University of Minnesota Press, 2002.

———. *A World of Becoming.* Durham, NC: Duke University Press, 2011.

"Constitution of the Republic of Ecuador." 2008. Political Database of the Americas. Edmund A. Walsh School of Foreign Service, Center for Latin American Studies, Georgetown University. https://pdba.georgetown.edu/Constitutions/Ecuador/english08.html.

Coole, Diana. "Agentic Capacities and Capacious Historical Materialism: Thinking with Materialisms in the Political Sciences" *Millennium—Journal of International Studies* 41, no. 3 (2013): 451–68. https://doi.org/10.1177/0305829813481006.

———. "Experiencing Discourse: Corporeal Communicators and the Embodiment of Power." *British Journal of Politics and International Relations* 9, no. 3 (2007): 413–33.

———. "Rethinking Agency: A Phenomenological Approach to Embodiment and Agentic Capacities." *Political Studies* 53, no. 1 (March 2005): 124–42.

Coole, Diana, and Samantha Frost, eds. *New Materialisms: Ontology, Agency, and Politics.* Durham, NC: Duke University Press, 2010.

Coulthard, Glen Sean. *Red Skin, White Masks: Rejecting the Colonial Politics of Recognition.* Minneapolis: University of Minnesota Press, 2014.

Cronon, William. "The Trouble with Wilderness, or Getting Back to the Wrong Nature." In *Uncommon Ground: Rethinking the Human Place in Nature,* edited by William Cronon, 69–90. New York: Norton, 1996.

Damasio, Antonio R. *Descartes' Error: Emotion, Reason, and the Human Brain.* New York: Harper Collins, 1994.

Delon, Nicolas, Peter Cook, Gordon Bauer, and Heidi Harley. "Consider the Agent in the Arthropod." *Animal Sentience* 5, no. 29 (July 29, 2020). https://www.wellbeingintlstudiesrepository.org/animsent/vol5/iss29/32/.

Demuth, Bathsheba. *Floating Coast: An Environmental History of the Arctic*. New York: Norton, 2019.

Denison, Jaime. "Between the Moment and Eternity: How Schillerian Play Can Establish Animals as Moral Agents." *Between the Species* 13, no. 10:60–72.

Derrida, Jacques. *The Animal That Therefore I Am*. New York: Fordham University Press, 2008.

de Waal, Frans. *The Age of Empathy: Nature's Lessons for a Kinder Society*. Toronto: McClelland and Steward, 2009.

Di Chiro, Giovanna. "Welcome to the White (m)Anthropocene? A Feminist-Environmentalist Critique." In *Routledge Handbook of Gender and Environment*, edited by Sherilyn MacGregor, 487–505. London: Routledge, 2017.

Dienstag, Joshua Foa. "Dignity, Difference, and the Representation of Nature." *Political Theory* 49, no. 4:613–36.

Disch, Lisa. "Ecological Democracy and the Co-participation of Things." In *The Oxford Handbook of Environmental Political Theory*, edited by Teena Gabrielson, Cheryl Hall, John M. Meyer, and David Schlosberg, 624–40. Oxford: Oxford University Press, 2016.

Dobson, Andrew. "Representative Democracy and the Environment." In *Democracy and the Environment: Problems and Prospects*, edited by William M. Lafferty and James Meadowcroft, 124–39. Cheltenham: Edward Elgar, 1997.

Dolgert, Stefan. "Sacrificing Justice: Suffering Animals, the Oresteia, and the Masks of Consent." *Political Theory* 40, no. 3 (March 19, 2012): 263–89.

Donaldson, Sue, and Will Kymlicka. *Zoopolis: A Political Theory of Animal Rights*. Oxford: Oxford University Press, 2013.

Dryzek, John S. "Institutions for the Anthropocene: Governance in a Changing Earth System." *British Journal of Political Science* 46, no. 4 (October 2016): 937–56.

———. *The Politics of the Earth: Environmental Discourses*. Oxford: Oxford University Press, 1997.

Eckersley, Robyn. "Ecological Democracy and the Rise and Decline of Liberal Democracy: Looking Back, Looking Forward." *Environmental Politics* 29, no. 2 (2020): 214–34.

———. *Environmentalism and Political Theory: Toward an Ecocentric Approach*. Albany: State University of New York Press, 1992.

———. *The Green State: Rethinking Democracy and Sovereignty*. Cambridge, MA: MIT Press, 2004.

Edelglass, William. "Rethinking Responsibility." In *Facing Nature: Levinas and Environmental Thought*, edited by William Edelglass, James Hatley, and Christian Diehm, 209–28. Pittsburgh, PA: Duquesne University Press, 2012.

Edelglass, William, James Hatley, and Christian Diehm, eds. *Facing Nature: Levinas and Environmental Thought*. Pittsburgh, PA: Duquesne University Press, 2012.

"Emancipate." In *Dictionary by Merriam-Webster*. Accessed July 5, 2022. https://www.merriam-webster.com/dictionary/emancipate.

"Emancipate." In *Online Etymology Dictionary*. Accessed July 5, 2022. https://www.etymonline.com/word/emancipate.

Ephraim, Laura. "Save the Appearances! Toward an Arendtian Environmental Politics." *American Political Science Review*, November 15, 2021, 1–13. https://doi.org/10.1017/S0003055421001180.

————. *Who Speaks for Nature? On the Politics of Science.* Philadelphia: University of Pennsylvania Press, 2018.

Esteva, Gustavo, and Madhu Suri Prakash. *Grassroots Postmodernism: Remaking the Soil of Culture.* London: Zed Books, 1998.

Feinberg, Joel. *Doing and Deserving: Essays in the Theory of Responsibility.* Princeton, NJ: Princeton University Press, 1970.

Fitzpatrick, Simon. "Chimpanzee Normativity: Evidence and Objections." *Biology and Philosophy* 35, no. 4 (August 2020). https://doi-org.revproxy.brown.edu/10.1007/s10539-020-09763-1.

Forrest, Adam. "Interview with Naomi Klein." *Big Issue*, October 28, 2014. https://www.bigissue.com/interviews/naomi-klein-3-day-week-will-help-save-life-earth/.

Forsyth, Tim. *Critical Political Ecology: The Politics of Environmental Science.* London: Routledge, 2003.

Fortescue, Elizabeth. "If a Polluted River Could Speak, What Would It Say? Sydney Biennale Gives Waterways a Voice." *Art Newspaper*, March 15, 2022. https://www.theartnewspaper.com/2022/03/15/its-only-natural-sydney-biennale-invites-rivers-to-take-part-in-2022-show.

Fox, Warwick. *Toward a Transpersonal Ecology: Developing New Foundations for Environmentalism.* Boston: Shambhala, 1990.

"Fracking in Montana: Asking Questions, Finding Answers." *Montana Farmers Union*, February 3, 2016. https://montanafarmersunion.com/experts-in-public-policy-environmental-issues-collaborate-on-report-exploring-fracking-in-montana/.

Fraser, Nancy. "Rethinking the Public Sphere: A Contribution to the Critique of Actually Existing Democracy." In *Habermas and the Public Sphere*, edited by Craig J. Calhoun, 109–42. Cambridge, MA: MIT Press, 1993.

Friedman, Marilyn. *Autonomy, Gender, Politics.* New York: Oxford University Press, 2003.

Fritsch, Matthias, Philippe Lynes, and David Wood, eds. *Eco-Deconstruction: Derrida and Environmental Philosophy.* New York: Fordham University Press, 2018.

Gabrielson, Teena. "Bodies, Environments, and Agency." In *The Oxford Handbook of Environmental Political Theory*, edited by Teena Gabrielson, Cheryl Hall, John M. Meyer, and David Schlosberg, 399–412. Oxford: Oxford University Press.

Gell, Alfred. *Art and Agency: An Anthropological Theory.* Oxford: Oxford University Press, 1998.

Gibson-Graham, J. K. *A Postcapitalist Politics.* Minneapolis: University of Minnesota Press, 2006.

Global Witness. "On Dangerous Ground." June 2016. https://www.globalwitness.org/en/campaigns/environmental-activists/dangerous-ground/.

Gómez-Barris, Macarena. *The Extractive Zone: Social Ecologies and Decolonial Perspectives.* Durham, NC: Duke University Press, 2017.

Goodin, Robert E., Carole Pateman, and Roy Pateman. "Simian Sovereignty." *Political Theory* 25, no. 6 (December 1997): 821–49.

Görg, Christoph. "The Politics of Science: Has Marcuse's New Science Finally Come of Age?" In *Critical Ecologies: The Frankfurt School and Contemporary Environmental Crises*, edited by Andrew Biro, 43–72. Toronto: University of Toronto Press, 2011.

Gourevitch, Alex. *From Slavery to the Cooperative Commonwealth: Labor and Republican Liberty in the Nineteenth Century.* Cambridge: Cambridge University Press, 2015.

The Green Belt Movement. "Who We Are." Accessed March 11, 2021. http://www.greenbeltmove ment.org/.

Guha, Ramachandra. *Environmentalism: A Global History.* New York: Longman, 2000.

Gunster, Shane. "Fear and the Unknown: Nature, Culture, and the Limits of Reason." In *Critical Ecologies: The Frankfurt School and Contemporary Environmental Crises,* edited by Andrew Biro, 206–28. Toronto: University of Toronto Press, 2011.

Hall, Cheryl Ann. *The Trouble with Passion: Political Theory beyond the Reign of Reason.* New York: Routledge, 2005.

Haraway, Donna J. *Staying with the Trouble: Making Kin in the Chthulucene.* Durham, NC: Duke University Press, 2016.

———. *When Species Meet.* Minneapolis: University of Minnesota Press, 2008.

Hardt, Michael, and Antonio Negri. *Assembly.* Oxford: Oxford University Press, 2017.

Hart, H.L.A. *Punishment and Responsibility: Essays in the Philosophy of Law.* New York: Oxford University Press, 2008.

Hayward, Clarissa Rile. "Responsibility and Ignorance: On Dismantling Structural Injustice." *Journal of Politics* 79, no. 2 (April 2017): 396–408.

———. "What Can Political Freedom Mean in a Multicultural Democracy? On Deliberation, Difference, and Democratic Governance." *Political Theory* 39, no. 4 (August 2011): 468–97.

"Health, United States, 2019: Table 17." Hyattsville, MD: National Center for Health Statistics, 2021. https://www.cdc.gov/nchs/data/hus/2019/017-508.pdf.

Hirschmann, Nancy J. "Disability as a New Frontier for Feminist Intersectionality Research." *Politics and Gender* 8, no. 3 (September 2012): 396–405.

———. "Disability, Feminism, and Intersectionability: A Critical Approach." *Radical Philosophy Review* 16, no. 2 (2013): 649–62.

———. "Feminist Thoughts on Freedom and Rights." *Politics and Gender* 8, no. 2 (June 2012): 216–22.

———. *The Subject of Liberty: Toward a Feminist Theory of Freedom.* Princeton, NJ: Princeton University Press, 2003.

Hirschmann, Nancy J., and Beth Linker. *Civil Disabilities: Citizenship, Membership, and Belonging.* Philadelphia: University of Pennsylvania Press, 2015.

Hochschild, Arlie Russell. *Strangers in Their Own Land: Anger and Mourning on the American Right.* New York: New Press, 2016.

The Holy Bible. King James Version. New York: Penguin, 1974.

Honig, Bonnie. *Antigone, Interrupted.* Cambridge: Cambridge University Press, 2013.

Horkheimer, Max, and Theodor W. Adorno. *Dialectic of Enlightenment.* Translated by John Cumming. New York: Continuum, 2002.

Howard, Sam. "AIDS Memorial Quilt Still Traveling 30 Years since First Unfolding." *UPI,* October 11, 2017. https://www.upi.com/AIDS-Memorial-Quilt-still-traveling-30-years-since -first-unfolding/1591507680588/.

Jamieson, Dale. *Reason in a Dark Time: Why the Struggle against Climate Change Failed—and What It Means for Our Future.* Oxford: Oxford University Press, 2014.

Jamieson, Dale, and Marcello Di Paola. "Political Theory for the Anthropocene." In *Global Political Theory,* edited by David Held and Pietro Maffettone, 254–80. Malden, MA: Polity, 2016.

Jaspers, Karl. *The Question of German Guilt*. Translated by E. B. Ashton. New York: Fordham University Press, 2000.

Jennings, Bruce. *Ecological Governance: Toward a New Social Contract with the Earth*. Morgantown: West Virginia University Press, 2016.

Johnson, Genevieve Fuji, and Loralea Michaelis, eds. *Political Responsibility Refocused: Thinking Justice after Iris Marion Young*. Toronto: University of Toronto Press, 2013.

Jones, Owain, and Paul Cloke. "Non-human Agencies: Trees in Place and Time." In *Material Agency: Towards a Non-anthropocentric Approach*, edited by Carl Knappett and Lambros Malafouris, 79–96. New York: Springer, 2010.

Kant, Immanuel. *Grounding for the Metaphysics of Morals*. Translated by James W. Ellington. Indianapolis: Hackett, 1981.

———. "Toward Perpetual Peace: A Philosophical Sketch." In *Perpetual Peace, and Other Essays on Politics, History, and Morals*, 107–43. Translated by Ted Humphrey. Indianapolis: Hackett, 1983.

Kateb, George. *Human Dignity*. Cambridge, MA: Belknap Press of Harvard University Press, 2011.

Knappett, Carl, and Lambros Malafouris, eds. *Material Agency: Towards a Non-anthropocentric Approach*. New York: Springer, 2010.

Krause, Sharon R. "Agency." *Political Concepts: A Critical Lexicon* 3, no. 5 (2016). https://www.politicalconcepts.org/category/issue-3/.

———. "Creating a Culture of Environmental Responsibility." *Cultural Values in Political Economy*, edited by J. P. Singh, 65–86. Stanford, CA: Stanford University Press, 2020.

———. "Environmental Domination." *Political Theory* 48, no. 4 (August 2020): 443–68.

———. *Freedom beyond Sovereignty: Reconstructing Liberal Individualism*. Chicago: University of Chicago Press, 2015.

———. "Political Respect for Nature." *Philosophy and Social Criticism* 47, no. 2 (2021): 241–66.

Kutz, Christopher. *Complicity: Ethics and Law for a Collective Age*. Cambridge: Cambridge University Press, 2000.

Lane, Melissa. *Eco-Republic: What the Ancients Can Teach Us about Ethics, Virtue, and Sustainable Living*. Princeton, NJ: Princeton University Press, 2012.

Latour, Bruno. *Facing Gaia: Eight Lectures on the New Climatic Regime*. Cambridge, UK: Polity, 2017.

———. *Reassembling the Social: An Introduction to Actor-Network-Theory*. New York: Oxford University Press, 2007.

———. *We Have Never Been Modern*. Translated by Catherine Porter. Cambridge, MA: Harvard University Press, 1993.

Lavin, Chad. *The Politics of Responsibility*. Urbana: University of Illinois Press, 2008.

Law, John, and John Hassard. *Actor Network Theory and After*. Hoboken: Wiley-Blackwell, 1999.

Law, John, and Annemarie Mol. "The Actor-Enacted: Cumbrian Sheep in 2001." In *Material Agency: Towards a Non-anthropocentric Approach*, edited by Carl Knappett and Lambros Malafouris, 57–78. New York: Springer, 2010.

Lazarus, Richard. "Rights for Lake Erie?" *Harvard Law Review Blog*. Accessed March 14, 2021. https://blog.harvardlawreview.org/rights-for-lake-erie/.

Legal Information Institute. "Strict Liability." Accessed March 8, 2021. https://www.law.cornell.edu/wex/strict_liability.

Leiss, William. *The Domination of Nature*. New York: G. Braziller, 1972.

———. "Modern Science, Enlightenment, and the Domination of Nature: No Exit?" In *Critical Ecologies: The Frankfurt School and Contemporary Environmental Crises*, edited by Andrew Biro, 23–42. Toronto: University of Toronto Press, 2011.

Leopold, Aldo. *A Sand County Almanac*. New York: Ballentine Books, 1966.

Levinas, Emmanuel. *Totality and Infinity: An Essay on Exteriority*. Translated by Alphonso Lingis. Pittsburgh, PA: Duquesne University Press, 1969.

Lindahl-Kiessling, Kerstin, and Hans Landberg, eds. *Population, Economic Development, and the Environment*. Oxford: Oxford University Press, 1998.

Linzey, Andrew. *Animal Theology*. Urbana: University of Illinois Press, 1995.

Litfin, Karen. "Ontologies of Sustainability in Ecovillage Culture: Integrating Ecology, Economics, Community, and Consciousness." In *The Greening of Everyday Life*, edited by John M. Meyer and Jens Kersten, 249–64. Oxford: Oxford University Press, 2016.

Locke, John. "Second Treatise of Government." In *Two Treatises of Government*, 265–428. Edited by Peter Laslett. Cambridge: Cambridge University Press, 1988.

Lovett, Frank. *A General Theory of Domination and Justice*. Oxford: Oxford University Press, 2012.

Luke, Timothy W. *Ecocritique: Contesting the Politics of Nature, Economy, and Culture*. Minneapolis: University of Minnesota Press, 1997.

MacGregor, Sherilyn, ed. *Routledge Handbook of Gender and Environment*. London: Routledge, 2017.

Mackenzie, Catriona, and Natalie Stoljar, eds. *Relational Autonomy: Feminist Perspectives on Autonomy, Agency, and the Social Self*. New York: Oxford University Press, 2000.

Mahmood, Saba. *Politics of Piety: The Islamic Revival and the Feminist Subject*. Princeton, NJ: Princeton University Press, 2004.

Mapes-Martins, Brad. "Household Maintenance and the Environmental Politics of Tending." In *The Greening of Everyday Life*, edited by John M. Meyer and Jens Kersten, 98–114. Oxford: Oxford University Press, 2016.

Marcuse, Herbert. *One-Dimensional Man: Studies in the Ideology of Advanced Industrial Society*. Boston: Beacon, 1964.

Markell, Patchen. *Bound by Recognition*. Princeton, NJ: Princeton University Press, 2003.

———. "The Insufficiency of Non-domination." *Political Theory* 36, no. 1 (February 1, 2008): 9–36.

Martínez-Alier, Joan. *The Environmentalism of the Poor: A Study of Ecological Conflicts and Valuation*. Cheltenham: Edward Elgar, 2002.

Marx, Karl. "Economic and Philosophic Manuscripts of 1844." In *The Marx-Engels Reader*, edited by Robert C. Tucker, 66–125. New York: Norton, 1978.

Massumi, Brian. *What Animals Teach Us about Politics*. Durham, NC: Duke University Press, 2014.

Matravers, Matt. *Responsibility and Justice*. Cambridge, UK: Polity, 2007.

McFarland, Sarah E., and Ryan Hediger, eds. *Animals and Agency: An Interdisciplinary Exploration*. Leiden: Brill, 2009.

McKibben, Bill. *The End of Nature*. New York: Random House, 1989.

———. "What Exxon Knew about Climate Change." *New Yorker*, September 18, 2015. https://www.newyorker.com/news/daily-comment/what-exxon-knew-about-climate-change.

Merchant, Carolyn. *The Death of Nature: Women, Ecology, and the Scientific Revolution*. San Francisco: Harper and Row, 1983.

———. "The Scientific Revolution and *The Death of Nature*." *Isis* 97 (2006): 513–33.

Meyer, John M. *Political Nature: Environmentalism and the Interpretation of Western Thought*. Cambridge, MA: MIT Press, 2001.

Michaelis, Loralea, and Genevieve Fuji Johnson. "Political Responsibility Refocused." In *Political Responsibility Refocused: Thinking Justice after Iris Marion Young*, edited by Genevieve Fuji Johnson and Loralea Michaelis, 3–20. Toronto: University of Toronto Press, 2013.

Mikati, Ihab, Adam F. Benson, Thomas J. Luben, Jason D. Sacks, and Jennifer Richmond-Bryant. "Disparities in Distribution of Particulate Matter Emission Sources by Race and Poverty Status." *American Journal of Public Health* 108, no. 4 (April 2018): 480–85.

Mills, Charles. "White Ignorance." In *Race and Epistemologies of Ignorance*, edited by Shannon Sullivan and Nancy Tuana, 11–38. Albany: State University of New York Press, 2007.

Montesquieu, Charles de Secondat. *The Spirit of the Laws*. Translated Anne M. Cohler, Basia C. Miller, and Harold S. Stone. Cambridge: Cambridge University Press, 1989.

Mooney, Edward F., and Lyman F. Mower. "Witness to the Face of a River." In *Facing Nature: Levinas and Environmental Thought*, edited by William Edelglass, James Hatley, and Christian Diehm, 279–300. Pittsburgh, PA: Duquesne University Press, 2012.

Morton, Timothy. *Hyperobjects: Philosophy and Ecology after the End of the World*. Minneapolis: University of Minnesota Press, 2013.

Myers, Ella. *Worldly Ethics: Democratic Politics and Care for the World*. Durham, NC: Duke University Press, 2013.

Naess, Arne. "The Deep Ecology Movement: Some Philosophical Aspects." Open Air Philosophy. https://openairphilosophy.org/wp-content/uploads/2019/02/OAP_Naess_Deep_Ecology_Movement.pdf. Originally published in *Philosophical Inquiry* 8, no. 1 (1986).

Nagel, Thomas. "Moral Luck." In *Mortal Questions*, 24–38. Cambridge: Cambridge University Press, 1979.

NFWF (National Fish and Wildlife Foundation). "Path of the Pronghorn." Accessed March 14, 2021. https://www.nfwf.org/programs/path-pronghorn.

Nixon, Rob. *Slow Violence and the Environmentalism of the Poor*. Cambridge, MA: Harvard University Press, 2011.

Nussbaum, Martha C. "Beyond 'Compassion and Humanity': Justice for Non-human Animals." In *Animal Rights: Current Debates and New Directions*, edited by Cass R. Sunstein and Martha C. Nussbaum, 299–320. Oxford: Oxford University Press, 2004.

———. "Foreword." In *Responsibility for Justice*, by Iris Marion Young, ix–xxv. New York: Oxford University Press, 2011.

Ober, Josiah. *Athenian Legacies: Essays on the Politics of Going on Together*. Princeton, NJ: Princeton University Press, 2007.

O'Donnell, Erin L., and Julia Talbot-Jones. "Creating Legal Rights for Rivers: Lessons from Australia, New Zealand, and India." *Ecology and Society* 23, no. 1 (2018): 7. https://doi.org/10.5751/ES-09854-230107.

Panagia, Davide. *The Political Life of Sensation*. Durham, NC: Duke University Press, 2009.

Pettit, Philip. *A Theory of Freedom: From the Psychology to the Politics of Agency*. Cambridge, UK: Polity, 2001.

————. *On the People's Terms: A Republican Theory and Model of Democracy.* Cambridge: Cambridge University Press, 2012.

————. *Republicanism: A Theory of Freedom and Government.* Oxford: Oxford University Press, 1999.

Plato. *The Republic.* Translated by Allan Bloom. New York: Basic Books, 2016.

Plumwood, Val. *Feminism and the Mastery of Nature.* London: Routledge, 1993.

Pollan, Michael. *The Omnivore's Dilemma: A Natural History of Four Meals.* New York: Penguin Books, 2006.

"Pope Francis's Speech to the UN in Full." *Guardian,* September 25, 2015. http://www .theguardian.com/environment/2015/sep/25/pope-franciss-speech-to-the-un-in-full.

Premack, David. "Animal Cognition." *Annual Review of Psychology* 34, no. 1 (January 1983): 351–62.

Press, Daniel, and Daniel A. Mazmanian. "Toward Sustainable Production: Finding Workable Strategies for Government and Industry." In *Environmental Policy: New Directions for the Twenty-First Century,* edited by Norman J. Vig and Michael E. Kraft, 239–64. London: Sage, 2016.

Purdy, Jedediah. *After Nature: A Politics for the Anthropocene.* Cambridge, MA: Harvard University Press, 2015.

Randall, Cassidy. "'They Won't Survive': Trump Gas Wells Would Block Pronghorn Migration Route." *Guardian,* February 24, 2020. http://www.theguardian.com/environment/2020 /feb/24/pronghorn-migration-gas-wells.

Rawls, John. *A Theory of Justice.* Cambridge, MA: Belknap Press of Harvard University Press, 1971.

Raz, Joseph. *From Normativity to Responsibility.* Oxford: Oxford University Press, 2012.

Regan, Tom. *The Case for Animal Rights.* Berkeley: University of California Press, 1983.

Reid, Mark D. "Moral Agency in *Mammalia.*" *Between the Species* 13, no. 10:1–24.

Robbins, Jim. "America's Gray Ghosts: The Disappearing Caribou." *New York Times,* October 3, 2016. https://www.nytimes.com/2016/10/04/science/endangered-caribou-idaho-british -columbia.html.

Roberts, Neil. *Freedom as Marronage.* Chicago: University of Chicago Press, 2015.

Roberts, William Clare. *Marx's Inferno: The Political Theory of Capital.* Princeton, NJ: Princeton University Press, 2018.

Rose, Tricia. *The Hip Hop Wars: What We Talk about When We Talk about Hip Hop—and Why It Matters.* New York: Basic Civitas, 2008.

Rossello, Diego. "The Animal Condition in the Human Condition: Rethinking Arendt's Political Action beyond the Human Species." *Contemporary Political Theory* 21, no. 2 (June 2022): 219–39. https://doi.org/10.1057/s41296-021-00495-9.

Salatin, Joel. *Everything I Want to Do Is Illegal: War Stories from the Local Food Front.* Swoope, VA: Polyface, 2007.

Salleh, Ariel. *Ecofeminism as Politics: Nature, Marx, and the Postmodern.* London: Zed Books, 1997.

Sapontzis, Steve. *Morals, Reason, and Animals.* Philadelphia: Temple University Press, 1987.

Schiff, Jade [J. L.]. *Burdens of Political Responsibility: Narrative and the Cultivation of Responsiveness.* Cambridge: Cambridge University Press, 2014.

————. "Power and Responsibility." In *Political Responsibility Refocused: Thinking Justice after Iris Marion Young*, edited by Genevieve Fuji Johnson and Loralea Michaelis, 42–62. Toronto: University of Toronto Press, 2013.

Schlingloff, Laura, and Richard Moore. "Do Chimpanzees Conform to Social Norms?" In *The Routledge Handbook of Philosophy of Animal Minds*, edited by Kristin Andrews and Jacob Beck, 381–89. New York: Routledge, 2017.

Schlosberg, David. *Defining Environmental Justice: Theories, Movements, and Nature*. Oxford: Oxford University Press, 2007.

Schlosberg, David, and Romand Coles. "The New Environmentalism of Everyday Life: Sustainability, Material Flows, and Movements." In *The Greening of Everyday Life*, edited by John M. Meyer and Jens Kersten, 13–30. Oxford: Oxford University Press, 2016.

Schlossberg, Tatiana. "English Village Becomes Climate Leader by Quietly Cleaning Up Its Own Patch." *New York Times*, August 21, 2016. https://www.nytimes.com/2016/08/22/science/english-village-becomes-climate-leader-by-quietly-cleaning-up-its-own-patch.html.

Scott, James C. *Domination and the Arts of Resistance: Hidden Transcripts*. New Haven, CT: Yale University Press, 1990.

Sen, Amartya. *Development as Freedom*. New York: Anchor, 1999.

Sen, Gita, Adrienne Germain, and Lincoln C. Chen, eds. *Population Policies Reconsidered: Health, Empowerment, and Rights*. Harvard Series on Population and International Health. Cambridge, MA: Harvard University Press, 1994.

Sender, Ron, Shai Fuchs, and Ron Milo. "Revised Estimates for the Number of Human and Bacteria Cells in the Body." *PLOS Biology* 14, no. 8 (August 19, 2016). https://www.ncbi.nlm.nih.gov/pmc/articles/PMC4991899/.

Shakespeare, Tom, ed. *The Disability Reader: Social Science Perspectives*. London: Cassell, 1998.

Shapiro, Paul. "Moral Agency in Other Animals." *Theoretical Medicine and Bioethics* 27, no. 4 (2006): 357–73.

Shelley, Mary Wollstonecraft. *Frankenstein: The 1818 Text*. New York: Penguin Books, 2018.

Shiva, Vandana. *Earth Democracy: Justice, Sustainability, and Peace*. Berkeley, CA: North Atlantic Books, 2005.

Shutkin, William A. *The Land That Could Be: Environmentalism and Democracy in the Twenty-First Century*. Cambridge, MA: MIT Press, 2000.

Siebers, Tobin. *Disability Theory*. Ann Arbor: University of Michigan Press, 2008.

Simmons, J. Aaron. "Toward a Relational Model of Anthropocentrism: A Levinasian Approach to the Ethics of Climate Change." In *Facing Nature: Levinas and Environmental Thought*, edited by William Edelglass, James Hatley, and Christian Diehm, 229–52. Pittsburgh, PA: Duquesne University Press, 2012.

Singer, Peter. *Animal Liberation: A New Ethics for Our Treatment of Animals*. New York: New York Review, 1975.

————. *The Life You Can Save: How to Do Your Part to End World Poverty*. New York: Random House, 2010.

Skinner, Quentin. *Liberty before Liberalism*. Cambridge: Cambridge University Press, 2012.

Smith, Kimberly K. *Governing Animals: Animal Welfare and the Liberal State*. New York: Oxford University Press, 2012.

Smith, Mick. "Earthly Politics of Ethical An-arche." In *Facing Nature: Levinas and Environmental Thought*, edited by William Edelglass, James Hatley, and Christian Diehm, 135–60. Pittsburgh, PA: Duquesne University Press, 2012.

Solomon, Julie Robin. *Objectivity in the Making: Francis Bacon and the Politics of Inquiry*. Baltimore: Johns Hopkins University Press, 1998.

Sommers, Tamler. "The Two Faces of Revenge: Moral Responsibility and the Culture of Honor." *Biology and Philosophy* 24, no. 1 (January 2009): 35–50.

Southside Community Land Trust. "Mission and Impact." Accessed March 14, 2021. https://www.southsideclt.org/mission-values/.

Spinka, Marek, and Francoise Wemelsfelder. "Environmental Challenge and Animal Agency." In *Animal Welfare*, edited by M. C. Appleby, I.A.S. Olsson, and F. Galindo, 39–55. Wallingford, UK: CABI, 2018.

Stengers, Isabelle. *In Catastrophic Times: Resisting the Coming Barbarism*. Translated by Andrew Goffey. Lüneburg, Germany: Open Humanities in collaboration with Meson, 2015.

Stone, Christopher D. *Should Trees Have Standing? Law, Morality, and the Environment*. Oxford: Oxford University Press, 2010.

Stout, Jeffrey. *Blessed Are the Organized: Grassroots Democracy in America*. Princeton, NJ: Princeton University Press, 2010.

Stow, Simon. *American Mourning: Tragedy, Democracy, Resilience*. Cambridge: Cambridge University Press, 2017.

"Sustainable Development Institute." Accessed March 14, 2021. http://sustainabledevelopment institute.org.

Sunstein, Cass R., and Martha C. Nussbaum, eds. *Animal Rights: Current Debates and New Directions*. Oxford: Oxford University Press, 2004.

Szerszynski, Bronislaw. "Technology, Performance, and Life Itself: Hannah Arendt and the Fate of Nature." *Sociological Review* 51, no. 2:203–18.

Taylor, Charles. "What Is Human Agency?" In *Philosophical Papers*. Vol. 1, *Human Agency and Language*, 15–44. Cambridge: Cambridge University Press, 1985.

Taylor, Paul W. *Respect for Nature: A Theory of Environmental Ethics*. Princeton, NJ: Princeton University Press, 1986.

Thompson, Charis, and Sherilyn MacGregor. "The Death of Nature: Foundations of Ecological Feminist Thought." In *Routledge Handbook of Gender and Environment*, edited by Sherilyn MacGregor, 43–53. London: Routledge, 2017.

Thoreau, Henry David. *Walden: Or, Life in the Woods*. Boston: Ticknor and Fields, 1854.

Toadvine, Ted. "Enjoyment and Its Discontents: On Separation from Nature in Levinas." In *Facing Nature: Levinas and Environmental Thought*, edited by William Edelglass, James Hatley, and Christian Diehm, 161–90. Pittsburgh, PA: Duquesne University Press, 2012.

Tsing, Anna Lowenhaupt. *The Mushroom at the End of the World: On the Possibility of Life in Capitalist Ruins*. Princeton, NJ: Princeton University Press, 2015.

Twenty-Third Biennale of Sydney. The Biennale of Sidney, José Rojas, Artistic Director. https://www.biennaleofsydney.art/biennale/23rd-biennale-of-sydney-2022/.

United Church of Christ Commission for Racial Justice. "Toxic Wastes and Race in the United States: A National Report on the Racial and Socio-economic Characteristics of Communities with Hazardous Waste Sites." Public Data Access, 1987. https://www.worldcat.org/title

/toxic-wastes-and-race-in-the-united-states-a-national-report-on-the-racial-and-socio
-economic-characteristics-of-communities-with-hazardous-waste-sites/oclc/16985343.

Vanderheiden, Steve. *Atmospheric Justice: A Political Theory of Climate Change*. Oxford: Oxford University Press, 2008.

Vázquez-Arroyo, Antonio Y. *Political Responsibility: Responding to Predicaments of Power*. New York: Columbia University Press, 2016.

Vogel, Steven. *Thinking Like a Mall: Environmental Philosophy after the End of Nature*. Cambridge, MA: MIT Press, 2015.

Voice, Paul. "Consuming the World: Hannah Arendt on Politics and the Environment." *Journal of International Political Theory* 9, no. 2:178–93.

Vrousalis, Nicholas. "Exploitation, Vulnerability, and Social Domination." *Philosophy and Public Affairs* 41, no. 2:131–57.

Warner, Michael. *Publics and Counterpublics*. New York: Zone Books, 2002.

Watts, Vanessa. "Indigenous Place-Thought and Agency amongst Humans and Non-humans (First Woman and Sky Woman go on a European World Tour!)." *Decolonization: Indigeneity, Education, and Society* 2, no. 1 (2013): 20–34.

Whatmore, Sarah. *Hybrid Geographies: Natures, Cultures, Spaces*. London: Sage, 2002.

White, Damian F., Alan P. Rudy, and Brian J. Gareau. *Environments, Natures and Social Theory: Towards a Critical Hybridity*. London: Palgrave, 2016.

Whiteside, Kerry H. "Worldliness and Respect for Nature: An Ecological Application of Hannah Arendt's Conception of Culture." *Environmental Values* 7, no. 1:25–41.

Whitman, Walt. *Leaves of Grass*. Mineola, NY: Dover, 2007.

Whyte, Kyle P. "Indigenous Science (Fiction) for the Anthropocene: Ancestral Dystopias and Fantasies of Climate Change Crises." *Environment and Planning E: Nature and Space* 1, nos. 1–2 (May 30, 2018): 224–42.

Whyte, Kyle, Chris Caldwell, and Marie Schaefer. "Indigenous Lessons about Sustainability Are Not Just for 'All Humanity.'" In *Sustainability: Approaches to Environmental Justice and Social Power*, edited by Julie Sze, 149–79. New York: New York University Press, 2018.

Wildlife Conservation Society. "Pronghorn Migration on the Path of the Pronghorn." Accessed March 14, 2021. https://northamerica.wcs.org/Wild-Places/Yellowstone-and-Northern -Rockies/Pronghorn-Field-Program/Pronghorn-Migration-Path.aspx.

Williams, Bernard. *Moral Luck: Philosophical Papers 1973–1980*. Cambridge: Cambridge University Press, 1981.

———. *Shame and Necessity*. Berkeley: University of California Press, 1993.

Williams, Melissa S. "Political Responsibility for Decolonization in Canada." In *Political Responsibility Refocused: Thinking Justice after Iris Marion Young*, edited by Genevieve Fuji Johnson and Loralea Michaelis, 78–101. Toronto: University of Toronto Press, 2013.

Williams ⸱ ⸱ry Tempest. *The Open Space of Democracy*. Eugene, OR: WIPF and Stock,

ʿ *Is Posthumanism?* Minneapolis: University of Minnesota Press, 2010.

ım. "Michael, a Pastoral Poem." 1800. In *Wordsworth's Poetry and Prose*,
⸱ W. W. Norton, 2014.

w of the Rights of Mother Earth." Accessed March 11, 2021. http://www
ʿProjects/Indicators/motherearthbolivia.html.

Wright, Anthony A. "Testing Complex Animal Cognition: Concept Learning, Proactive Interference, and List Memory." *Journal of the Experimental Analysis of Behavior* 109, no. 1 (January 2018): 87–100.

Young, Iris Marion. "Responsibility and Global Labor Justice." *Journal of Political Philosophy* 12, no. 4 (2004): 365–88.

———. *Responsibility for Justice*. New York: Oxford University Press, 2011.

Zerilli, Linda M. G. *Feminism and the Abyss of Freedom*. Chicago: University of Chicago Press, 2005.

Zheng, Robin. "What Is My Role in Changing the System? A New Model of Responsibility for Structural Injustice." *Ethical Theory and Moral Practice* 21, no. 4 (August 2018): 869–85.

INDEX

Abram, David, 16, 29, 44, 48, 161n27
abyssal rupture, Derrida on, 21, 75, 82–83
accountability: in actions against injustice,
    118; distinctive capacities of humans and,
    44, 50; for environmental domination, 47;
    global inequality and, 99; nonsovereignty
    of agency and, 37–38, 48; norm-responsive
    agency and, 45–46; in public rituals of
    mourning, 96, 98; responsibility and, 63,
    103, 108–9, 110–11, 114–15, 122, 176n29,
    177n38; sovereigntist agency and, 35, 36
Ackerly, Brooke, 22, 102, 110, 117–19, 177n33
acknowledgment, Markell on, 163n36
actants, Bennett's concept of, 41, 45
activism: catalyzed by rights and represen-
    tation, 148; changing public attitudes, 5,
    116; connected, 22, 102; disruptive politics
    and, 102; force used against, 57; of garment
    workers, 117–18; for human rights, 102;
    institutions and, 73, 149; responsibility
    and, 115. See also mobilizing for eco-
    emancipation; protests
actor network theory, of Latour, 166n65
Adorno, Theodor W., 13, 20, 58–59, 61, 66,
    115, 135
agency: as capacity of nonhuman beings, 17,
    18, 30–31, 46–47, 166n82; deeply mislead-
    ing ideal of, 29–32; individual vs. collective,
    163n23; Kant's misconceptions of, 76;
    Kateb on, 31, 32–34; materially distributed,
    40–44, 45; moral and political standing
    and, 49; norm responsiveness and, 45–48;
    porosity of, 16, 29–30, 31, 44, 78; power

differentials and, 18; responsibility and,
    104, 108, 111; socially distributed, 34, 35,
    36–40, 105, 163n25 (see also nonsovereign
    agency); summary of, 50–51; unintentional
    outcomes and, 34–35. See also nonsover-
    eign agency; sovereigntist conception of
    agency
agriculture: alternative economic frame
    works for, 144, 149; decisions about animal
    well-being in, 92; industrialized, 6, 7, 135,
    138, 144, 149; organic, 139, 149; of Salatin's
    Polyface Farm, 142–43, 181n68; sustainable,
    153, 154. See also factory farms; food systems
AIDS quilt, 96–97
air pollution, 35, 126
alterity: of Derrida's cat, 83, 84; Levinasian
    concept of, 21, 75, 84, 85, 86, 89
alternative energy, 6, 35, 176n29. See also
    renewable energy
alternative modernities, 11, 140, 159n16
animal rights, 35, 92, 94–95, 145–46, 160n18,
    173n68
animals. See nonhuman beings and things;
    suffering of animals
animal welfare, 92, 160n18
Anker, Elizabeth, 42–43, 125
apparel industry, 106. See also garment
    worker activism
Arendt, Hannah: on freedom, 123–24; on
    natality, 173n59; nonhuman nature and,
    41, 164n45; nonsovereign agency and, 16,
    18, 30, 36, 41, 163n25, 163n30, 163n32; on
    power, 116

Niger delta: Ken Saro-Wiwa in, 134; oil companies and, 126, 127, 129

Nixon, Rob, 154–55

nonhuman beings and things: agentic capacities in, 17, 18, 30–31, 46–47, 166n65, 166n82; as catalysts of ethical epiphany, 89–91; conceptions of freedom and, 125; conflict with, 21–22, 70–71, 93–94, 100; constitutional protections for, 4, 92, 146, 147–48, 159n7; Dienstag on care for, 167n83; disavowal of, 91, 125, 173n72; domination of, 54–55, 170n71 (see also domination of nature); as Earth others, 159n12; eco-emancipation and, 49, 124, 130–34, 140–41, 150; eco-responsibility in relation to, 113, 119; as ends in themselves, 31, 77, 80–81; epistemologies of ignorance and, 120; human agency embedded with, 48; humans' necessary use of, 3, 21, 53–54, 65, 70–71, 80–81, 96, 98; human vulnerability to, 90, 173n71; institutional change and, 141, 142–43, 145; irreducible alterity of, 86–87; Kateb on, 31, 32, 33–34; materially distributed agency and, 41–44, 45; as participants in art, 136; representation for, 10–11, 92, 146–48; responsiveness to, 84, 92; rights for, 10–11, 92, 145–46; in simulated climate negotiation, 157; wilderness within and, 139–40; worldmaking in tandem with, 24, 124, 125, 149, 150, 155. See also animal rights; animal welfare; political respect for nature; suffering of animals

nonsovereign agency, 16–17, 36–44; accountability and, 37–38, 48; animal agency as, 47; Arendt and, 16, 18, 30, 36, 41, 163n25, 163n30, 163n32; eco-emancipation and, 38, 50; materially or corporeally distributed, 40–44; new exceptionalism and, 17–18, 31–32, 44, 48–49; old exceptionalism and, 30, 31, 36; responsibility and, 22, 23, 101–2, 105, 163n36; social inequality and, 38–39, 164n38; socially distributed, 36–40; of wilderness within, 139–40

nonsovereign institutions, 141–42, 147, 149

nonsovereignty of eco-emancipation, 133–34

norm responsiveness, 45–48, 50, 71

Nussbaum, Martha, 88, 173n68, 176n22

Occupy movement, 120

Oedipus, 37–38, 39

oil companies: advertising campaigns of, 6; Niger delta and, 126, 127, 129; pronghorn migration and, 156. See also petrochemical industry

old exceptionalism: blind to addresses of nonhuman others, 91; distribution of agentic capacities and, 17; Ephraim's Arendtian environmentalism in, 165n45; epistemologies of ignorance and, 120; justified by human distinctiveness, 49; justifying environmental domination, 163n25; limits of sovereignty and, 32–36; nonsovereignty of agency and, 30, 31, 36; porosity of agency and, 29–30, 44; posthumanism and, 161n33

Padres Hacia una Vida Mejor, 149

pandemics, global, 52

Paris climate accord of 2015, 6, 156

patriarchy, 19, 23–24, 54, 56, 124

Pericles's funeral oration, 96

petrochemical industry, 114, 126, 129. See also oil companies

Pettit, Philip, 25, 55, 66–69, 162n22, 168n25, 170n65

planned obsolescence, 8, 72, 127

plastics, 8, 61, 119

Plato, 3, 104

Plumwood, Val, 13, 60

political community: creating new modes of, 149, 150, 177n33; garment worker activism and, 117; historically identified with equality, 91; human beings' distinctive place in, 10–11; iterative and inclusive deliberation in, 95; making freer forms of, 27, 28, 51; more-than-human forms of, 49; reconstructing the concept of, 26; rights for Earth others and, 145

A NOTE ON THE TYPE

This book has been composed in Arno, an Old-style serif typeface in the
classic Venetian tradition, designed by Robert Slimbach at Adobe.